D1384438

Information Revolution and Global Politics

William J. Drake and Ernest. J. Wilson III, editors

Transforming Global Information and Communication Markets

The Political Economy of Innovation

Peter F. Cowhey and Jonathan D. Aronson
with Donald Abelson

The MIT Press
Cambridge, Massachusetts
London, England

Acknowledgments

We owe thanks for suggestions and tolerance to all of the usual suspects—family, friends, colleagues, and research assistants. We particularly want to recognize and thank three of our colleagues in ICT policy. Milton Mueller was a co-author on an earlier paper on which chapter 9 draws heavily. Donald Abelson joined us as a co-author of the summary. John Richards was the perfect sounding board, agreeing and disagreeing with our arguments and provoking us to refine our thinking as the chapters took shape. Chapters 8 and 9 also draw heavily on papers that he co-authored with us. And he read the final manuscript and provided us with insightful suggestions and criticisms. Many people shared their ideas with us; a substantial number did so "off the record." We thank those anonymous sources and these who were on the record: Don Abelson, Francois Bar, Michael Borrus, Carlos Casasus, Manuel Castells, Bob Conn, Cory Doctorow, Kenneth Cukier, Pierre de Vries, Gerald Faulhaber, Eric Gan, Don Gips, Scott Harris, Reed Hundt, David Hytha, Mimi Ito, Michael Kleeman, Zhong Yuan Li, Paul Maritz, Cory Ondrejka, Robert Pepper, Peter Preuss, Nicholas Pujet, Howard Rheingold, Gregory Rosston, Sachio Semmoto, Larry Smarr, Simon Wilkie, and John Zysman. We also thank Cindy Hwang, Piyoo Kochar, Emilie Lasserson, Federica Marchesi, and Meg Young for research assistance. None of these friends and critics is responsible for any errors of fact or argument that may remain.

For family (Margaret, Megan, Joan, Adam, and Zach) and mentors (Robert O. Keohane and in memory of Ernst B. Haas). All of them "inflection points" in our lives.

Transforming Global Information and Communication Markets

Introduction

As 2009 nears, the world is in a time of gloom and panic. Will global governance and the global economic order survive? In retrospect, some saw the collapse of the dot com bubble as a portent of the financial meltdown and the collapse of confidence in the future. In the United States there is a dour bipartisan consensus that escalating special interest politics, budget deficits, economic insecurity in the midst of more consumption, environmental and energy policy gridlock, and deep uncertainties about national-security strategy point to intractable problems in the design and conduct of public policy. In other countries the specific bill of complaints may differ, but a similar uneasiness is widespread.

Although we can gripe as well as anyone about the world's follies, this book is more upbeat. Since World War II, a planet-straddling information and communications technology (ICT) infrastructure has created a global information economy at an ever-accelerating pace. A radically different model for competition and public policy for this infrastructure was introduced that is far sounder than its predecessor. More remarkably, countries agreed to rewrite the basic international agreements governing commerce for the communications and information infrastructure in a way that makes more sense than the consensus that was forged immediately after 1945.

For once, the transformation in governance and technology is not just a tale of the prosperous states doing better. These changes boosted the economic takeoff of India and China and other emerging powers, and also brought a much greater level of digital connectivity to the poor than anyone dreamed of in the late 1980s. Much remains to be done in poor countries, but an expanding record of successes now exists. For example, banking done over mobile phones ("m-banking") is taking off faster in developing countries, which lack well-developed financial markets, than in wealthy countries.

This book explains how and why a combination of technological innovation, market strategies, and political entrepreneurship propelled these developments, first in the United States, Europe, and Japan and then in the rest of the world. Public debates sometimes grow cynical about big successes in public policy because of their preoccupation with the flaws that are inherent to even the best of policies. Although we note bad news when it occurs, we emphasize the larger story of accomplishment.

Policy is imperfect because too little is known to understand all the dimensions of an issue, because the tools for intervening in markets lack the precision of a surgeon's scalpel, and because significant compromise is necessary in political and economic bargaining. Politics is not pretty and often leads to absurdities, but it can also fundamentally redirect outmoded compromises that hamper market efficiency. "Pretty good" governance should be a goal, not a disappointment.

The current ICT infrastructure required a policy revolution to introduce competition in telecommunications markets. By correcting existing inefficiencies, this policy reversal created an innovation space that had high returns in the market for long-distance phone and data communications. In contrast with the few other countries that quickly followed the lead of the United States, the US formula eschewed most limitations on the number of entrants or the number of business models, thereby nudging diverse business strategies. Just as crucially, the policy's political coalition pushed policy in a way that favored experimentation and innovation in the closely complementary markets of computing and global information systems for large users. This tilt in favor of entrepreneurs in computer networking led to broad commercial deployment of the Internet and the Web, to e-commerce, and to the mixing and mingling of digital applications (including broadcasting, videoconferencing, and collaborative computing).[1]

But, as is typical even of successful public policy, the redefined market was hardly ideal. The political compromises that enabled the policy shift still restricted certain forms of freedom of pricing and competition in order to ensure stable pricing of local phone services. These restrictions led to a less-than-ideal market and triggered a cascade of academic criticism in the 1980s and the 1990s. However, in our view, empowering the coalition favoring technological innovation through policy was more crucial than getting all the details correct. The policy compromise defined a robust new market in which the most important options for technological innovation could be pursued competitively.

Still, basking in pleasure over past good judgments is perilous. No successful policy comes with a lifetime warranty. To paraphrase the warnings in advertisements for mutual funds, strong past performance of a public policy is no guarantee of future returns. We believe that the world's information economy is at an inflection point. A productive shift in the direction of the world market is possible if we can adapt national and global public policies prudently. The innovation space that nurtured change in the 1980s and the 1990s is becoming less fertile. The telecommunications ("telecom") market is significantly more efficient today, and the major potential for creative political economic bargains that would open major markets for growth (through gains of efficiency and innovations) lies elsewhere. Can the domestic and global governance of the ICT infrastructure adapt to seize these opportunities?

The chapters in part I explain the political economy of domestic ICT infrastructure policy.

Chapter 1 provides a brief overview of the argument.

Chapter 2 establishes a base line for the change by reviewing the first two eras of ICT development; it also explains the technological and political economic factors that drove the shifts in the American market from the 1950s until 2000.

Chapters 3 and 4 explain how an inflection point emerged after 2000, examine the technological drivers and changes in the global supply chain that make the inflection point possible, and strongly dispute popular assumptions about the technological and economic dimensions of the market's future. For example, since the 1970s market dominance first rested with AT&T and IBM, then moved on to the regional Bell operating companies and "Wintel" (Microsoft and Intel), and now seems to be heading toward Google. But the inflection point means that the last passing of the torch of market dominance will take a different form.

Chapter 5 describes the changing political economy of policy in the United States (the global pace setter). It re-examines the political and economic logic of debates over telecom competition policy, such as the debates over "net neutrality," content, and information-market policies.

Part II, a theoretical interlude, explores the political economy of global ICT evolution since the 1950s. It consists of a single chapter, which provides an analytic framework for understanding how and why global market governance rules and institutions change and which also examines the architecture of governance.

Part III comprises three case studies that take a finer-grained look at global market governance. In chapter 7 the general rules governing competition and pricing of global networks are considered. That chapter examines why governments moved as much authority over these issues from the International Telecommunication Union to the World Trade Organization as they did, and the international consequences that arose.

Chapter 8 considers the specialized world of standard setting and spectrum policy and the raw politics that shaped the infrastructure of wireless communications. Chapter 9 examines why the choices about institutional delegation for governance had important implications for the evolution of the Internet and for the creation of new global resources for networking.

The central question of the concluding chapter is "What should be done next?" In light of the political economy shaping policy options, how should prudent policy makers approach global market governance? In this chapter we set forth principles and norms for organizing decisions and provide examples of how programs might implement them. Our goal is not to lay out a detailed manifesto, but rather to sort out first principles for policy and then begin to imagine how innovations might turn principles into market realities.

The MIT Press has agreed to make the entire text of the book available online at the time of publication. Supplementary materials on the website explore topics touched on in the book in greater depth and provide background and explanatory materials. The online material is available at http://irps.ucsd.edu/globalinfoandtelecom/.

I   The Inflection Point

1 The Next Revolution in Global Information and Communication Markets

This book focuses on the ICT infrastructure, the intersection of communications networks with the infrastructure and applications of information technology. The networked information infrastructure that blends computing and communications is the largest construction project in human history. The money and the effort required to build this infrastructure dwarf what was needed to erect the pyramids of Egypt or the Great Wall of China. The initial investment created a huge global market for information and communications technology, estimated to grow to almost $4 trillion by 2009. (Figure 1.1 tracks the growth of the hardware, software, services, and communications market segments from 1999 to 2009.[1])

An inflection point, according to former Intel chairman Andy Grove, "occurs where the old strategic picture dissolves and gives way to the new."[2] Today we are at a new inflection point for the ICT infrastructure. All the components of the infrastructure are becoming modular, and powerful broadband networks are becoming ubiquitous. When we speak of modularity, think of Lego building blocks of many shapes that can be easily mixed and matched because they have standardized interfaces to stick them together. ICT technology is becoming both modular and radically cheaper. The equipment industry knows this path well, as is evident in consumer electronics. But now software and content are following the same path. At the same time, ubiquitous wired and wireless broadband can meld these ICT capabilities together into far more powerful applications, and these applications can escape the boundaries of office buildings and literally be everywhere.

Modularity and broadband mean that convergence of services and equipment will defy traditional market boundaries. Television programs seen in the United States may originate on French television broadcasts and be delivered to American viewers by broadband Internet. The distinctions between telephone and data services are rapidly disappearing. Decisions

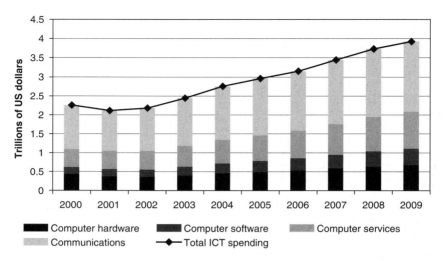

Figure 1.1
Total ICT spending, 2000–2009. Source: *Digital Planet: The Global Information Economy* (2006 report by World Information Technology and Services Alliance), at http://www.witsa.org.

on whether to store data on networked databases or on inexpensive home terminals are a matter of design form and function, because storage is cheap and Web browsers make it easier to switch between data formats. Players in ICT markets are scrambling to adapt to this rapidly emerging environment. Many of their assumptions about how ICT markets operate—assumptions based on competitive experience—will not be accurate guides to the future. Meanwhile, government policies have segmented the markets in ways that do not fit the new realities. In the absence of significant policy reforms, global economic prospects will diminish, perhaps markedly. This challenge raises the central question we address in this book: How can national and global policies best fulfill the promise of this inflection point in the global ICT infrastructure?

We are especially concerned with public policy because it was, and will continue to be, a critical driver of the ICT infrastructure's evolution. This may surprise some in the technology community, because it has a habit of retrospectively assuming that the march of technology was inevitable. But this view conveniently forgets the many battles over policy and markets that shaped the market's path. Consider, for example, the history of international long-distance services. In 1949, Wall Street attorneys still considered it a status symbol to "reserve" an operator-assisted call from New York to London. By 1979, you could punch a few numbers and the right phone would ring thousands of miles away, but high prices kept international calling a luxury. It was not until 1999 that the price of global calling plunged to the level of the mass market. The 20-year lag between techno-logical capability and attractive pricing was a product of policies and cor-porate strategies that propped up the cost of international calling. To change pricing required major shifts in national competition policy and in world trade rules. (See chapter 7.)

In 1967, television still offered only 5–10 channels, and programming was geared to the median viewer. In 2007, more than 100 channels appealed to minutely dissected audiences, such as aficionados of trout fishing or cooking. The proliferation of channels was stimulated by government poli-cies that limited the ability of a few networks to lock up programming rights. The growth of cable television, in turn, created a competing infra-structure for broadband computer networking. Today most channels still are national, but a combination of hardware and Web innovators is making a television program offered in any local market instantly available glob-ally. Dealing with the clash of digital universality and regulatory national-ism will require policy choices.

In 1984, telephone companies thought of computer networking as just another extension of phone calling, and they projected a computer network, operating at low speed, that would be rolled out at a stately pace. Computer networking and online commerce would look vastly different today if public policy had not cumulatively tilted in favor of the engineers and entrepreneurs who became the pioneers of the Internet architecture and its applications. The policy decisions that spurred network competi-tion accelerated the commercial deployment of email and hastened the triumph of the Internet. The Internet's roots rest firmly in a government-funded research community that was forced to become a protagonist in conflicts over ICT infrastructure policy. (See chapter 9.) Their engineering and policy triumphs made it possible for email messages, instant messages, and Web-based e-commerce using the Internet protocols to seamlessly tie the world together at a fraction of the price of phone calls. By 2007, YouTube and its Web rivals were serving up the personal videos of millions of amateur auteurs and traditional media companies were posting vignettes from their most popular broadcasts, thus setting the stage for policy con-tests over the control of intellectual property on the Web.

The triumph of the Internet, the increase in broadcast alternatives, and the dizzying flow of innovations on the Web are not the happy endings of a Hollywood tale of "white hats" and "black hats." The Internet did not emerge simply because wise engineers won support from enlightened government technocrats. It also depended on support from companies with particular competitive interests and from political leaders who wanted to position their parties as champions of the computer industry. In short, in today's world many different private interests back different visions of the public interest. Complex political bargaining and business strategizing produce politically inspired guidance of the modern ICT infrastructures. This is more than a struggle pitting the public interest against special interests.

We emphasize the importance of politics and policy because of the broader historical record. Throughout recorded history, governments have claimed a prominent role in shaping the infrastructure. Their specific roles changed over the centuries as enterprising rulers tried to consolidate their power by providing critical infrastructures (such as roads, water, energy, and communications) to promote security, health, and commerce.[3] Often, governments owned and operated these infrastructures.

Today, the private sector often owns and operates ICT infrastructures, and markets have become more competitive. Governments' interest remains strong, but competition and privatization have reoriented their role. ICT infrastructures, for example, have special economic characteristics that invite oversight by competition authorities. Moreover, all governments pursue other goals, among them universal service, industrial policy, national security, network reliability and security, and consumer protection. For example, balancing the efficient provision of the infrastructure and its services with social objectives (e.g., universal telephone service) has led to large distortions in ICT markets.

Governments' rules for ICT infrastructures rest on complex political and economic bargains, not always formally proclaimed. Some economists decry most government regulation, but the politicians' romance with intervention is (to borrow a phrase from Cole Porter) here to stay.

If politics shape important policy choices, whose politics matter the most for the world market? We argue that until about 2025 the United States will be able to lead, but not to dictate, the world's choices about future policies. China, India, and other countries will grow in influence, but the United States will remain the pivot for global choices.

What Is at Stake? The Implications of the Inflection Point

The future of the ICT infrastructure matters because during the last two decades ICT and an accompanying revolution in logistics (e.g., the advent of containerization) fundamentally reshaped the global economy. The production and the distribution of goods changed fundamentally as complex global supply chains changed where and how the world undertook these functions. The services supporting and complementing the "goods" economy, ranging from research and design through finance and logistics, became the dominant share of the world's output, and all these activities grew markedly more global, more information intensive, and more communications intensive. These upheavals resulted in a significant increase in the world's productivity and wealth.[4] The large stakes assure ICT of a prominent place on the global economic policy agenda for the foreseeable future. Chapter 2 explains the political economy of the revolution in ICT policy that was fundamental to these structural changes in the world economy.

Today's inflection point poses further challenges and opportunities for the ICT industry. Chapters 3 and 4 argue that several simultaneous changes in ICT alter the way in which the industry will operate and the potential for economic and technological innovation. Modularization is the increasing ability to mix and match individual terminals and sensors, pieces of software, massive computational capability, media, and data sources flexibly and experimentally. The emergence of ubiquitous broadband communications capabilities through flexible hybrids of wired and wireless networks greatly increases the potential scope of information-technology solutions. Together these changes constitute an inflection point that has two consequences.

First, the inflection point significantly changes competitive opportunities in the ICT industry. The niches of dominance for winners will continue to narrow. Historically, the high cost of entry, coupled with the economics of delivery and limited global markets for many ICT elements, meant mass market goods and services dominated markets. This created a limited set of "winner-take-all" firms with broad footprints across specific parts of the ICT stack.[5] Modularization allows greater convergence among functional capabilities. It lowers development costs and enables faster development. It also reduces the chance of vertical and horizontal leveraging of a strong market position. Economies of scale do not disappear with modularity (as exemplified by large-scale data storage and the economies of chip making), but market entry for many functions is much less expensive than it was in 2000, making competitive advantages less secure even if it remains lucrative in narrow niches or over the life span of a "hit" product. As a result, competition is waged on all fronts. Within product and service markets, the ability to enter and to challenge market leaders is, on the whole, greater. As computers challenge televisions, and as mobile phones challenge computers, there also is more competition over defining the market. Suppliers may dominate the market, but they may see its nature changing rapidly before their eyes.[6]

Second, the inflection point breaks ICT out of geographic and functional boxes, thereby opening new frontiers for applications. Put differently, it creates new models for technological and commercial innovations by permitting IT services to expand horizontally (e.g., outside large office buildings) and vertically (e.g., into the warehouse and onto the factory floor, or from the doctor's examining room and into sensors planted in the human body). The inflection point will prompt changes in high-end applications and then in mass applications of ICT. For example, even in industrial countries, experts report that higher-end broadband information services remain clustered in large commercial users. Factory floors often do not have routine provision of company email accounts. Further, although low-bandwidth applications are becoming available by wireless, the innovation space for imagining information services remains stunted outside the commercial centers because powerful computing and bandwidth are not cost effective.[7]

At the high end, grid-style computing networks for supercomputing, ultra-broadband networks, and new imaging tools are revolutionizing the foundations of science. Scientists envision a new generation of technological innovation as they deploy protocols to bind together supercomputing, advanced visualization tools, large-scale data gathering by billions of sensors, and ultra-broadband networks to enable real-time virtual collaboration among labs around the world.

Typically, the networked ICT experiments in the research community reach high-end commercial applications within 7 years and the mass market in about 12 years. In 2008, the largest traffic flow on fiber-optic networks was illegal movie sharing. By about 2020, it will be massively interactive applications combining video, data, and computing. Imagine truly interactive, remote medical examinations that make current efforts look like silent movies. Think of the shift in aerodynamic design of objects for energy conservation that will occur because communities of individual experimenters will share costs through ultra-broadband access to "community" wind tunnels and high-end simulation facilities. Or picture hundreds of thousands of interactive "Web channels" blossoming as the cost of virtual video productions plummets and as computing drives production values up and costs down. Visualize what will happen when the successors to Google Earth go far beyond searching websites for satellite images. These sites could gather live feeds from neighborhood cameras and individual cell phones, assimilate data on personal preference patterns of network users in a region, and deploy formulas dissecting time-of-day behavior in neighborhoods to help a person decide where to spend a Saturday night.[8]

Each of these innovations requires modular combinatorial advances from the inflection point and also requires policy decisions that stimulate competitive ICT infrastructures to cut prices and to be responsive to users' experimentation with the network. They also require policies that enable privacy, intellectual property, and traditional broadcast content to be "diced and spliced" while meeting agreed-upon public standards of protection.

Why Global Politics and Policy Matter

Even among those passionately concerned about technology, many also assume—wrongly, we think—that if governments stand aside, the technology will sweep away all obstacles and bring widespread worldwide prosperity. Others assume that the real challenge is to get governments out of the pockets of large corporations and to unleash digitally enabled "people power." Although the follies of government can be incredible and the lobbying muscle of big business often is immense, these views are mistaken.

We have already explained why ICT infrastructures are inherently political. It is equally important to grasp why its policies and politics are inherently global. Marketplace reforms at home demand complementary actions at the global level. And global governance is deeply entangled with power and politics.

The Global Dimensions of ICT Network Governance
There are at least four reasons why the domestic governance of ICT infrastructure depends on global arrangements. First, network externalities ensure that networks are more valuable when they connect more users. National networks gain even more value if they connect internationally. Making that feasible when there is divided governance requires negotiation among national authorities. These issues are tied both to the cost of connecting to foreign users and to the technology and technical standards needed to make this possible. Second, economies of scale still apply in similar ways to the engineering and the economics of networks. This invites the growth of regional and global suppliers whose fate partly

depends on the rules governing the provisioning of networks. The supply base influences the characteristics of innovation and cost for the national ICT infrastructure. Third, the pricing of networks usually is affected by governments, but even when prices are determined entirely by markets, a raft of unusual strategic dimensions arise because of the particular features of network economics. As a result, the pricing for connecting domestic networks internationally often displays unusual characteristics that matter to many political stakeholders. Changes in global circumstances can cause major strategic shifts in the marketplace. Fourth, concerns over sovereignty issues make it likely that the public holds government responsible for the quality of networked infrastructures. Political leadership encourages this equation, ensuring that the national control of networks becomes highly political. This has major consequences for the performance of networks.

Power Politics and Global Coordination about Networking

No government begins by asking "How can we optimize efficiency and equity for global networking?" Rather, responsible governments begin by seeking ways to improve their public and national interests. They ask "What set of global arrangements complement existing or desired domestic arrangements?" Many of the regulatory arrangements for world markets look odd and haphazard from the viewpoint of functional efficiency because they were political first and functional second.

Powerful markets get more of what they seek than weaker ones. Since World War II, the United States, the most powerful economic actor, usually has played the leading role in the story of global transformation. For that reason, we focus on how America's domestic political economy shaped its policy choices and on how these decisions have bent the direction of global governance of ICT infrastructures in surprising ways since 1945. The new policy choices posed by the inflection point will occur before 2025, while the US is still the world market's political, economic, and technological pivot.

Our assertion about US predominance will strike many as controversial. The global market for ICT will grow rapidly, with a continuous stream of new technological frontiers opening. The United States will not be the leader in every market segment. Digital technology and modular production systems will reinforce the segmentation and diversity of market leadership. Skype's software came out of Estonia and Sweden, not Silicon Valley. China's and India's supply and demand advantages (low-paid engineers and vast untapped consumer markets) will be formidable. Many expect their challenge to US dominance to ascend from the lower end of the market into higher, value-added layers, and to ensure their supremacy by 2020. Continental Asia, led by Huawei and other Chinese producers, could displace the United States, Europe, and Japan as the largest center for growth of network equipment.

However, the United States dominates the market segment and the technology innovations that drive the inflection point. The US is at the forefront of major breakthroughs, including the combination of grid computing systems with powerful wireless broadband and the creation of remote sensor networks. It remains the undisputed leader in software innovation. US venture funding far outstrips international spending.[9] A powerful research infrastructure will feed these breakthroughs, propelling a newly integrated market for business and consumer services. Furthermore, these breakthroughs will yield critical competitive and innovation dynamics that cater to the strengths of the US if inept policies do not critically undermine the potential of the US for leadership.

We have emphasized the pivotal role of the United States because to do otherwise would be to ignore strategic realities underlying long-term calculations of global stakeholders. But, with apologies to *Damn Yankees*, we are not simply telling a story of "what the US wants, the US gets." Although the US plays a pivotal strategic role, other countries are influential. Just as crucially, the rules for global decision making rarely conform to the straightforward logic of fulfilling the wishes of the strongest country. Indeed, market governance in a world of decentralized authority and imperfect information about motives and behavior profoundly slants the organization of global networking. Global networking has a political economic architecture as well as an engineering architecture. In this book, we explain the implications of this architecture.

Market Governance and the Policy Implications of the Inflection Point

If the political economy of the ICT market shapes the direction of technology and the market through policy choices, how do we grasp the essentials of the policy mix underpinning the market? The legal rulebooks governing ICT infrastructures are ponderous, and the interpretative analyses of them are numbingly complex. It is easy to lose the structure in the thicket of individual issues. To make the issues analytically tractable, we identify their central features using the concept of market governance.[10]

Global market governance is the mixture of formal and informal rules and the expectations about how markets should logically operate. These "principles" and "norms" embraced by active stakeholders govern expected behavior. The stakeholders are the actors and groups with strong interest in governance. A major function of governance is to convey an understanding of these expectations and their implications for all stakeholders.

international policies. The growth of stock markets (specialized, privately controlled, transaction-based institutions that were accountable to governments) was analogous.[11] Global governance will require more reliance on non-governmental institutions to coordinate and implement global policy. These institutions should be accountable to governments and should be transparent, but they can be more effective than traditional international organizations. At the same time, the new governance regime should flexibly reshuffle the mandates of inter-governmental arrangements. For example, we consistently advocate an expanded role for trade institutions as appropriate forums for setting governance rules for the inflection point. The World Trade Organization, in a way little noticed by those outside the community of trade specialists, has evolved special arrangements for the information economy that can accommodate sophisticated compromises on governance that allow national flexibility on policies while providing essential global accountability. Even if negotiations on global trade agreements bog down as they did in Geneva at the end of July 2008, the new tools for governance eventually forged at the WTO can inform the options used in other international arrangements, such as the Asia-Pacific Economic Community.

Whatever the specific policy choices, this book explains the logic of changes in political economy and the architecture of global governance that shape the world's choices for ICT infrastructure policy. It grounds this explanation in an analysis of the inflection point in the technological frontier that will force those with commercial interests and those who analyze ICT policy to reconsider past assumptions and policy compromises. Not every piece of our analysis will prove right. That's the nature of exploring frontiers. Our goal is to clarify the underlying foundations of thousands of technological developments and policy spats so as to illuminate a path to a revised governance structure for the ICT infrastructure that is reshaping the world.

2 The First Two ICT Eras

The organization of the global ICT infrastructure shifted dramatically from the mid 1950s through the end of 2000. Technology and policy changes drove the shift.

In the early years, ICT was essentially two markets: a monopoly telecom marketplace and a distinct, concentrated computer and software industry centered on mainframes and mini-computers. During the 1960s and the 1970s, the growth of data networking and nascent competition in equipment and value-added services led to increased value-added competition in both services and equipment as a limited exception to monopoly. As networking matured, it gradually brought these two markets together into an integrated ICT market. This ultimately led to the breakup of AT&T (which occurred on January 1, 1984) and to the introduction of more sweeping competition and subsequent innovations in the market, particularly in the United States. The introduction to the mass market of the first model of the IBM personal computer (in August 1981) accompanied increasing competition and innovation in the telecom markets.[1] The deployment of the PC across the business and consumer landscape fueled the growth of client-server architecture, created new packaged software markets (enterprise resource planning, productivity software) and consumer uses (word processing, graphic design), and defined the architecture for a generation of devices and applications. The network's scope, its performance, and market-based networked applications continued to evolve in response to the growth of the Internet during the 1990s.

This chapter outlines the evolution of ICT markets during two distinct periods since the 1950s. The first period begins during the early postwar years and extends to the breakup of AT&T. The second period stretches from 1984 to about 2000. (The post-2000 period is discussed in chapters 3–5.)

Before plunging into the details, it is useful to mention three long-term trends in the ICT infrastructure. The first trend involves the end points on the ICT networks: What is their number, scope (ubiquity), and heterogeneity? How many and what type of processors and data sources connect at the edge of the network? Consider the evolution of terminals. First there were voice-only dumb terminals, then there were dumb data terminals, and finally powerful networked PC terminals emerged. The second trend involves the price point for a specific speed or quality of service in ICT markets. This point determines which applications might be usefully deployed across a network. Sometimes performance levels are not available. (During the 1980s there was no commercial 256K data transport.) At other times the main issue is price and therefore widespread deployment. (Home broadband networking was too expensive during the late 1990s for many applications that were emerging in 2005.) The third trend involves the breadth of applications that are supported by the network, as determined by the processing capabilities, the location of the processing and application logic, and interoperability across the network. Mainframes were limited in their processing power and in their ability to run applications that relied on data from multiple systems and resources. Client-server architectures continue to evolve. Cable televisions running on cable networks once mainly relied on dumb data-entry terminals. But as applications increasingly run partly in "the Cloud" and partly on devices at the edge (see chapter 4), additional flexibility and resources both at the edge and in the network will be needed.

Here, two policy elements are highlighted: (1) The ICT industry gradually grew more modular since the 1950s. The 1968 Carterfone decision was especially momentous in extending modularity. It introduced disruptive new rules that allowed firms to connect equipment to the public network so long as it caused no harm.[2] The slow march toward greater modularity continues and may be accelerating. (2) In parallel, governments undertook pro-competitive policies. They increasingly embraced policy interventions that promoted competing infrastructures to enhance service competition and, also pressured competitors to embrace modularity. For example, the AT&T breakup, the IBM plug-and-play intervention, and the Microsoft antitrust case all aimed at limiting the ability of leading firms in important network segments to leverage their positions in one network element into downstream or upstream elements.

Technology and Market Evolution: 1950s–1983

The first phase of convergence of computing, software, and communications began in the mid 1950s and extended through 1983. Except in the

United States and a few smaller countries, the telecom market was characterized by government ownership of monopoly carriers with extensive cross-subsidies to achieve universal voice access. Transmission quality and throughput were optimized for voice networks, which made adding networking capabilities difficult and expensive. Until the mid 1970s, network intelligence was expensive and highly centralized in order to concentrate network switching at the top of a hierarchy of switches.[3] Network transmission capacity was sparse, expensive, and specialized. This meant that intelligence in the network was limited and that expanding intelligence was expensive and physically difficult. Early networking services were geared toward large business users and were slow. Quality voice services required 64 kilobits per second; data rates on these circuits were far slower and less reliable. As a result, networking focused almost exclusively on large business centers. Telecommunications and broadcast required separate transmission networks. Even the introduction of two new broadcast infrastructures, cable and direct satellite broadcast to the home, were dedicated specialized infrastructures. When computer networking took off, issues involving the quality, the speed of transmission, and related technical issues made the traditional networks' practices inadequate for the new data networks.[4]

This era was characterized by limited deployment of low-performance IT. Most systems had limited processing capacity and dedicated linkages across hardware and software elements. Early on, the major IT users were governments and large enterprise buyers. Even after the 1956 IBM "Plug and Play Compatible" antitrust decision partially separated the hardware and software markets, IT was mostly dominated by significant data processing applications for the largest government and enterprise buyers. The 1969 IBM consent decree finally decoupled hardware and software, opening the door open to a stand-alone software industry separate from hardware vendors.

During the 1960s, stresses to this structure emerged as the speed of networks increased. New industries appeared that sought entry into various parts of the market.[5] Rivalry for the terminal equipment on the communications network emerged in the late 1950s as large users sought specialized functions that traditional telephone networks had trouble meeting. More stresses emerged as the speed of networks increased. New industries appeared and sought entry into various parts of the market. The initial introduction of what is now called "modularity" provided the conceptual policy breakthrough that helped address potential conflicts between those intent on connecting equipment to the network and those demanding the protection of network integrity. It quickly became evident that transparent network standards for interfacing with equipment could allow a variety of manufacturers to supply equipment and evolve new technical features.

On the computing side, the mainframe computing experience produced a growing pool of programmers who could write code independent of the big computer companies. US public policy helped drive this market evolution. Specifically, the government antitrust suit against IBM led to the decoupling of hardware and software. This promoted the take-off of an independent software industry featuring packaged software,[6] a software industry quite different from the one associated with the PC industry. Still, this development started to erode IBM's dominance and contributed to the move toward modularity in computing hardware and software.

Changes in network performance and the emergence of a stand-alone software industry were important, but the most disruptive development during the 1960s and the 1970s was the rise of computer and corporate networking. Networking opened new markets for firms, sparked new demands from users, and required new policy responses. Policy makers recognized that the status quo was no longer sustainable. On the telecom side, new rules made it easier to attach terminal equipment to the telecom network, liberalized entry into data networking, and allowed private corporate networks for voice and data services. In services, the new entrants slowly undercut AT&T's dominance in long-distance and data transmission facilities and services. Prices responded; service innovations followed.[7] The United States was the exception during this period. Most of the world's markets were dominated by vertically integrated, government-owned firms with close ties to vertically integrated equipment providers.

The following is a summary of what happened from the 1950s through 1983:

• The number, ubiquity, and heterogeneity of network end points accelerated as PC connections to the Internet proliferated and as voice and data mobility spread.
• The price for services of comparable quality and speed declined sharply. The decline in cost structures spanned applications and services.
• The breadth of applications supported by the network increased substantially.

Technology and Market Evolution: 1984–2000

The second phase of convergence of computing, software, and communications began with the breakup of AT&T in 1984 and extended through

2000. The gathering momentum of the microprocessor revolution for personal computing, competition in communications networking, and a second generation of computer networking architecture shifted the market horizon again. By the mid 1980s, the semiconductor industry began to enable deeper network architecture changes and revolutionize ICT devices' power at the edge of the network. Telecommunications switching grew more sophisticated, but this happened more slowly than intelligence could be incorporated in computers and other devices operating at the network's edge. This "flipped" the logic of network architecture even as Moore's Law took hold and the spread of PCs in business and consumer arenas created new demands for networked applications and services.

The telecommunications market was characterized by the gradual but forceful introduction of competition in all infrastructure, hardware, software, and services segments. Two important consequences were the build-out of narrowband dial-up networking in the consumer marketplace and the beginning of broadband to the home. Dramatic improvements in the capacity and cost of lasers and electronics and the explosion of data traffic they prompted led to the build-out of backbone fiber and broadband to more business users. Another result was the beginning of metropolitan fiber networks and broadband consumer networks. Transmission capacity expanded dramatically, from snail-paced modems dripping out data at 128K to the T3 (45 megabits per second) connections that became routine for larger enterprises.[8]

Another major development was the explosive growth of mobile wireless. In developing countries mobile wireless connections rapidly overtook wireline connections when the introduction of second-generation ("2G") systems greatly upgraded capacity and quality while reducing costs. By 2000, mobile communications had emerged as a vertically integrated competitor to the wired network in all market segments except for data.

The Internet and its commercialization also were hugely important. The Internet revolutionized the architecture and underlying capacity of the network. The beginnings of inter-networking dated from the mid 1980s (Cisco shipped its first router in 1986), when companies and network providers began to "inter-connect" their networks. In 1991 US policy changes enabled the commercial use of the Internet. This set the stage for the ICT growth of the 1990s. By 1994, the Internet swamped commercial email services. In August 1995, Netscape went public, igniting the "dot com" boom. In the United States, and to a limited extent elsewhere, new Internet services providers (AOL, MSN) and later large content and e-commerce applications (Yahoo, @Home, eBay) aimed to take advantage of the network's power and scope. A myriad of smaller, more specialized applications also emerged that built their businesses on powerful, cheaper PCs, broadband networking at the office, and widespread narrowband networking in the home.

The burgeoning PC market, advances in the PC's operating systems, and the growth of networked enterprise computing supported the development of new, packaged, mass consumption, software applications and attracted enormous investment in, and innovation around, PC-based software.[9] Declining price/performance ratios spurred widespread deployment and adoption of vast enterprise software packages to manage enterprise-wide processes and data. Packaged software for PCs opened the way to greater complementarity of software products, particularly between the Microsoft software platform and specialized software applications. This strengthened Microsoft's position by creating a new set of hardware and software industries focused on the PC ecosystem, from mice to games to semiconductors. The emergence of the Internet and in particular a new PC application used to "browse" content and services, reinforced the client-server architecture that dominated enterprise architectures.

In the mid 1990s, serious challenges began to undermine the existing technology, economics, and policy equilibria. Technologically, the growth of Internet standards, data protocols, and Application Programming Interfaces (APIs) outside the control of any single platform vendor created momentum for more open APIs. On the PC, Microsoft defined the APIs that other applications used to interact with Windows. Microsoft's power provoked strong opposition, which led to intense commercial rivalries and disputes. From the Microsoft litigation an important legal right emerged that allowed software developers to reverse engineer software interfaces to create complementary and substitute software.[10] Limitations on the extent of Microsoft pricing flexibility across original equipment manufacturers and the requirement that Microsoft publicly share terms of OEM agreements were related and equally important parts of the Microsoft antitrust settlement. This limited the ability of Microsoft to "punish" OEMs for inclusion of competing software on Windows machines or for shipping non-Windows computers.

The emergence of the Internet provided Tim Berners-Lee with the base from which he launched a suite of software applications—now known as "the World Wide Web"—that further altered these dynamics.[11] HTML, the programming language that enabled the Web, consciously avoided the Microsoft approach and embraced open APIs. Netscape's Web browser and the subsequent inclusion of Microsoft's browser in Windows sounded the death knell of Internet Service Providers (ISPs) that forced consumers to rely on proprietary software systems to access the Web.[12]

Another major change was the quiet but fundamental transformation of the ICT production system. Traditionally, vertically integrated firms in both telecom and IT delivered complete systems (hardware, software, integration services, and support) to customers. By the late 1980s, international challenges from Japanese electronics vendors and the growth of the software industry created pressures[13] and opportunities for vertical disintegration, commoditization, co-competition in equipment and services, and a dynamic of user co-invention of breakthroughs.[14] The breakup of AT&T began the dynamic vertical disintegration of the telecommunications network into local and long-distance services. In the 1990s, the advent of a new class of specialized fiber-optic transport networks, of which Level 3 was the most prominent example, segmented the market further.[15] Forces for commoditization and competition augmented those of vertical disintegration. Barriers to entry generally declined and global production networks increased the universe of potential entrants in one niche after another.[16] Speed and declining barriers to entry meant that the life cycles of products became shorter and the ability to maintain premium pricing declined rapidly for most products. Demands from sophisticated IT and telecom users also began to set the agenda that new vendors scrambled to meet. They illustrated the forces of co-invention by users of digital technology.[17] The evolution of more flexible and less expensive modular systems made it easier for users to innovate in critical technologies directly or by working intensively with suppliers. The rebellion of the office floor against centralized computing proved a springboard for local area networking of desktop computers. The growth of the Web browser and the Web opened a mass consumer market. Amazon, eBay, and others introduced another set of complementary users and vendors built around e-commerce. This dynamic played out first and proceeded furthest in the United States, but other countries moved down the same path.[18]

Meanwhile, after several fruitless efforts to mandate standards for computer networking, Western Europe reluctantly made plans for wide-ranging competition in the wired network infrastructure. The cost efficiencies and technology and service innovations that occurred in the United States eluded Europe.[19] With the notable exception of Finland, most of Europe did not introduce general wired network competition until 1998. Mobile competition (usually in the form of duopoly) sprang up earlier, but few in Europe believed that this limited competition would have major implications for the wired network.

Broadband networks for households became common in Asia, in Europe, and in North America during the late 1990s, causing many countries to rethink their policies. The crucial point in broadband deployment was the determination of most countries to close the gap with the United States in Internet connectivity (using telephone dial-up modems) and to leapfrog it as broadband deployed. This is precisely what occurred. In mid 2007, the top five world leaders in fast, affordable broadband networks were Denmark, the Netherlands, Switzerland, Korea, and Norway. In June 2007, the US ranked 15th globally in broadband Internet penetration. From June 2006 to June 2007, the number of broadband subscribers in OECD countries grew by 24 percent, from 178 million to 221 million.[20] These shifts were caused as much by policy and politics as by the technological decisions discussed in later chapters. The same dynamics almost certainly will drive broadband for wireless and mobile services. Historic broadband penetration from 2001 to 2007 for the OECD countries as a group and for the major countries is tracked in figure 2.1.

The Political Economy of Marketplace Change in the United States

At the core of our argument about the political economy of markets are political institutions and their impact on the incentives and authority of elected politicians to shape marketplace outcomes to the advantage of specific sets of constituents. In view of the importance of the United States in global ICT markets and the centrality of the American institutional argument for later chapters, this section sketches our institutional argument in the context of the first two ICT eras in the US.

The American political system has three salient features relevant to communications policy: the division of powers, the majoritarian electoral system, and federalism.[21] First, the division of powers in the US government was designed to make it difficult to initiate major policy changes but also difficult to rapidly undo major commitments. The division between the president and Congress (and between the two houses of Congress, one based on population and the other on equal representation for each state) creates many points during the decision process at which an initiative can be stopped.[22] This hampers the passage of major changes in laws that have sweeping geographic consequences and a wide range of winners and losers. Only two major US telecommunications laws were passed during the twentieth century: one in 1932 and one in 1996. Thus, much of the decision making about federal policy resides at the Federal Communications Commission, which is charged with implementing the acts.

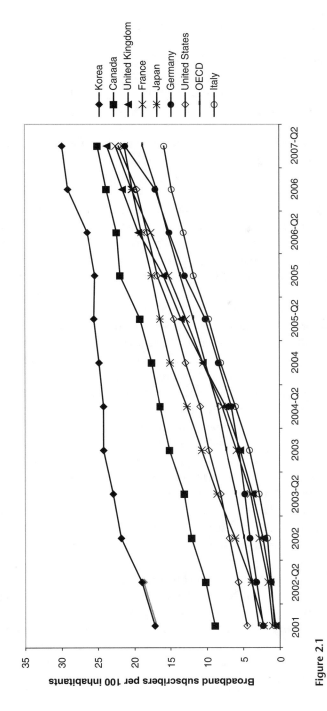

Figure 2.1

Broadband penetration, historic G7 countries plus Korea. Source: "OECD Broadband Statistics to June 2007," Organization for Economic Cooperation and Development, October 13, 2007.

The inherent conflict between the executive and legislative branches means that Congress is less willing to grant the kinds of discretion to executive bureaucracies that are found in parliamentary democracies, where the division between the executive and the legislature is more blurred.[23] In some areas Congress recognizes the need for a substantial amount of expert bureaucratic authority. Thus, the FCC is allowed to deal with complicated issues where many of the detailed political costs and benefits are difficult to determine. Congress then uses a variety of devices to delegate power to the bureaucracy with specialized controls.

Congress confirms FCC commissioners nominated by the president and stipulates a 3–2 split of commissioners, with the president's party holding the majority and the chairmanship. The political sensibilities of the major parties thus are replicated in the FCC's majority voting system. (Commissioners are political appointees, but usually are more technocratic and less ideological than members of Congress.) Congress also uses the power of the purse by threatening to use its budgetary powers to instruct the FCC on certain issues—for example, barring the FCC from using public funds to create rules to auction communications satellite spectrum. Similarly, it mandates elaborate FCC procedures to ensure transparency in decision making so that all interested parties will have access to the decision process. Members of Congress can observe the process with an eye to politics, and can try to influence FCC if there is a compelling political interest.[24] These complexities constrain the FCC's flexibility and complicate its ability to focus on competition problems when they arise. Thus, when such problems are identified, the FCC relies more on elaborate "ex ante" rules than on ad hoc solutions. The net result is that the FCC responds to presidential and congressional politics but is legally empowered to make important discretionary policy. It is subject to judicial review for its adherence to a reasonable reading of the underlying law. It bases its decisions on its analytic judgment, the evidence on the public record developed in each procedure, and an instruction to use this discretion to serve the public interest. These expert and transparent but politically informed decisions influence market dynamics.

A second feature of the US political institutions is that presidential and congressional elections are based on winner-take-all voting. Analysts of electoral systems have shown that this voting system builds a strong interest in "brand identity" for political parties. Despite the role of lobbying and campaign contributions, parties invest to develop a reputation with policy initiatives on broad issues that they believe will mobilize elite and mass electoral support.

Telecommunications policy traditionally influenced the high technology industry and research communities. It achieved broad political salience to the voting public in two ways: (1) To promote equity, there was continuing sensitivity to telephone pricing, and now broadband pricing. (2) It was part of the broader debates over economic policy, including the debates over "deregulating" the American economy and the creation of the "new" or "Internet" economy to stimulate growth. Thus, the Clinton administration highlighted its telecommunications policy to polish its reputation as pro-competition and pro-innovation.[25] It bragged about early US leadership in the mass adoption of the Internet. Similarly, the George W. Bush administration worried about the potential embarrassment of America's lagging position on deployment of broadband.

A third feature of the institutional context is federalism, the division of authority between the federal and state governments. The US Constitution reserves all powers not given explicitly to the federal government for the states. Moreover, each state is allocated two senators, regardless of its population. This increases the power of low-population farm and mining states at the expense of heavily populated, urbanized states. Federalism matters for telecommunications policy directly and indirectly. It directly impacts the subsidy of rural communications users and providers, which powerfully constrains all regulatory policies influencing pricing and competition. Federalism indirectly provides a foundation for strong competition policy. State authorities used competition policy to shelter local competitors from dominant national competitors that held various advantages over them and smaller firms would enlist the support of their senators. The pivotal role of rural states in the Senate also heightened interest in competition rules that emphasized consumer welfare because those states have less interest in industrial policy favoring national champions.[26] The result was an economy with broad geographic scope for its competitive firms and far less concentration in its major industries, including telecommunications and electronics, than its counterparts in other major countries.[27] The US also had a telecom market whose behavior was skewed by a pricing structure that bore little relationship to efficient costing. The implications for telecommunications policy were profound.

The Political Economy of the First Era (1950–1983)

As was demonstrated many times between the 1950s and 2000, even with divided powers, policy evolution can move quickly if economic interests and political institutions are aligned. In this era, the United States was by far the largest ICT market and its economy had a continental scope. As it became evident that there was strong political support for policies strengthening competition, the scale of the American market allowed pro-entry policies to open the market to new entrants while simultaneously retaining market scope for incumbents. New services became available for large enterprise users that were deploying ICT to help enable new production and service processes that they needed to stay competitive nationally and internationally. Large enterprise buyers also began using long-distance telephony to increase branch coordination.[28] This produced a group of large potential customers concerned with the market's organization among sophisticated firms and guaranteed an environment favorable for political entrepreneurship. Thus, policy changes unfolded faster in the United States than elsewhere.

The role of large users mattered because they were transformed by ICT and intensified their policy advocacy. Eventually, ICT became more than a cost factor for US-based multinational firms. In response to rising competition, US financial institutions and many manufacturing firms evolved into information analysis companies that deliver information in the form of, for example, a global financial or engineering product. Global banks no longer focus mainly on checking or mortgages. Their edge comes from complex and ultimately riskier financial products that rest on high levels of computing and global information operations that are rolled out quickly on a global scale over their ICT infrastructures. Multinational manufacturers understand that the cost and quality of production are important, but the information intensive, global design and service functions are their critical edge. Boeing executives sometimes joked that an airplane is a flying software stack because there is more value added in the complex programming than in the sophisticated airframe.[29] This fundamental shift in the strategic use of ICT persuaded these firms to become committed advocates for changes in ICT markets.

The political institutional legacy of the American market structure shaped the way that emerging interests played out. No firm legal basis for AT&T's national long-distance monopoly existed, and many smaller telecom carriers remained in small states and rural areas. This lacuna arose because it always proved politically difficult to craft legislation to authorize (or, later, to preserve) a monopoly. In addition, previous antitrust actions created huge electronics firms that rivaled AT&T and lusted to supply equipment to American telecommunications networks. In 1956 their limited antitrust victory forced Bell Labs to license its technology to them at little or no cost. Meanwhile, federal power sharing with the states with regard to telecom pricing and a sympathetic Senate restricted AT&T's ability to lower long-distance costs so that the transfer of funds to support smaller rural carriers could continue.[30] AT&T offered special discounts to large corporate customers, but could not offer true cost-related pricing. Thus, large customers continued to seek market change.

The growth of computer networking, especially by IBM's smaller rivals, created another powerful set of motivated allies that were unhappy with AT&T's dominance.[31] An IBM "plug compatible" industry grew up that targeted the networking market. This led directly to the formation of a "corporate competition coalition" made up of computer companies that wanted to create customized computer networks or feared AT&T's entry into the computer equipment market. The computer companies were joined by large corporate clients, smaller electronics equipment vendors, would-be resellers of basic phone services, and government agencies, all seeking better deals.[32]

Increasingly, governance was guided by a new principle: modularity. It became common to distinguish among "basic phone services" provided over the general public network, the equipment that enabled it, and new advanced communications and equipment functions made possible by new electronic and computing technologies. Momentum grew to competitively deploy new "value-added" services and equipment.

Four important norms emerged that enabled greater modularity. The roots of the first norm came in 1956, when the limited liberalization of attachment of terminal equipment was allowed. Twelve years later, the Carterfone decision opened the way toward full freedom of competition in equipment attached to the network by creating the first norm to implement modularity. The FCC held that new equipment attached to the network was acceptable if it did "no harm to the network." The FCC recognized that the demands for computer networking required less restrictive equipment markets.[33]

The "no harm to the network" norm implied a freedom of choice that grew into a second norm, technology neutrality that resonated with US political and market institutions. The US rarely picks civilian technology champions. Its diverse economy usually does not generate political agreement on a single technology path for any market. Further, by the 1980s US policy makers questioned whether they could readjust their direction if they chose the wrong technology path. For these reasons, neutrality seemed a sound policy norm with political merit.[34]

At the same time, the FCC lurched toward allowing competition in the provision of networked computer data services. In 1959, AT&T Long Lines established a discount rate for its largest corporate and government

presidential and congressional political agendas. Political parties strive to be national policy entrepreneurs. Democrats and Republicans both saw deregulation as a way to show their commitment to revive the American economy.[38] The political economic interests of the corporate competition coalition reinforced their enthusiasm for deregulation.

Renewed antitrust action during the Carter administration set the stage for the breakup of AT&T during the Reagan administration. The decision reflected American political institutions. First, the courts followed established antitrust law that arose from the US political economy and favored a consumer-welfare standard. America's federal system produced this legal approach and a court system with the latitude to back it up. Second, the president and Congress cannot easily take decisive legislative action to steer an industry because it can be blocked at many points. This structural factor sidetracked AT&T's attempt to legislatively assert it monopoly, repulsed increasing pressure from MCI and other upstarts, and convinced a generation of entrepreneurial politicians that identification with AT&T's critics was politically advantageous. Even the Democratic Party, predisposed to supporting organized labor and therefore a likely ally of AT&T and its union members, spawned a generation of "Atari Democrats" critical of monopoly. Economic conservatives in the Republican Party joined them. This coalition sufficed to block pre-emptive legislation to preserve the phone monopoly. Third, although the president and many in Congress were wary of the AT&T antitrust decision, they did not try to overturn it because they saw it as politically risky to favor monopoly.[39] Fourth, the settlement made sense because it could withstand political pressures to protect incumbents before and after the AT&T breakup. The long-distance competition by the new AT&T and monopoly phone services for the new regional Bells mandated by the court protected both local and rural telephone service pricing. The FCC and state public utility commissions could mandate cross-subsidies from long-distance carriers to local phone monopolies and still allow competition to improve services and lower long-distance pricing. Lower long-distance prices appealed to the middle class that tended to vote more than other Americans. Because it did not unwind local subsidies quickly, network competition also appealed to the corporate competition coalition by providing a strong, politically sustainable competition platform.[40]

The outline of a new managed-entry regime that would dominate the United States and then prevail globally emerged from the struggle over the fate of AT&T. The principle of favoring competitive network infrastructures led to the extension of the earlier norm that forced dominant networks that controlled essential bottleneck facilities to share their capabilities with new rivals to promote rapid industry entry. This required detailed FCC supervision of interconnection by dominant carriers. The challenge was to police against bottlenecks in a way that allowed market forces to rationalize costs, staffing, and prices. Tools such as price caps and dominant carrier regulation were designed to foster pro-competitive interconnection with new entrants and allow pricing rationalization.

Three norms supplemented this competition principle and made it politically practical. First, regulators should adjust prices of local services, without allowing rapid price escalation. Competition had to be reconciled with this goal. Second, to cash in on the political promise of competition, regulatory reforms should promote technological and service innovation for ICT, including lower prices. Economic theory argued for maximizing consumer welfare. This norm clarified what political leaders meant by "consumer welfare." Third, policy makers should be sensitive to employment effects. They could allow labor staffing to decline in dominant incumbents, but needed to cushion job losses by encouraging the entry of new companies which might offset the downsizing of old incumbents.

This mixture seemed politically successful. Prices for long-distance and data services decreased significantly. Service innovation climbed. Initially, computer networking rose and then soared as the importance of the Internet spurted. Politicians could boast that new entrants helped revive American fortunes in the computer and computer networking equipment markets. But trouble was brewing.

The push for technological and economic efficiency ultimately raised two issues. The first issue was purely a product of technological innovation: How should the potential for mobile wireless networks be used to boost competitive network infrastructures? Second, what role should the Bells play? Why should they be barred from entering the long-distance market when their entry might further reduce prices? But how could complete network innovation and competition be achieved in the absence of contestable markets for local communication services and infrastructure? This huge market still wore a regulatory straitjacket.

Originally, mobile services were offered as a duopoly in the United States and most other industrial countries; invariably the local phone company received one of the licenses.[41] The introduction of second-generation wireless services in the 1990s permitted more competition. More competition promised the political benefit of better prices and services for consumers. The largest telecom carriers and equipment suppliers sought lush new growth markets. And, to the hidden relief to all involved, mobile services still seemed a luxury good that would not significantly substitute for wired voice services. So mobile seemed an area ripe for political profit and innovation. But how?

Policy experts in both political parties favored auctions to more efficiently assign spectrum licenses. The principle was that a properly organized system of market bidding provided more accurate cues for assigning and valuing a scarce national resource (government-controlled spectrum) than discretionary decisions by government officials. This option was embraced because auctions would be easier for new entrants, which might be less connected politically before the auction, but would be grateful afterwards. National spectrum auctions also promised to reduce the federal budget deficit by raising large sums of money. This was a goal of both political parties, of the president, and of Congress.

When the FCC designed its auction system, it envisioned obtaining four to six competitors in every American market.[42] The FCC reasoned that if four to six competitors each had enough spectrum to support a significant network and service offerings, none could dominate. Although continued scrutiny of the interconnection of wireless with wired networks might be necessary, regulators expected that the interconnection rules for wireless networks could be much lighter than those for wired networks. Uniquely, the FCC mandated very low wireless-wire interconnection charges. Only the United States had a multi-firm market and low fees. Other nations slowed the growth of wireless by imposing high fees wireless paid to wire. (The EU imposed high fees, but offset them with limited wireless competition that let wireless carrieers flourish financially.) These differences mattered when there were few wireless customers and almost all their calls went to wire. Now wireless talks to wireless, and this starter move matters less than it once did.[43] Thus, wireless presented a glimpse of what ICT markets after the end of dominant control of bottleneck facilities might achieve.

The other important wireless choice involved technology policy. As with computing and terminal equipment for wired networks, on wireless the FCC adopted a norm of technology neutrality. The deployment of multiple architectures resulted. Although the timing varied by market segment, the cost of diverse architectures caused some confusion and delay in deployment of features requiring mass scale. This tracked exactly earlier computer industry developments. Originally, the United States trailed other countries in this field. Eventually, after a shakeout, US reforms led to increased technological innovation and experimentation with equipment, software, and service application mixes and some closing of the gap on wireless with

Europe and Asia. Pricing is much lower and volume usage for voice and data much higher in the US than in the European Union, for example. But penetration remains lower.

Meanwhile, all agreed that the Internet and the Web would lead the next boom in communications and IT investment. The major corporate players wanted to be ready. The bargain leading to the 1996 Telecommunications Act was struck between a Republican Congress and a Democratic White House, each of which had reasons for wanting to reach an agreement.

Predictably, the politically muscular regional Bells, which operated in every congressional district, wanted permission to compete in all markets. Republicans sided with the Bells because their strength was greatest in the West and the South, where the Bells were especially influential, and because the Republicans had won control of Congress in the 1994 election. Most Democrats, including the president, depended on a strong urban base and lined up with the long-distance carriers that had cultivated ties to large urban users and the computer industry.[44] The long-distance companies recognized that pressures for Bell entry were enormous, but they counted on the Clinton administration's support on the terms for their cross-entry into local services. The White House did so; however, Democrats also were re-branding themselves as the pro-competition champions of the information economy, and they did not want to oppose allowing the Bells to compete.[45]

During the legislative bargaining, the Bells rejected a deal that guaranteed them entry into the long-distance and data markets 3 years after passage of the act. Instead, they opted to meet a "check list of obligations" that allowed them fully into long-distance and data only after they demonstrated that their territories were open to local service competition. They made this choice because they believed, wrongly it turned out, that congressional pressure on the FCC would help them gain entry in less than 3 years. However, the Democratic FCC, with strong White House support, interpreted the act to call for strong interconnect obligations for the Bells at long-run incremental costs. This formula enraged the Bells and the Republican Congress.

Many economists, wary of major government regulation, worried that the FCC's terms for interconnection might discourage investment by the Bells and induce inefficient, subsidized entry that rested on the Bells' unrealistically priced facilities.[46] The Bells launched a full-scale legal counterattack on FCC rules. Because American administrative bureaucracies enjoy less latitude than their counterparts in parliamentary democracies, court challenges tied up portions of the interconnection regulation. Still, market bargains were struck because the Bells wanted to claim that they had fulfilled the 1996 act's checklist.

In the later 1990s the emergence of new ICT competitors and the Web bubble led to a huge investment boom in fiber-optic networks. By late 2001 the boom had fizzled and most Web start-ups had crashed, but across the United States and under the Atlantic and Pacific Oceans a huge new installed infrastructure remained. This infrastructure helped kill the pricing structure for traditional long-distance carrier's voice and data transport offerings.[47] It also prompted the US government to exempt Internet "backbone" traffic from regulatory scrutiny, thereby creating an international controversy. Only a proposed merger of MCI and Sprint, then two of the largest backbone providers, prompted regulatory intervention to ensure that competition in the backbone market was not substantially curtailed.

The introduction of infrastructure competition in telecommunications raised worries that incumbents might leverage their control of bottleneck facilities and led to more detailed governance to manage market entry. The same concerns soon extended to the mass consumer infrastructure for networked information technology when email and the Web emerged as a high-profile focus of technology politics and policies.

Until 1994, the ICT infrastructure relied on proprietary email systems (such as MCI Mail and AOL) and computer network formats (such as IBM's System Network Architectures protocols). There was some grumbling about the lack of interconnection of these proprietary, "value-added" services, but this was still a small market for large institutional users and a relatively small technophile population. The proliferation of the Web escalated the commercial stakes and attracted political attention. The Web proved transformative because its simple path to interconnecting all networks quickly overwhelmed existing formats underlying uncompetitive "walled gardens" for data networking and email.[48]

The story was different at the intersection of networking and desktop computing. The Internet also transformed computing and software strategies in the marketplace thereby focusing attention on the logic of market governance built on vertical integration and the control of market power from bottleneck facilities. Thus, in theory Microsoft might leverage its PC operating system (a bottleneck facility) to unfairly enhance its competitive Internet position at the expense of competition and consumer welfare. Worries increased that Microsoft would use its Internet browser packaged with Windows to promote its own software add-ons and content. The political economy logic of the Microsoft antitrust action tracked the history of US electronics policy. Many rivals located outside the Pacific Northwest began a campaign to capture the attention of state and federal authorities. The same issues were raised over the AOL-TimeWarner merger.[49] Although in that case the operational remedy was restrained, the basic issue of leveraging bottleneck facilities was identical because the US political logic then favored such government decisions.

Change in the broadcasting arena preceded more slowly during the first two policy shifts. Traditionally, broadcasting embraced separate networks (optimized for point-to-multi-point transmission). It was subject to specialized regulation that was shaped by vigorous lobbying (broadcasters controlled congressional members' access to their district's airwaves) and by fierce voter demands for television services at "affordable" prices. The political and cultural sensitivity of broadcast content reinforced the level of arbitrary regulation. The United States maintained a public interest standard for broadcasting that purportedly protected the public interest no matter how difficult that was to define or enforce.[50] Other countries had the added burden of broadcasting rules that tried to protect national culture through various content quotas.

The emergence of cable television as a rival platform also was of great significance for the ICT infrastructure. Cable began as a series of locally granted franchises and quickly won legislative favor as a way of delivering television to rural areas or urban areas where there were reception problems. The industry profited from the same antitrust legacy that shaped telecom policy when, in 1953, the Department of Justice forced RCA, the dominant equipment supplier for cable, to divest itself of network holdings. (The Department of Justice made an ownership share into a condition of supply.) Finally, in 1984, as access to cable became a popular grassroots issue in both Republican and Democratic districts, Congress passed a bipartisan Cable Act that systemized the terms on which towns and cities could grant cable franchises, ended local price regulation, and banned the Bells from purchasing cable systems. This propelled the growth of cable operators around the country, but especially in the West. The legislative leader was Representative Tim Wirth, a Democrat from Colorado.[51]

As cable became a powerful industry with revenues far exceeding those of the three large broadcast networks, it also sparked consumer ire. When prices climbed rapidly and service was undependable, two-thirds majorities in the House and the Senate passed the Cable Rate Act of 1992 and overrode President George H. W. Bush's veto. The act capped cable rates, insisted that cable make its programming available to its broadcast satellite competitors, and stipulated that cable had to pay for retransmitting broadcast programming. (The cable operators often "paid" broadcasters by agreeing to carry their new cable networks.) Despite this setback, cable's technical infrastructure had the potential for providing broadband to the home but needed massive capital investment to upgrade it. The cable industry's entrepreneurial leadership mixed financial acumen with a poker-playing style as it played off major IT companies (e.g., Microsoft) and telecom companies (e.g., AT&T) to fund its investment model. (AT&T's investment in TCI ended up costing it dearly.) Eventually, cable emerged as a rival network platform for home data services. This revitalized the industry.

The growth of US cable television and satellite broadcast networks also began to fragment the broadcast markets into numerous specialized channels and market niches. Mass audiences began shrinking. This set the stage for a restructuring of the content industry after 2000.

Parallel Changes around the World

As US policy change progressed, parallel changes were underway elsewhere. Usually changes originated first in the United Sates, but not always. A significant exception, discussed in chapter 8, was the takeoff of the mobile wireless infrastructure more rapidly outside of the United States.

The analysis of trade policy in chapter 7 examines the critical role of US bargaining with the world over the introduction and consolidation of ICT transformation in the late 1990s. The US sought two global changes. In the first era it wanted to extend internationally the competitive provision of value-added networks and the creation of private corporate networks (internal communications). It also promoted policies similar to Carterfone to allow modularity for terminal equipment attached to the telecom network. Germany and the US had spirited, sometimes bitter negotiations over these goals. The US also began pressing Japan to open its international value-added networks to greater competition, a crucial wedge for US multinational firms operating there. The idea was that value-added competition in Japan would boost IBM and other US computer firms that were struggling against a Japanese industrial policy determined to overtake America's lead in semiconductors and computing. Eventually, these bilateral and regional (e.g., NAFTA) negotiations moved to the multilateral trade level.

After the decision to break up AT&T, the US government began to preach the virtues of facilities-based competition.[52] This caused stakeholders elsewhere to revisit their own political economic calculus.

We call the period 1984–2000 an era of "managed competition" because during that time the United States allowed unlimited entry in long-distance but, until the Telecom Act of 1996, retained a monopoly on local phone services. Even then, it micro-managed its markets by implementing detailed regulations that addressed the market power of the dominant carriers (AT&T and the Bells). (The FCC declared AT&T dominance on long distance to be over in 1996.) They were forced to share their networks so that new entrants could rent detailed technical elements.

Other countries introduced their own competition schemes, but few of them went as far as unlimited entry doctrines of the United States. The timing varied substantially. The United Kingdom, Canada, Australia, New Zealand, Hong Kong, Singapore, Japan, and South Korea followed closely on the heels of the US. Except for mobile wireless, until the official liberalization of European telecommunications on January 1, 1998, the general policy of many EU members was to experiment with value-added competition. Even the countries that allowed facilities-based competition approached managing competition in different ways. For example, Japan limited the number of entrants in network facilities to minimize "disruptive" competition that might endanger the incumbent.[53] This was a popular solution elsewhere too, as in Britain's late 1980s duopoly policy. Many countries also divided the domestic and international markets, and Japan and some other countries maintained elaborate controls on pricing to make sure that all major players showed profits. Others remained committed to active industrial technology policies even after introducing competition.

In addition to the policy changes on market entry and pricing in the 1980s and the 1990s, many advanced economies began separating government from market supply, by fully or partially privatizing their telecommunications industry. Slowly, they also began to substitute arms-length government rule making for management of the market by the former monopoly carrier. In the negotiations that led to the 1997 WTO Basic Telecom Agreement, countries that had recently adopted such changes—worrying that this process easily could go wrong—enshrined the creation of independent regulators in the WTO accord.

The changes in telecom were far more sweeping than those in broadcasting. In broadcast, most advanced economies allowed limited entry for broadcast satellite services, but there was no generalized entry policy. The fate of cable television franchises was uneven. Both satellite and broadcasting changed the economics of media markets by creating options that expanded and fragmented the broadcast channel universe. A more profound change occurred in countries with extensive growth of cable television because it could be upgraded to handle other services, especially broadband data and telephony. Cable emerged as the only credible local infrastructure platform for wired networks fighting entrenched phone companies. During the 1990s, a major divide in national networking emerged between countries that evolved a relatively ubiquitous cable

cheap enough, for it to become, like electricity, a general-purpose technology generated by large "power plants" and distributed over long distances.[2]
Related, but generally not explicitly outlined in these predictions, is
Google's leadership position in online advertising—both in terms of search
monetization and the syndicated ad network (Adsense) that brings advertisers and third-party sites together (with Google taking a cut, or "vig," of
the fees for placing the ad).

In some respects, this reasoning captures critical aspects of the technological frontier. Today, new computing and information architectures—
e.g., "the Cloud" and "the Grid"—implicitly rest on a much different set
of capabilities and market organization than in the past.[3] These architectures assume that powerful broadband networks intersect with two other
emerging trends: (1) the integration of massive and inexpensive information storage with network architecture and services and (2) the emergence
of virtual computer systems that collectively and flexibly harness many
computers, including high-end supercomputers, to mesh on demand to
meet user needs. For example, the Cloud could reorganize companies'
vastly underutilized ICT infrastructure for efficiency gains sometimes estimated at 50 percent or more.[4]

The Cloud's building blocks demonstrate the major changes since the
late 1990s. Then, Oracle championed "thin client" computing tied to the
emerging popularity of laptop computers that relied heavily on networked
processing and storage. But storage and computing costs on a networked
basis were expensive. Bandwidth also was costly, inflexible, and not always
available until after 2000. Further, the absence of industry-wide data standards and open protocols precluded full use of the proposed thin clients.
Until recently EDS and other vendors coped with proprietary software
standards and major jerry rigging of hardware from different vendors that
did not easily mesh. Enterprises now demand that Grid and "Services-
Oriented Architecture" (SOA) offerings mix and match data from different
systems and meld them to enable business decision making.[5]

The Cloud's implication is that there are huge economies of scale in
storage and computing that favor a company with an economic proposition that supports giant scale. Google, with ad-supported revenues propelled by a dominant search engine (and with capitalization soaring as a
result of huge stock appreciation), seems the logical candidate. In 2006
interviewees suggested that Google was buying 15 percent of the servers
sold in the US market. By early 2007, Google was rumored to operate on
500,000 servers in its data centers! Google then used its own proprietary
architectures to organize the data that fed its search-engine results and

many of the applications built on them. Google apparently envisions a virtual private network built within, and fully interoperable with, the inter-networking of the Internet.[6] At best, telecom carriers are partners in this private network (by building the initial supply of dark fiber). Thus, as a corollary, the utility metaphor suggests that value added comes primarily from the value added of search and the biggest applications of (ad) revenue that it fuels. The rest of the ICT infrastructure businesses tend to be commoditized.

Google's dominance in horizontal search, the largest source of ad revenue, could create a virtuous cycle. It may reinforce Google's leadership in search and advertising placement because economies of scale and cost advantages in networking, data storage, and processing capabilities allow faster and more powerful searches and better targeting of ads to individual users. If this analysis is correct, there may be a potential for dominance across a broader array of services both in ICT end markets and in online advertising networks.[7] More searches provide more inventory for ads and more insight into consumer behavior. This enables better ad targeting (on both Google and third-party sites via Adsense), thereby making Google more attractive to advertisers.

At the same time, dominance in search, and thus dominance of ad revenues, might make Google into a software powerhouse akin to IBM in the mainframe era. Clearly, Google derived economies of scope from the skills it developed in search software for becoming an alternative source of complex application software. More important, Adsense, a leading ad network, is essential to many developers of ad-funded applications.

Google's leadership position in search and online advertising is significant and reflects two major developments in the economics and technology of ICT. Their leadership position could increase Google's ability to leverage into related major markets in a manner analogous to the way that ICT giants in the previous two eras ascended—but this rests on two premises: (1) the implied advantages that accrue to Google across the landscape for online software (from email to complex enterprise applications) from its current scale in infrastructure and (2) the network externalities associated with Adsense and the online ad network it provides for advertising and third-party sites.

By modifying the scenario slightly, we could imagine somewhat fiercer competition among a handful of oligopolists that dominate the strategic heights of the global ICT infrastructure. Once again, if giant economies of scale exist for some market segments, three or four giant search and ad platforms could emerge globally because scale matters, especially in this market. The huge size might lead to rivalry between search giants and other entrants. For example, some telecom carriers may learn to use their networks' information and billing systems to target ads and searches.[8] Nokia also is investing in this set of capabilities from their position of strength on the handset.[9] Immediately after Microsoft's early-2008 bid to acquire Yahoo, one analyst foresaw Nokia, China Mobile, and a partnership of Apple and Disney as a possible cluster of giants.[10]

To summarize the logic of the utility metaphor: The Cloud makes economies of scale (infrastructure) and scope (ad network and software) into critical competitive assets. Inexpensive broadband allows vast computing centers to deliver at long distances. The ad revenues from search can fund building to scale, and then scale economies reinforce leadership in search while commoditizing the infrastructure and most of the equipment business.[11] Ad leadership provides more data for targeting and more reach for advertisers. Indeed, search in itself may have properties of a virtuous circle—more searches lead to better searches and improved targeting of ads. In addition, there are economies of scope that create assets for being a leader in ad placement that may create a strong ecosystem centered around ad networks and related capabilities (analytics, targeting). Taken together, this mix of scale, scope, and control of the ad revenue stream allows the leader(s) in search to leverage their dominance into other parts of the ICT infrastructure.

In the next two sections, we suggest an alternative to this utility metaphor. First, we argue that the dynamics created by the rise of modularity in the ICT infrastructure's building blocks—microelectronics, broadband networking, software, and digital content—are more about increasing speed and power with plunging costs, flexible combinations of inputs, and the spread of ICT intensive processes to a new universe of applications than they are about economies of scale. Scale matters, but is less important in the overall picture than the utility metaphor suggests. Second, we draw out two other metaphors for the future of the industry: the "systems engineering" metaphor and the "fashion industry" metaphor. Both of these, we suggest, offer a broader range of insights into the implications of modularity.

Modularity and the Inflection Point

The "information utility" metaphor rightly suggests that the global information economy—including telecommunications, information technology, and increasingly all forms of copyrighted content—is at an inflection point. At the inflection point, if policy permits, a shift in the strategic context of the market invites a new direction in networked ICT infrastructure.[12] But we believe that the leverage points are different than the ones that the utility metaphor suggests. The two critical factors are pervasive modularity in ICT capabilities and ubiquitous, inexpensive broadband networking.

At an intuitive level, think of modularity as turning ICT capabilities into Lego bricks that can be assembled in any number of ways. More technically, modularity means that components that work together interoperate through transparent, nondiscriminatory interfaces. Interoperability requires (1) the technological capability to build separable inputs at competitive prices and (2) making design choices that ensure that interfaces connect seamlessly.[13] As we noted in chapter 2, modularity first became important in terminal equipment and then became central to computing, storage, and networking elements. Now it is emerging as a defining characteristic of software and content, as well as ad networks and online payment systems.

Modularity has three crucial first-order implications. First, as a central design feature it facilitated the "Cheap Revolution" (to be discussed shortly), which changed the price and performance frontiers for ICT infrastructure. For example, modularity enabled many specialized market strategies that thrived with varied scale economies. Fueled by vigorous competition, the early trailblazers in modularity—terminal equipment and component markets—marched quickly towards more specialization and faster innovation rates. Second, modularity allowed the building blocks of ICT to be mixed and matched more cheaply, quickly, and efficiently in end-to-end service and equipment packages than was imagined even at the turn of the millennium. Third, modularity plus ubiquitous broadband will extend intensive networked information applications beyond traditional business and academic centers.

Modularity's cumulative effect on the market goes beyond the first-order effects. It accelerates the growing significance of "multi-sided" platforms that alter pricing and competition dynamics in ways not found in most non-digital environments. A multi-sided platform serves two or more distinct types of customers that are mutually dependent and "whose joint participation makes the platform valuable to each."[14] Network externalities are direct and indirect. Thus, more Palm users directly increase the value to these users and to the Palm programming community. Cheaper computer printers indirectly make PCs more valuable, and more PCs expand the value of the printer market. Windows is a three-sided market because the software platform is deeply interdependent with application developers, end users, and hardware producers.[15] The main implication of these multi-sided platforms is that pricing is optimized across the several sides of the platform. Some pieces of the platform may be priced below cost or subsidized because it is more profitable to charge more on other segments.[16] This strategy can increase revenues and maximize the collective value of the platform for all stakeholders.

Modularity is important for multi-sided platforms because it increases the incentives to experiment with novel combinations of prices, inputs, and applications in ways that will subvert many players' traditional business models. For example, a Web service may provide Voice-over-Internet Protocol service at little or no charge because the traffic, customer base, or complementary uses of VoIP offset its free provision.[17] Yahoo provides a variety of free services to authors and other users to build original content that attracts traffic and generates ad revenues. Google and Microsoft have experimented with launching inexpensive communications networks in several cities to entice broadband wireless users to their search services. (Broadband significantly increases the level of search activities and hence their ad revenues.) The same is true for mobile data services. Indeed, Google (and presumably AT&T) was astonished and at first suspected an error when it saw "50 times more search requests coming from Apple iPhones than any other mobile handset."[18] Similarly, the legacy telecom giants may raise the price of underlying broadband data capacity to allow cheaper, more flexible pricing of the services offered over broadband.[19] This multi-sided strategic logic does not preclude anti-competitive behavior, but limits the incentive of suppliers to harm consumers, a major concern for policy. Inflated pricing or predation is more difficult to sustain when the potential routes to providing a service become so varied.

Modularity is important for multi-sided platforms, and thus for the information utility model, because it multiplies the potential routes for providing a service or function. Today, at the inflection point, the potential for full modularity and ubiquitous broadband is close at hand. The dawning of an ICT market with separate ICT capabilities (e.g., networking, processing, storage, application logic, content, and terminal devices) that can more readily be mixed and matched is evident. Often these capabilities will be integrated into stickier, bundled groupings (e.g., an iPod-like combination of storage and terminals). However, flexible, powerful building blocks allow diverse architectures, easier rival substitutes, more variety in pricing schemes, and simpler interoperability of complementary products and services than previously. They also permit dramatic new applications that will further disrupt the marketplace. Ubiquitous broadband means that all devices and spaces can be smart and networked, thereby changing how information in complex applications are gathered and used and enabling more innovation on the terminal as "cloud services" become an integrated part of the hardware "terminal."[20]

Modularity and the Cheap Revolution

Modularity thus has both first-order and cumulative effects. The first-order effects are the Cheap Revolution (lower price and higher performance), interoperability, and extension of the ICT infrastructure into a more pervasive penetration of all facets of the human experience and environment. The cumulative effect is accelerating the import of multi-sided platform logic for ICT markets.

This section spells out the implications of the Cheap Revolution. This pithy sobriquet, coined by Rich Kaarlgard, captures the consequences of the cumulative impact of (1) the dizzying price-performance dynamics ranging from microelectronics innovations involving computer chips through data storage, (2) innovations in regard to fiber-optic and wireless bandwidth, (3) changes in software design and costs, and (4) the emerging cost and delivery structure of digital content.[21] All four of these processes reflect the advantages of modularity, but software and content were the slowest to yield to the logic of modularity.

The Microelectronics Revolution

The microelectronics revolution extends from computer chips (e.g., memory and processors) through their specialized applications (e.g., to mobile terminals) to hybrid systems of magnetic and optical data storage. Famously, Intel co-founder Gordon Moore predicted that processors would double their price-to-performance ratio every 18 months. After more than 20 years, the cumulative effect of Moore's Law is huge and unrelenting. That cumulative effect is manifested in the inexpensive computing power harvested by the Cloud.

The power of Moore's Law is not limited to computing. Makers of other ICT terminals bank on the same logic. Mobile terminals, for example, are evolving rapidly as prices plunge, processing power increases, and information storage is added. These changes enable multi-purpose terminals. Cell phones, personal computers, iPods, and iPhones can serve as partial or full substitutes. Sophisticated recording devices for cable television can allow customers to watch television programs when and where they wish.

Cell phones could soon rival computers for many remote information applications. But the engineering logic is little understood. Less than
one-fourth of the space on the Qualcomm chip set for a 2006 cell phone
was dedicated to the radio. The remainder supports other capabilities.
The terminal's design is essentially modular so independent add-ons to
support specialized functions are likely. This will become a major growth
area in ICT, although the precise path of change will depend on policy
choices.[22]

The takeoff of inexpensive specialized radios and sensors is just as dramatic. Radio-frequency identification devices (RFIDs) for tagging mer-
chandise achieved economies of scale that lowered the prices of these
micro-radios to about 20 cents per unit in 2007.[23] As they become ubiquitous, new markets for their functions emerge, such as electronic chains of
documentation and custody for global commerce.[24]

The cost of sophisticated electronic sensors on a radio also is decreasing,
thus leading to many more sensors on a single chip in a fashion similar
to Moore's Law. For instance, monitoring air quality once required $400,000
computer stations; now $150 mobile terminals are deployed, and soon
10-cent computer chips may perform the same function.[25] Homeland security systems, such as those for atmospheric monitoring for biological
weapons, are accelerating development of these technologies.

Breakthroughs in data storage are even more dramatic. The cost of data
storage per megabyte is falling faster than the cost of processing power.
In 2006 memory was about 4,000 times cheaper per bit than in 1985.[26]
Centralized storage's plunging costs opened up the mega-data sites on
the Web.

The changes in data storage performance have another implication that
runs directly counter to thinking about the Cloud. These improvements
mean that there is tremendous capacity to both decentralize and centralize
data storage. Large-scale storage on individual terminals permits mobile
digital libraries (8 gigabits on the "iPod nano" by 2006) and the growth of
home storage, led by the US market.[27] Thus, the role of the Cloud's storage
will vary in future product and service offers depending on business model
and performance design goals.

To summarize: The microelectronics revolution enabled the Cloud architecture, but also spawned two other forces. First, terminals became more
powerful and escaped the desktop. For information services providers,
mobile terminals are just one more entry point to its cloud, but these terminals now have the capability to drive functions, not just to rely on
centralized computing and storage. (The terminal's own computing and

storage powers are pivotal).[28] Second, terminals and devices on the edge of the network, as exemplified by RFIDS and sensors, open entirely new applications and architectures with huge growth potential.

The Network Revolution

A second driver of the Cheap Revolution is the ubiquitous broadband packet-switched network, often dubbed the Next-Generation Network, which will stimulate network traffic and the geographic spread of ICT applications in unexpected ways. It had been agreed since the 1990s that the predominately wireline, circuit-switched, telephone architecture was in rapid decline. Incumbent networks and their suppliers had vested interests in slowing the transition in network architectures, but after 2000 the legacy networks became too complex and too slow to support major new applications.[29] Now this transformation is beginning to take hold of the general telecom infrastructure. A major transition to next-generation packet networks is underway.

Broadband service will become faster, ubiquitous, and a hybrid of many network infrastructures.[30] Two points are worth considering. First, modularity allows different networks, with different design features, to meld their capabilities more flexibly. Second, modularity's acceleration of the microelectronics revolution boosts the power and lowers the price of electronics that upgrade copper lines (to Asymmetric Digital Subscriber Lines, abbreviated ADSL), improve cable networks, "light" fiber-optic networks, or enable new wireless networks to transform rapidly. The result is a plunging cost per bit and, in Japan, best-effort speeds of 50 (ADSL) or 100 megabits per second (fiber) to the home. Figure 3.1 illustrates the Nippon Telegraph and Telephone Corporation's claims about the declining costs of fiber to the home in Japan. Although we should treat NTT's cost estimates for after 2004 cautiously, the pertinent point is that ADSL and cable are getting so fast and so cheap that they are forcing carriers to find a more economic plan for fiber if they are to have a viable business case.[31] Figure 3.2 provides a rough comparative estimate of the dramatic decrease in costs and increasing capacity for mobile data. This combination of lower costs and greater capabilities in next-generation networks will support new information services, a dizzying array of applications, and content delivery to an ever growing number of subscribers.

Every facet of the inputs to advanced networks responds to galloping technological progress. Stubborn "non-digital" realities spurred policy controversies that we examine in the next chapter. It is expensive and slow to deploy new fiber or coaxial-fiber hybrid networks because construction is

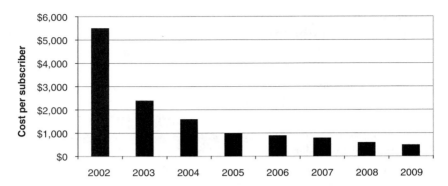

Figure 3.1
The falling cost of fiber. Source: "FTTH Worldwide Market & Technology Forecast, 2006–2011," *Heavy Reading* 4, no. 9 (2006). Based on NTT East costs (construction and equipment) per subscriber (estimated for 2005–2009).

difficult. Spectrum also remains an input to wireless networks that is subject to constraints of physics and politics. So for now, we examine the impact of the changes as the networks are deployed.

Everyone acknowledges the importance of the switch in fixed network architecture. Business commentaries obsess about whether 12-, 45-, or 100-megabits-per-second options for data and video will ultimately be needed to meet consumer demand for video applications on fixed networks.[32] This obsession with bandwidth throughput on fixed networks misses the big picture because two parallel transformations receive too little attention.[33] The first of these is the emergence of mobile terminals with multimedia capabilities that are changing the landscape independent of fixed bandwidth constraints. Wireless networking is evolving into hybrid systems that combine mobile and fixed wireless with different technologies on many bands to provide broadband. In early 2008, Japanese third-generation ("3G") systems delivered downloads at speeds up to 7 megabits per second (3 megabits per second measured by average throughput, the best indicator of performance). Upgrades of 3G scheduled for 2009 will have peaks of 24 megabits per second. The future wireless terminal will seamlessly integrate the multi-band, multi-technology network as advanced 3G evolves by incorporating other technologies for mobility and as complementary technologies (e.g., WiMAX) emerge. Speeds of 50–70 megabits per second (average throughput) may emerge, especially because of military applications.[34]

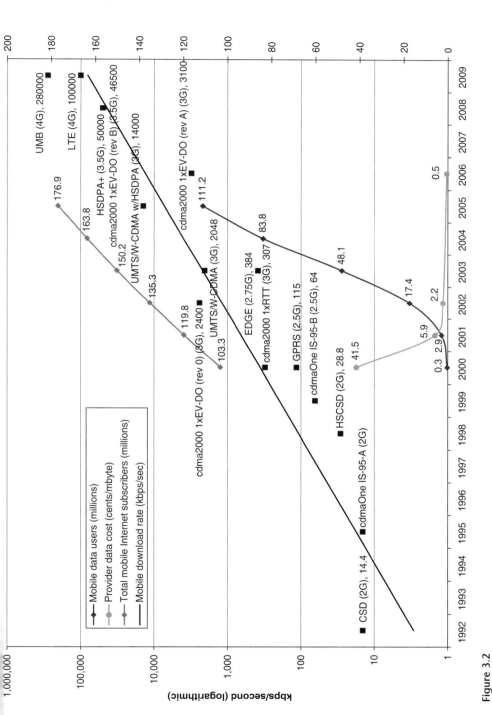

Figure 3.2

The mobile network revolution begins. Sources: http://www.chetansharma.com (mobile data users and total mobile internet subscribers); http://www.cdg.org (provider data costs and mobile download rate).

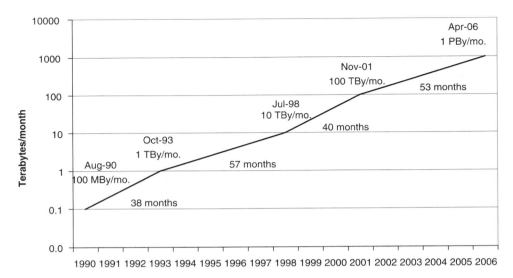

Figure 3.4

Log plot of total ESnet traffic since 1990. Data approximated from William E. Johnston, "ESnet: Advanced Networking for Science," *SciDAC Review*, summer 2007, p. 53.

increasing share of the traffic on networks will be machine to machine, as witnessed by the growth of networked data from industry and vehicles (figure 3.5).[46]

In sum, broadband ICT deployment is occurring on a very large scale. One dimension is the upgrading of home and small and medium enterprise capabilities on fixed networks. But the complementary dimensions, the interaction of wireless broadband with new generations of terminal devices, and the deployment of ultra-broadband networks for innovative applications fueled by the university research system may be even more significant.

The amount of digital network capacity and the new applications and architectures make pricing and service segmentation shakier, as we expect with multi-sided platforms. This has two implications. First, massive, sophisticated networking capacity may be more fully available on demand for specialized players than the "information utility" metaphor suggests. Second, this networking revolution is reshaping the debate over the ability of local communications carriers to manipulate the market for information services.

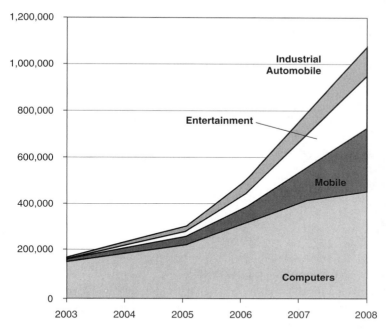

Figure 3.5
The growth of networked data, as illustrated by the amount of data received or transmitted by device (petabytes/day). Source: Krishna Nathanson, "From RFID to the Internet of Things: Bridging the Gap between Research and Business in the On Demand Era," presentation to EU IST Conference, 2006.

The Software Revolution

The third part of the Cheap Revolution is software. Although modularity began when IBM broke up the integration of its hardware and software components (which led to the creation of an independent software industry), modularity has been slower to come to software. Software is becoming more open and modular, especially at the infrastructure layer, in part because the rise of the Web propelled changes in software design (and associated standards) and in part because of market pressures.

The first change is the growth of multiple operating systems as a reality that informs any major suppliers to the enterprise IT market. Figure 3.6 shows the stunning impact of OS-Agnostic Applications on software.[47] A huge percentage of the applications routinely run on Windows. The inflection point means that applications can run on anything. The complexities

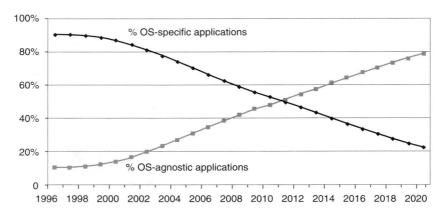

Figure 3.6
The growth of agnosticism. Source: Gartner Research 2005.

of the individual operating systems still pose challenges for vendors, but the emergence of multi-OS applications is the market direction.

Why has this occurred? No single technological driver is responsible. A big impetus was that large users demanded that their huge investments in heterogeneous software systems, each installed for a special purpose, become interoperable.[48] In addition, independent e-commerce and information services opened vast new markets within ICT that were not dominated by network providers or established platform vendors. The new separate market for innovation, for example, sought tools that worked across all software. They demanded modularity.

Modularity played an additional role. Since the late 1990s, the growth of more open and standardized Applications Processing Interfaces (APIs) and data standards facilitated the emergence of more heterogeneous architectures across all elements of the IT stack. The browser (and the standard html and data formats underpinning it) quickly emerged as the de facto interface for most consumer applications and more and more corporate applications. This undercut the ability of any piece of the software platform to exert leverage over other pieces of the platform.

Put simply, the standards encapsulated in "the browser as standard application interface" enable different operating systems, computing environments, services, and data sources to interoperate.[49] These developments helped facilitate the rise of independent Web-based information and technology providers (from e-commerce providers to portal leaders and eventually to services providers. The creation of a new, distinct set of Web-based competitors not tied to network providers (telcos) or existing software vendors further set the stage for the emergence of "the Web" as a set of standards and "ICT assumptions" that both buyers and sellers take advantage of in ICT markets. Salesforce.com, for example, assumes a broadband network and a browser interface and rests on a new business model and delivery vehicle for delivering Enterprise Resource Planning (ERP) applications.

Modular architectures also spur complementary, specialized, software supply communities featured in "Web 2.0." Websites that are "mash-ups" combine the capabilities of other websites into new, hybrid services more quickly and inexpensively.[50] Data are more easily available and freely shared online because data and software remain discrete and data are formatted to be interoperable with varying ranges of standardized software. Really Simple Syndication (RSS), for example, allows bloggers, catalog marketers, enterprise sales portals, and other data owners to "publish" a data source that anyone with a browser can "subscribe to" for regular content updates.[51] It sounds simple, but RSS rests on the xml data standard and the ability of any html browser to render the data in a consistent format. It also launched a modular way to aggregate content inside large enterprises that depends less on the traditional closed software for enterprise data systems.

A growing diversity of ecologies for software developers was made possible by modular interfaces. For example, in 2007 Facebook began to support a new array of developer tools and code libraries so that its social network could become a platform for third-party applications to use the Facebook "social graph" to quickly distribute their applications. This triggered a major new, ad-funded developer ecosystem where each individual developer is responsible for making decisions about which ad network to choose and how to monetize the real estate within their application (which runs inside the Facebook "experience" but is owned by the third-party developer).

The pioneering application developments whose economics rest on advertising stimulate the diversity of the developer ecosystems. Any content owner (Google, Amazon, Microsoft, virtual worlds such as Second Life, or diverse start-ups) can aspire to build applications and earn revenues from advertisers. This enables a "garage store" approach to becoming an applications developer because anyone can build an application, register with one of the ad networks, and be paid (by the ad network that sells ads) for click-throughs in their applications rather than having to build a sales system based on package software.[52]

The ad model is in its infancy. Strong funding supports a flood of new start-ups focused on disparate niches of advertising platforms (mobile, in-games, specific targeting technologies, etc.). Continued innovation and better targeting is guaranteed going forward given the size of the overall advertising market and the lack of data inherent in non-digital advertising. Coupled with experimentation among large and small advertisers (which see TV advertising as an increasingly incomplete model for their needs), and the promise of better targeting that comes with Internet protocol (IP) being the lingua franca of digital content, advertising as an economic engine for ICT is only beginning. Many new applications will flow from combining interoperability enabled by the presence of cross-platform standards, the ubiquitous standards-based browsers, and the powerful inexpensive hardware that is built for IP-based traffic. Open-source software communities are a complementary force for these developments.[53]

In summary: The full import of modularity came slower to software than to equipment markets, and it is still imperfect. New areas of software, notably online ad networks and software experiences that capture or store user data, are generating debates over leverage and lock-in that are reminiscent of those over traditional packaged software. That said, the center of gravity of the market has changed. Large users demanded interoperable operating systems, a goal facilitated by the emergence of the Web browser as the common interface for commercial and consumer applications. The development of open, transparent APIs propelled the emergence of "Web 2.0," with its extensive mash-ups, data syndication, and developer communities clustering around many new forms of online activity. Change was further speeded by a new "economic engine" in the form of ad-funded applications and experiences coupled with the plunging cost of development. The net effect of these changes is to make it more difficult to lock in around software systems and to leverage dominance in one software system on other software segments. The diversity of software ecosystems also is now much greater.

These dynamics undercut "information utility" metaphors in two ways. First, dominance of search (and shares of total ad revenue) does not translate into a model that weakens innovations by others. Second, dominance of the search environment does not lend itself to control over software ecosystems. Interfaces are fundamentally more open than in the past, and, if anything, modularity is accelerating the variety of software ecosystems.

Media Content

The logic leading toward powerful modularity is moving beyond hardware, software, and data. A parallel change is underway in media content. For decades television broadcasting was highly vertically integrated. RCA owned consumer equipment and NBC. The most important remaining question was whether broadcast networks should control the production and ownership of programming, a subject of intense debate for competition policy at the time. Today, digital modularity is transforming the media content market in three ways.

First, digital content is more convertible across networks and terminal systems. As the media industry is disaggregated, screens for television shows are migrating to mobile phones, computers, and iPods. The distribution pipe includes broadband, cable, satellite, and now mobile broadband. Smart terminals plus broadband are challenging media stalwarts. TiVo, a sophisticated digital video recorder, allows a remote PC on a broadband network to download programs, thereby allowing a PC user in Paris to watch local baseball games broadcast in Los Angeles.[54] These devices challenge the geographic boundaries of traditional broadcast models.

Second, content aggregators are extending beyond broadcast networks and cable channels. A television channel is a branded content aggregator. Today, similar exercises in aggregation are emerging on the websites anchoring peer-to-peer networks.

Joost is a good example of the potential for modular innovation and its implications. In January 2007 the co-founders of Kazaa and Skype announced plans for Joost, a new peer-to-peer television service over the Internet. It is the logical successor of the model honed for music and user-generated video clips. The founders claimed that open-source software available on the Web served as modular building blocks for about 80 percent of the system's code and thus shortened their development process to about a year, thereby cutting costs substantially. The processing, storage, and networking demands for Joost's server needs would have been unthinkable in 2001. (Joost runs as a peer-to-peer network, so storage and transport are shared among many machines tied together by software code.) In the beta design, the service required about 250 megabits of data per hour.[55] The proliferation of consumer broadband networks made the service possible, if still difficult.

In short, Joost rests on the Cheap Revolution of plunging costs for rapidly increasing computing, storage, and bandwidth capabilities combined with modular software and open APIs. As a result, Joost can, in theory, transform local broadcast content into universally available content on the Web, thus breaking old market and regulatory boundaries. And, as a rule of thumb, as the number of distributional channels (e.g., networks) proliferates, the business model changes. The television writers' strike of 2008 in the United States was precisely over how to share revenues from changes in the sales and distribution of media content as a result of digital modularity. The difficulty is that big change seemed clear to all, but the new financial model was still murky.

Joost is a pioneer. It may be some other entrant that gets the precise strategy and offering correct. But Joost illustrates the implications of modularity in a second dimension—the transformation of content production. Joost or a similar service could easily become a social network or even a platform for "plug-in" content interacting with its broadcast offerings. Content creation has recently transcended established traditional studio electronics, making possible high-quality, low-price productions. For example, a new series titled *Star Trek New Voyages* that features the original 1960s characters of *Star Trek* is produced only for the Web. It surpasses the technical quality of the original broadcast network series, and it is made with voluntary labor and a small budget of donated funds in a New Jersey warehouse. "Franchises" such as Star Wars and Star Trek have long had user-driven content as part of their mix—witness "fanzines" with stories by amateur writers and fan conventions. But now the fan community builds digital programming, much as major software games have generated online markets for "add-ons."

User-driven and social network content will not destroy all high-end productions, and the "long tail" (many products with very small markets) may never fully dominate the market. There is evidence that expensive content, backed by big financing, will still hold the major share of digital content markets for a variety of reasons.[56] But modularity introduces new ways to create content and to complement traditional content that will change business models in the future.

The third modular driver of the market, the ability to do visual searches, is emerging. As digital visual content becomes more central to the applications of the Web, visual search becomes more critical. The immediate objective is to engage with popular consumer culture's imagery. But, as we noted about the import of the "Internet of things," searches for detailed visual observational data for engineering and other purposes soon will be common. (Or, to be bleaker, the search could be to identify your individual travel patterns.) Right now, search engines are primarily optimized for word texts. Everyone is scrambling for more effective search techniques for images. Indeed some see this as a potential vulnerability of Google.[57] For now, the main point is that improved visual search will further change how we use digital content.

Modularity for digital media content means an expansion of distribution channels and a redefinition of market segments geographically and by product category (e.g., what constitutes broadcast content). More crossover of distribution networks and changing geographic reach of any offering require new economic models. Meanwhile, the plunging costs of creating digital content and the ability to interact with established content mean that user experimentation will generate a new universe of hybrid content with major commercial value. Improved visual search will further heighten its significance. This, in turn, matters for the ICT infrastructure, because the consumer marketplace will be a significant driver of innovation because of its large size and the lower costs of innovating to serve many of its new segments.

The trends in digital content market also illustrate the limits of the "information utility" metaphor. To begin, the challenges of visual search open the way to alternative approaches for search, a dynamic that could weaken the hold of all text-based approaches. Perhaps more significantly, this market also points to the diversity of advantages for content. Social networking and Amazon's affinity searches ("customers like you buy this video") are two alternatives for supplying and finding digital media, as well as two models emphasizing significantly different (and successful) economic propositions.

In sum, modularity reinforced the promise of digital technology in ways that enabled the microelectronic revolution of diverse processing power with inexpensive powerful terminals and massive storage to provide a powerful infrastructure for centralized and decentralized IT applications. When combined with ubiquitous ultra-broadband networks ICT becomes capable of new scale and scope of applications and new forms of network and application architecture. Now, software is in a modular transformation that changes the model and price of innovation. Trailing software, but no less being reshaped by modularity, is digital content.

4   Modularity and Innovation

The implications of modularity undercut the utility metaphor in important ways. Modularity and interoperability of capabilities signal the demise of the utility model that depends on quasi-monopoly or duopoly in major software and service platforms. Various competitive strategies and architectures are emerging. The inflection point puts large parts of the industry's value added in play.

The exploration of the implications of modularity begins with a closer look at how different competitors interpret the strategic import of the utility metaphor. These observations are then extended into a broader reflection on important competitive advantages by offering a "systems integration" model of ICT competition. Systems integration focuses on the building of complex, large-scale applications and capabilities. But does even that revision capture the real equilibrium for the ICT industry? To see whether it does, we conduct a thought experiment, using the "fashion industry" as a metaphor for market change and technological innovation. In this exercise we put aside the political economic controversies that will influence the equilibrium of the next generation of the ICT infrastructure, although we do flag some policy choice points.

Murky Clouds and the Systems Integration Metaphor

Consider Google's and Microsoft's visions of the implications of the Cloud. Both firms see the shift from desktop computer (or wireless terminal) to the Internet "Cloud" as a foundation for future of information architectures. Apparently Google embraces a "thin client" computing model where most of the data and application logic and computing functions reside in the Cloud and are available from any terminal. In contrast, Microsoft's vision of "software plus services" assumes that the Cloud will be powerful and flexible enough to provide software services and storage on demand, but that much of the action will remain on individual terminals because of design optimization, reliability, quality of experience, or security considerations. This view reflects one implication of the Cheap Revolution; the terminal is powerful enough to play a larger role in defining functional service packages.

Microsoft's aborted 2008 bid to acquire Yahoo underpins the importance of advertising and the scale implied in ad networks. Microsoft's attempted takeover was an effort to buy more "eyeballs" and a broader ad network. It was trying to buy "audience" and the ad engine to "monetize" this audience. The reactions to the proposed merger by industry analysts questioned whether Microsoft could catch Google with this strategy. But many observers welcomed the idea of Google facing a stronger rival in search. Yahoo promised to deliver an ad-network capability superior to Microsoft's, not just eyeballs. This would then launch a struggle pitting Google's leadership in horizontal search against Microsoft's leadership on the desktop (and, to a lesser degree, its strong position in enterprise systems and in particular servers).

That IBM is a third aspirant to "Cloud" leadership is sometimes lost in the frenzy that surrounds the Microsoft-Google rivalry. IBM's approach shows that the Cloud also can enable another class of strategies built on extremely large-scale specialized platforms. In recent years, IBM has strategically acquired an extensive software portfolio focused primarily on middleware and complex integration capabilities for applications. IBM's competitive strategy rests on integrating complex elements of enterprise applications into a single end-to-end solution that takes advantage of service-oriented architecture (SOA) to deliver unique (and sticky) value to its customers. IBM's bet depends on a "systems engineering" metaphor; value comes from mastering complex integrated integration of many functions into complex applications.

IBM emphasizes open-source software for customer front ends and servers. They seek to neutralize entry from the customer interface (e.g., Windows) backward into the middleware. This approach also appeals to the software community worried about Microsoft's market power.[1] More important, the complex corporate solutions delivered by IBM rely on heavy use of mainframe computing power; thereby creating an internal "grid" that maintains demand for IBM's mainframes. Indeed, the "ownership" of the mainframe platform is crucial because many of the functions envisioned for the Cloud are easy to launch from a mainframe architecture that respects enterprise security and existing IT architectures. Moreover, if its competitors' analyses and the conventional wisdom of the industry are correct, IBM makes modest returns on the sale of services. Services are a tool for generating hardware sales, leasing computing capacity (in lieu of hardware purchases), and selling some middleware.[2]

In short, IBM is betting on large customers' desire for systems integration and sufficient scale. IBM believes that existing large-scale grid implementations using mainframes will trump the lures of modularity for major customers, hold off encroaching general-purpose Web platforms, and strengthen its traditional mainframe-based offering. IBM's approach rests on "good enough" implementations, not on actually being "good enough" for demanding corporate customers that require specialized solutions.[3]

IBM is not alone in using this approach. Cisco is placing a similar wager. It also dominates a critical ICT infrastructure platform, the router. Cisco's goal is to work from the router into complex service applications. For instance, it seeks greater success in selling its routers to telecom carriers by creating enterprise application solutions that give a larger role to the carriers in the total system solution. This would provide telecom carriers with a larger piece of the Cloud and make Cisco the mediator between the telecom Cloud and the IT applications.

Earlier we noted that "systems integration" was one way to describe industry competition in the unfolding era. Some industry insiders wager that a "systems integration" strategy based on the tradition of large-scale project engineering will lead the future for ICT. If this is correct, then contractors will use modularity and broadband to build extremely powerful new solutions and then manage to make the whole package resistant to two competitive challenges. First, leaders with a dominant position on one critical piece of the ICT infrastructure try to work toward systems solutions from that base. Second, the sheer complexity of applications and solutions in terms of both architecture and stakeholders mean that in-market offerings can be sticky for extended periods of time.

The "systems integration" metaphor can be used to reinterpret the evolving Google-Microsoft story. Each firm controls a platform. Each wants to reach related market spaces with entries that build on their market strengths. The margins on both platforms remain healthy, but likely will be less spectacular than previously because of cross-entry and continued new entry along the margins of the platform (enabled by modularity). Scale and scope matter—particularly for ad networks—but it is not self-evident that it is the decisive factor in the adjacent market spaces for each company.

An Alternative Metaphor: The Fashion Industry

The high-end fashion industry provides an alternative metaphor for understanding how modularity could open new patterns of innovation and redefine markets.[4] The fashion industry metaphor is as imperfect as the utility or systems engineering metaphors but it captures dynamics that are critical for modularity. On the supply side, the fashion industry is characterized by complex, disaggregated global supply chains where design, production, and distribution are tied together by global networks. These global networks feature flexible specialists that contribute modules (such as textiles, cutting, buttons, zippers, and leather) that can be assembled and distributed as needed on a seasonal basis in a "vertically integrated product" (a suit). Some specialists are large and capital intensive (fine textiles are products of complex production centers), but many of the inputs are on a smaller scale and emphasize specialized skills. There also is an element of Hollywood in that the fortunes of specific vendors rise and fall from season to season based on the continual search for short-lived "hit products." There also is minimal lock-in of any single component (fabric, buttons), but there are significant scale and scope economies in distribution, branding, and design.

Modularity means that the fashion industry metaphor is salient even to the heart of the search and ad markets because these markets do not define the industry's architecture in the same way that the IBM and Wintel (Microsoft-Intel) architectures did in their prime. So long as public policy reinforces modularity, all pieces of the ICT infrastructure will remain fundamentally (but not perfectly) interoperable, because programming languages and Web browsers are now standard on all major products and systems. Since all major vendors anticipate that significant elements of the overall system will be heterogeneous, they are increasingly building applications and services that rely on commonly accepted and used standards—even for important assets.[5] This allows easier substitutability among applications, making it difficult for market leaders to leverage leading positions in one segment/application into neighboring segments/applications. Moreover, the cost of designing innovative Web services is declining because of the ability to "recycle" code embedded in common building blocks. In addition, new Web applications may be embedded with specialized terminals that are not controlled by the search and software giants (examples: the iPod and iTunes). Leading terminal makers also are increasingly entering services and software markets (examples: Amazon's Kindle and Nokia's purchase of Navteq), and that is contributing to a diverse strategic landscape.

Economy-of-scale advantages from the Cloud are likely to be more limited than most observers believe. This matters. Many in the industry that believe that Google's scale in search will enable it to use its infrastructure advantages to lead in other information services markets. We disagree. Our scan of the landscape suggests that the scale required for search may not be replicated across information markets. In addition, many of the global system integrators already are delivering cloud services for enterprise clients at global scale, These more traditional, "boring" elements of the Cheap Revolution do not make headlines, but they suggest that scale will not be the key variable in the migration to the cloud. Indeed, inexpensive storage and computing make it easier for specialized players to match the giants' economics when building to target specialized markets in information services.[6] Modularity makes it easier to mix and match ICT infrastructure elements. Modularity brings carrier economics into play by marrying technology and new forms of financial engineering and business models. For example, application providers might flourish by purchasing services (e.g., Amazon's S3 and EC2 Cloud) that already serve specialized Web businesses.[7] GSX (a company spun off from GE) already provides major outsourcing of enterprise-scale Cloud infrastructure for electronic data interchange and supply chain management. And smaller companies can replicate many of the advantages of big firms that control private fiberoptic networks by using new peer-to-peer models for sharing inexpensive dark fiber capacity.[8]

All these forces are making "long-tail" niche markets more prominent, even in search. Specialized providers such as Kayak.com are offering niche search services and capturing significant query volumes. Their ranks will grow because of specialized demands in regional global markets and the many networked applications where specialized capability may outweigh general functionality of leading "cloud" companies. Modularity is opening the way to search capabilities geared to video, vertically specific applications, and people. As targeting and ad networks become more specialized, these more focused offerings are likely to command higher per-click prices than horizontal offerings and therefore could capture an increasing share of overall ad spending.[9]

Salesforce.com exemplifies the rise of focused solutions providers that leverage modular software and hardware. It also creates a dynamic ecology for developers. Salesforce.com assembled network and storage vendors to provide inexpensive on-demand computing and storage via the Web. Its competitive advantage does not rest on infrastructure control. Its advantage is at the applications layer, where it developed a programming language to allow firms to build customized, on-demand business applications. This creates a platform for other software add-ons.[10] Other firms may use the features of mash-ups and ad revenues to build specialized applications combined with "leased" ICT infrastructure. MySpace, Facebook, and other social networking spaces also have promoted a complementary community of programmers and information services.

To illustrate the potential of the fashion industry metaphor, we examine four elements of current ICT markets: Apple and the terminal market, convergence and content, the rise of the "Personal Network Platform," and fundamental R&D systems.

Apple and the Terminals Market

This subsection tells the story of Apple and how it informs the fashion industry metaphor. In some respects the iPod perfectly exemplifies the fashion industry metaphor. The extended iPod supply chain resembles value creation in the high-end fashion industry. Both depend on specialized inputs and high-end assembly, but integrate everything around a high-quality, high-concept fashion product.[11] Apple vertically integrates all of the value added from the website through the hardware device drawing on a modular supply base.[12] Integration provides an end-to-end experience with integrated end-to-end design and better ease of use.[13] Despite the usual assumption of the business press that hardware is just a commodity, the most profitable aspect of the iPod package is its hardware, and the iPod is definitely a fashion accessory.

The discussion that follows makes three main points. First, Apple's leadership position in digital music players (terminal and terminal software) has not translated into advantages in other content markets. Second, competition in music players and related segments (online services) remains rich because global supply chains have lowered barriers to new rivals constantly experimenting with alternatives to the iPod. Third, Apple—like Motorola with the RAZR—has limited capacity to sustain strong changes in fashion or a miss in the next product cycle. (Apple TV is widely considered a miss.)

The iPod also helps clarify the issues of leveraging and hardware competition in a modular world. For all its success, the iPod illustrates the limits of leveraging one element in the value chain (in this case the terminal) into adjacent market segments (digital content). The competition issues play out differently than in the 1990s. The iPod's current dominant position creates network effects. and its software makes it impossible for alternative formats (MP3) to interconnect. Thus, iPod users benefit from more swapping opportunities as the pool of iPod users grows. This network effect produced pressures from European authorities to open iPod's platform.[14] In addition, iPod's dominant market share worries others because the 1996

Digital Millennium Copyright Act (DMCA) makes it illegal to interoperate with the iPod without Apple's permission.[15] These concerns help clarify what is and what is not feared about Apple's market position. As late as the 1980s, iPod's success might have spurred a fear of Apple acquiring economies of scale that would lead to advantages in other markets. In the 1980s the mastery of one advanced manufacturing process with huge economies of scale provided advantages for attacking adjacent markets. At that time, this expertise propelled the Japanese economy.[16] Over time, this advantage diminished because Dell, Ericsson, Motorola, Hewlett-Packard, and other end-system producers developed competitive responses. They created design, production, and distribution chains with improved efficiencies and cost savings derived from outsourcing to sophisticated manufacturing specialists. Eventually these firms evolved into today's sophisticated original design manufacturers (ODMs). Collectively, these specialists mean that ICT firms can develop sophisticated make (build it yourself) or buy decisions when designing and marketing new products.[17]

The iPod also reveals how the Cheap Revolution is redefining hardware value. Networked services now are more central to hardware and software value because modularity helps equipment better respond to service designs from the ground up. Networked ICT once struggled to stitch together proprietary hardware platforms with complex code and clunky networks. Today, hardware design is planned as part of an overall applications package.[18] This is the promise of both the iPod and Amazon's Kindle. Both of these offerings are vertically integrated to deliver a compelling experience (hardware, software, and services complement). This is an important function of corporate strategy and design, but not a requirement for the products.

Modularity makes it possible for the system designer to mix and match where functionality resides. Routers had a relatively narrow functional mission to keep prices down while providing enough capacity to handle large traffic volumes. For example, Cisco now is investing heavily in health services management on the theory that the router and the software/service design can be optimized jointly in powerful combinations. The implications of these changes are explored shortly.

Another dimension of the iPod story is the increasing share of data in the total value of a hardware/services package. Users' inability to easily port data or iPod content to other applications may become a major ICT issue. It is the prime competition accusation made about the iPod. But modularity also undercuts the ability for iPod policies to seriously harm consumers on a sustained basis even with locked in content.

Digital content systems are abundant and market innovation for networked digital content takes many forms that are at least partial substitutes. (Many of the rivals embrace multi-sided platform strategies.) As demonstrated by YouTube's growth, the iPod world does not dominate all online media experiences.[19] Moves by NBC and Fox to launch their own websites and online services offerings and pull back content from Apple are proof of this concept.[20] Moreover, customers swap out consumer electronics quickly and reasonably close substitutes are available if Apple makes mistakes on pricing or product.

The iPod case illustrates a major implication of modularity: pressure on market leaders in every ICT equipment and software segment is increasing. These changes undercut traditional advantages enjoyed by systems vendors. This weakens the certainty of strategies that are based on the "systems engineering" metaphor. For example, Cisco does not have a platform for Internet routers as Intel once did for integrated circuits for PCs. Cisco enjoys scale economies, rapid innovation of devices that support complementary hardware communities, and brand reputation, including for customer service. However, the leverage from its proprietary technology (its software code) over others is limited because the interface between the router and other network functions and servers is open and modular. Its efforts to build vertical applications out from the router also face rivalry from expanding substitution possibilities by players in adjacent markets or new entrants. Cisco allows VoIP to ride on its routers as a software application that may pressure traditional telecom service and equipment offerings. Meanwhile, IBM mainframes can provide both VoIP and router capabilities.

A further implication of modularity is that tensions could flare between terminal and network suppliers. As convergence and modularity progress, pricing and functionality can be strategically located, thereby creating new rivalries between terminal providers and telecom networks. For example, mobile network operators may respond by working directly with the Taiwanese suppliers, to create handsets that deepen the carriers' control over customers' experience.[21] In response, traditional handset leaders, including Nokia and Motorola, may back public policies that weaken the control of mobile networks over their terminal equipment. Simultaneously, software vendors use ODMs to enter the mobile terminal market. Microsoft relies on HTC, a Taiwanese firm, for a significant share of Windows Mobile phone production. Google is giving "Android" (a Linux software package) to mobile phone suppliers that will feature Google at the center of the experience.

The iPod demonstrates three elements of the fashion metaphor. First, product life cycles are short; even leaders face substantial competitive pressure. Second, the iPod assumes a cloud-based services component (music, content) to complement the terminal, thereby enabling rapid innovation and choices between what forms and functions the terminal takes versus what relies on the cloud. Finally, the iPod also demonstrates the complex competitive landscape created by the presence of a sophisticated supply chain and the convergence of competitors from multiple geographies and segments in a single "market."

Convergence and Content

As services convergence approaches, the rise of a true Internet Protocol (IP) network and broadband will restructure service and content markets. Large changes in pricing and geographic market segmentation are on the horizon. The major competitors in networking pursue single packages of wired, wireless, and video services running on IP networks. Substituting among modes of exchanging information, including email, voice, messaging, video, and data sharing from multiple sources is getting easier. As content and information services markets grow, for example, it becomes possible to deliver telecom services alongside high valued content. This means conventional "pricing" for individual services is under increasing pressure from cross-industry entry across the board. It also means that geography is a less significant barrier to entry—either on the supply side (the creation of new services) or on the demand side (in the consumption of services).

Convergence already has transformed telecom pricing. Where competition and government rules permit, the long-distance market for domestic calls is fast becoming a residual. The marginal cost of a long-distance call is close to zero. The rise of VoIP illustrates this point. By operating as a data service, VoIP arbitrages the remaining legacy costs of older telephone networks, including their marketing and labor costs. VoIP avoids the cross-subsidies included in long-distance prices that government regulators mandated. US cell phone systems already offer a single bundle of local and long-distance services. Local phone services, spurred by new deals offered by hybrid cable telephone services, are following suit. The further collapse of phone pricing matters because voice remains the largest revenue generator for networks. The introduction of 3G, IP-based wireless networks migrate this pressure to the mobile wireless space. In 2008 a smaller Japanese carrier, eMobile, offered $55 per month pricing for unlimited data use on networks delivering downloads at 1.4–3.0 megabits per second and providing VoIP. These practices are a challenge to older carriers and

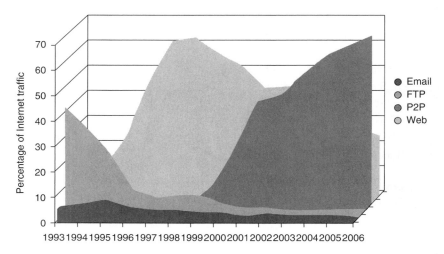

Figure 4.1
Internet protocol trends, 1993–2006. Source: CacheLogic Research, 2006.

governments because margins on cellular subsidiaries were propping up the carriers' business cases. Moreover, the rise of VoIP with true global numbering plans will allow much of the value added in voice telephony to be provided by global companies, such as Skype.

When combined with multi-band, all-purpose, digital appliances, new IP broadband networks also undercut the control of rigidly structured, terrestrial and satellite broadcast networks or cable television networks.[22] This calls into question the assumed dominance of point (headquarters) to multi-point distribution and content models. Broadband content distribution further erodes the control of siloed, point-to-multipoint business models.

Peer-to-peer connections will weaken program syndication and media business advertising models because they rely on running the same programs and charging for separate ads in multiple geographic markets.[23] As figure 4.1 shows, peer-to-peer traffic far exceed Web traffic on the Internet. Interviews confirm the Web folk wisdom that 5 percent of users generate more than half of the US Web traffic. Much of its content involves commercial media (including pornography) that often is copied illegally.[24] Illegally copied content is becoming a convenient, close substitute for copyrighted material. Consequently, producers of copyrighted material are under pressure to substantially alter pricing, reduce the availability and dissemination of material (using DRM or other systems), or move to an entirely different revenue stream. Britain funds the BBC through a tax on televisions. Music companies might embed their content with ads.[25] The European antitrust debate over iTunes is part of this broader discussion of how the future business model for digital music might look.[26]

Unlike the music industry, the worldwide film industry's box office revenues increased dramatically since 1990, especially outside North America. Between 1990 and 2005 global box office more than tripled from just over $7 billion to more than $23 billion. During the same period, however, the U.S. share of global box office fell from about 70 percent to about 40 percent of the total. Figure 4.2 shows that these trends continued between 2002 and 2006, Although the American and Canadian markets remained nearly stagnant at just over $10 billion during this period, box office revenues increased in Europe, the Middle, Africa, Latin America, and the Asia Pacific during the same period from about $9.6 billion in 2002 to about $15.6 billion in 2006.[27]

A further consequence is that lower entry barriers for applications and content are creating new global content markets. The mass consumption, broadband market empowers a new set of lead users in households (not large businesses) that use technology to co-invent new digital applications. This is reflected in the mobile services being pioneered by Asian teenagers.[28] It is also promotes thriving new niche markets such as Facebook, which began as a digital college yearbook and is now a major Web phenomenon. Critically, broadband networks make alternative programming and social communities possible. Online gambling and online gaming are

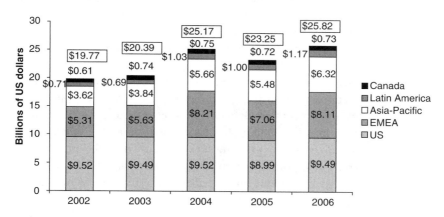

Figure 4.2
Global box office revenues, 2002–2006. Source: "MPA Snapshot Report: 2006 International Theatrical Market," Motion Picture Association, April 2007.

growing rapidly in popularity worldwide. Online gambling is growing exponentially outside the United Stares (where it is legal) and significantly in the United States (where it is not legal). Online gaming was projected to triple from $2.5 billion annually in 2004 by 2007.[29] At the end of January 2008, World of Warcraft, a hugely popular online video game, topped 10 million active subscribers worldwide—slightly more than half of them in Asia, one-fourth in North America, and slightly more than one-fifth in Europe.[30]

It also is becoming easier to share and build social networks around user-generated content.[31] The growth of YouTube is fueled by tens of millions of viewings of amateur music and video makers.[32] In October 2006 Google paid $1.6 billion for YouTube, a stunning assessment of the power of this blend of multimedia and social networking.[33] As tools for building communities and monetizing user-generated content evolve, the scale and depth of this content will soar.[34]

The Long Tail thesis applies to more than lowering the costs of mar-keting niche media products.[35] It also applies to other markets where global demand is not homogeneous. For example, scale economies no longer preclude smaller markets from achieving world-class production values. For example, SK Communications, the huge online Web and gaming provider, is Korean.[36] The quality of its software games rivals Hollywood movies, but its lower distribution costs mean that it is easier to market to Korean speakers in the United States. At the same time, the cost of converting content for other language pools is declining.[37] The Chinese video game market is dominated by local producers and, to a lesser extent, Korean producers. Localization dynamics in growing markets meant that in mid 2006 only one of the 45 games most popular games in China (World of Warcraft) was produced by a Western vendor.[38]

If convergence means that the line between high value content and user-generated content is blurring (yielding to the "co-created application" with producers and consumers delivering the experience), then it is also blurring and pushing change in global advertising markets. Table 4.1 suggests that online advertising is growing at the expense of traditional, offline advertising. (From 2006 through 2008, the number of digital ads increased from about one-tenth to about one-seventh of the number of traditional ads.) As people spend more time online, marketers move online because they can earn a higher return on investment and benefit from better performance data that can be captured online. And the ad market is so large (more than $380 billion in 2008) that it is a huge incentive for new digital applications that can lure ads. Although the United States clearly is at the epicenter of this transformation (with more than 50 percent of every digital category), the pie is so large and growing so fast that it can fuel innovation in applications and content across major global markets (especially in view of the low cost of entry provided by the Cheap Revolution.

The growth of converged, online content markets and experiences spurred online ad networks for both large and niche online experiences. Google's Adsense, the best-known example, sells ad placement to advertisers and places ads across the Web (on third-party websites that sign up for the service) in exchange for a fee (or vig). As people spend more time online, the opportunities for online ad networks to monetize these experiences will grow. Ad net works have opened up new economic models on the Web that react to what has come to be called "the attention economy."[39] This make ad networks the center of large amount of venture capital investments (such as targeting technologies, micro-payments, and niche markets) and the source of furious innovation. This "economic engine" is forcing three further changes.

The first implication is that ad-funded experiences (and online ad spending) will grow at the expense of offline spending. Traditional ads are a relatively inefficient way for advertisers to reach consumers. Online ads are more targeted and therefore more efficient for both consumers and advertisers. The initial search on a topic (e.g., searching for consumer reports on dishwashers) is a better "signal" of consumer interest for the seller than traditional "signals" (e.g., income or neighborhood). The ads triggered by the search are also likely to be more pertinent to the consumer's interest. Thus, both the consumer and the producer can both potentially capture value from the exchange.

A second implication is that while the initial package of horizontal search and online ads was a great success, over time the degree of its preeminence will ebb. The reason is simple. Horizontal ad networks (Google or Yahoo) are unlikely to realize the click-through rates that more focused ad networks can deliver.[40] Just as coupons evolved into loyalty programs and other ways for producers to capture data about consumers, ad networks are likely to become more sophisticated.

Modularity enables the growth of innumerable specialized services that support niche communities of consumers. Consider the many organizations that create both social bonds and consumption needs, whether they may be bowling leagues or bird watchers. Information services for these communities are being created, serving specific functional needs for their organizations. Although their business models vary, our interviews with

Table 4.1
Global advertising market by format, category, and region. Sources: PricewaterhouseCoopers; analysts' reports.

Format	Category	Region	2006	2007	2008	2009	2010
Digital	Paid listings	LA	101	134	173	215	259
		APAC	2,041	2,648	3,383	4,172	4,989
		EMEA	3,266	4,241	5,376	6,492	7,530
		North America	6,748	8,312	10,097	11,748	13,306
	Paid listings total		12,156	15,335	19,029	22,627	26,084
	Display ads	LA	81	104	127	154	179
		APAC	1,632	2,042	2,483	2,983	3,451
		EMEA	2,611	3,270	3,946	4,642	5,209
		North America	5,396	6,410	7,412	8,400	9,204
	Display ads total		9,720	11,825	13,969	16,180	18,043
	Local search (incl. Internet YP)	LA	51	70	92	117	145
		APAC	1,038	1,385	1,791	2,270	2,786
		EMEA	1,662	2,218	2,847	3,532	4,205
		North America	3,433	4,347	5,347	6,392	7,431
	Local search (incl. Internet YP) total		6,185	8,019	10,076	12,311	14,567
	Classified	LA	40	52	66	81	97
		APAC	810	1,034	1,287	1,576	1,875
		EMEA	1,295	1,656	2,046	2,453	2,831
		North America	2,677	3,246	3,842	4,439	5,002
	Classified total		4,822	5,989	7,241	8,550	9,806
	CGM ads	LA	11	17	28	44	68
		APAC	213	337	537	845	1,302

Table 4.1
(continued)

Format	Category	Region	2006	2007	2008	2009	2010
		EMEA	340	540	853	1,315	1,965
		North America	703	1,058	1,602	2,379	3,472
	CGM ads total		1,266	1,953	3,020	4,582	6,807
	Mobile advertising	LA	9	19	31	47	64
		APAC	187	373	606	908	1,242
		EMEA	299	597	962	1,413	1,874
		North America	618	1,170	1,808	2,556	3,311
	Mobile advertising total		1,112	2,158	3,407	4,924	6,491
	Digital total		35,262	45,279	56,741	69,173	81,798
Physical	TV network advertising	LA	7,751	8,259	9,348	9,875	11,299
		APAC	33,434	35,377	39,457	41,200	44,862
		EMEA	41,733	44,057	47,387	50,081	53,751
		North America	75,000	77,619	84,528	86,420	92,163
	TV network advertising total		157,918	165,312	180,720	187,576	202,075
	Newspaper advertising	LA	3,821	4,097	4,371	4,646	4,920
		APAC	23,700	24,832	27,138	28,009	29,636
		EMEA	38,846	40,138	41,502	42,918	44,369
		North America	47,575	47,827	48,321	48,347	49,016
	Newspaper advertising total		113,942	116,894	121,332	123,920	127,941
	Magazine advertising	LA	1,127	1,219	1,311	1,402	1,498
		APAC	6,698	7,054	7,493	7,772	8,121
		EMEA	21,164	22,000	22,940	23,890	24,838

Table 4.1
(continued)

Format	Category	Region	2006	2007	2008	2009	2010
		North America	25,307	26,601	28,125	29,289	30,084
Magazine advertising total			54,296	56,874	59,869	62,353	64,541
Radio and out-of-home advertising	LA		264	285	309	332	356
	APAC		5,403	5,715	6,161	6,369	6,767
	EMEA		8,385	9,055	9,767	10,454	10,454
	North America		7,121	7,681	8,322	8,982	9,763
Out-of-home ads total			21,173	22,736	24,559	26,137	27,340
Physical total			347,329	361,816	386,480	399,986	421,897

the applications providers indicate a common dimension—specialized ad systems designed for these vertical niches.

The appeal of vertical niches is that user activity in these niches is an even better signal than a general horizontal search of a user's interest in specialized sales offerings. Users' activities on the application site can even be a stimulus for them to make the purchase decision at the time. (As an analogy, the sales of branded souvenirs and CDs at concerts of successful rock bands are predictably even more profitable than ticket revenue because attending the concert is a stimulus for consumption.) Thus, advertisers are willing to pay several times more than standard online rates for ads on these application sites. (A multiple of four is not unusual for strong sites.) This specialization in application services, and development of niche user communities, enables specialized search and ads as a significant rival to horizontal search ads. Modularity facilitates both the application and the specialized ad network.

The growth of vertical applications and ad networks is already emerging. A third implication of this economic engine is more nascent. Ad-funded software is a relatively imprecise way for consumers or small suppliers to "sell" their data to advertisers or larger service providers. Aspiring musicians complain that numerous social networking sites use their content to promote the popularity of the site, and thus generate ad revenue, without any form of compensation for the musician.[41] Consumers involved in new websites that provide organization, storage, and even some analysis of personal medical information (including data supplied by the user, not just the doctor) will worry about more than privacy. They will eventually realize that this information is valuable to the website to sell targeted ads for medical services and products. At a minimum, they will become interested in what economic benefit accrues to the user for providing this information. (See the following discussion of the Personal Network Platform.) As we discuss in the concluding chapter, policy and technology innovation will create new forms for consumers and producers to "exchange and price consumer data."

The Emerging Personal Network Platform

The ICT market traditionally divided into the enterprise and consumer/ small business markets. Enterprises' spending fuelled long-term ICT infrastructure innovation, but the mass market for ICT created a second innovation stream. Modularity will produce a crossover between the personal mass market and the enterprise market. Consumer email service already is making its way into the enterprise and public institutions. The

Table 4.2
ICT spending by government, business and consumer segments. Source: *Digital Planet: The Global Information Economy* (2006 report by World Information Technology and Services Alliance), at http://www.witsa.org.

ICT spending for 2005	$ billions	% of total
Government (government, transport/ communications, utilities)	815.1 (505.2, 250.5, 59.4)	27.50
Business (finance & business services, manufacturing, trade, other services, construction, agriculture, mining)	1,474.6 (481.5, 433.1, 292.2, 201.9, 36.6, 12.5, 16.8)	49.76
Consumer	673.7	22.73
Total	2,963.5	

eventual result will be the emergence of the Personal Network Platform (PNP).

As table 4.2 demonstrates, the enterprise and government markets still dominate in ICT spending. But the jumping-off point today is the consumer market's social networking, instant messaging, and user-generated content (of all types—from shopping reviews to personal videos). There already are aggregators, which connect existing data and micro-applications to function as "live portals" that connect various sources in a single place. VodPod and other companies aggregate online video sites, and Spokeo brings together social networking sites.[42] Netvibes quickly built a base of roughly 10 million users, mainly by providing the ability for non-technical users to quickly connect data fields from across the Web into a single interface.

The Personal Network Platform represents two intersecting forces creating a new synthesis. First, as Netvibes, Pageflakes, and the three major portals (Google, Yahoo, MSN/Live) illustrate, the flow, the form, and the diversity of user information have expanded tremendously. Users no longer just track and "file" their own information. They act more like firms of the past—huge assimilators of third-party information that is mixed and matched with their own creations. Users also access and manipulate information across many locations and devices. This requires powerful organizational capabilities for individuals that are tied to more than the PC.[43] Second, the enterprise and public sector are following the consumer space experiments with "Web 2.0" capabilities.

A more flexible ICT network infrastructure allows enterprises to respond to "consumer-driven" innovation in the firm.[44] Employees use software and services at home and expect similar levels of services at work. To attract and keep talent, enterprises must respond. They also can make business gains by deploying basic services across all segments of the workforce and new, specialized information services to specific user segments.

Consider the routine issue of calendaring. Employees want to reconcile their personal and office calendars, so some are turning to Web-based calendars on their cell phones to handle feeds from both. This raises new privacy challenges. For example, the details of a weekly McKinsey partner call found their way onto the Internet via a partner's Web-based calendar.[45]

Consolidated calendaring is a start. Sales personnel want routing that optimizes the list of best sales prospects, a trip to the dentist, and a stop for dinner.[46] Personal and business data must be mingled to optimize the lives of professionals away from their offices. Customer contact software for sales people began as a niche but evolved into customer management systems that provide a new way to organize work. Taken together these niche market applications are transformative.

The hallmark tools of "Web 2.0" also are migrating to business-to-business ("B-to-B") applications. Firms are using "wikis" and social networking tools to build links across disparate work groups and with their suppliers and customers. (Individuals can do the same thing using wetpaint.com.) Motorola's decision to use a wiki[47] for customer support for the Q phone illustrates how even customer support for leading consumer electronics devices with short product life cycles is increasingly bottom-up from corporate employees and customers, instead of top-down from customer support staff. This explosive growth will propel more mingling of personal and business applications, periodically vexing chief information officers.

Web platform companies once focused mostly on consumers but now are entering the enterprise through offerings that combine personal services for employees and support of "Web 2.0" tools. Another example is Amazon's S3 (Simple Storage Service) and EC2 (Elastic Compute Cloud) service, which provide online storage and processing. This online storage can be configured for backup capabilities if a firm's internal storage is not sufficient for a specific application. This service highlights the blurring of boundaries across the Web, storage, bandwidth, and enterprise/consumer scenarios as new applications and services emerge.

The concentration of high-bandwidth IT in a limited set of business and personal arenas has received limited attention. Consider the factory floor. In 2000 it was unusual for a majority of factory workers to have corporate email accounts. Firms have scrambled to correct this but try to cut the costs of building new IT infrastructure. One emerging option is that Web firms can deliver and support email and information services infrastructure as a "white label" for the corporate host.[48] This is a search for eyeballs that generate ad revenue and data sources that can be sold to other specialized information services suppliers.

These beginnings may lead to a single "personalized network platform" (PNP) built on Web technologies that combine the performance and security of corporate applications with the ease of use, flexibility, and personal scope of Web applications. The PNP would integrate the traffic, content, and applications of individual consumers as they participated in the corporate world, and vice versa.

The PNP will require innovations in ICT capabilities and business and government policies. For example, it would require powerful tools for managing identities. Suppose you are Maggie to family members, Margaret to business colleagues, Shop Wiz to e-commerce vendors, and Girl Scout to online game players, and that you maintain separate emails and profiles for each identity. A PNP would require public and corporate policies to manage the negotiation of the disclosure and sharing of privacy information. An employment contract would probably have to contain terms for sharing private information on the corporate networked applications (e.g., human resources access to certain health information).[49]

The PNP is part of a new innovation system that illustrates the horizontal widening of networked ICT outside traditional locations (e.g., office buildings) and the vertical application into a new hybrid of business, social, and personal processes.[50] As with all technology edges, it is unclear how these changes will develop, but its early manifestations are becoming apparent.

Less bandwidth-intensive examples show the horizontal potential of the wireless revolution. Existing services already spur users, including low-income ones to invest in connectivity. SMS, for example, is a valuable resource in medical emergencies in poor rural areas. Farmers worldwide increasingly use cell phones to check market prices offered in nearby towns. China Mobile, for example, provides farmers with the prices of different crops at different regional markets to help them guide planting and marketing decisions.[51] These low bandwidth innovations will multiply. The implications at the inflection point will be profound. The "precision agriculture" movement will move to poorer countries as the cost of "smart" tractors or plows decreases and broadband wireless emerges. These packages will deploy sensors and feed information on soil conditions to artificial intelligence systems that advise farmers in the fields as they decide on plowing and fertilizers. Large agriculture supply companies will share their ICT capabilities with their customers as a marketing tool. ITC, an Indian tobacco and agricultural supply company, is already a leader in deploying rural ICT data services of this type.

The vertical potential already is evident in existing rich media applications. They can pull audio, video, and data from disparate sources and at the same time request data from corporate databases. Now, think of what nike.com could be like if, instead of pulling data out of inventory files, a PNP pulled data from an individual's health monitoring files and suggested an appropriate shoe to buy for workout routines.

Even as large players expand into this space, modularity opens the way for an explosion of new, niche applications to serve the "long tail" of demand for software and services.[52] Standardized software components and data that can be combined into new applications yield a proliferation of micro-apps focused on ever-smaller slivers. As barriers to entry to software production fall, "user-generated software" proliferates, but not the software created by vendor developers or designers.

As the PNP evolves, it provides incentives for both producers and consumers to enter into sophisticated "bargains." For example, chain grocery stores lure customers with loyalty cards that promise lower prices on some items. This allows the store to create more accurate user profiles. Such developments have complicated consequences. In this instance the grocery industry becomes more efficient, thus lowering its cost structure, which is beneficial both for the stores and consumers. But critics note that it would be more accurate to state that stores are raising prices for the discounted items and charging a premium to customers who will not join the program. Consumers increasingly must choose between sacrificing their privacy if they permit purchases with smart tags to be tracked or paying a premium for products and services.[53] Concentrated vendors may sometimes wield so much market power that their influence over customers is significant and easy remedies do not exist.

Nonetheless, consumers may gain important benefits as well. Unified medical databases may help save lives.[54] Or, health insurers might charge patients more unless they are allowed to track their compliance with prescription medication regimens. This may help guarantee that patients take their medicine, but it also provides insurers with a reason to cut off benefits for noncompliance. At a time when insurers are accused of not extending benefits or cutting them off if treatment is expensive, this could raise concerns. To safeguard against possible abuses will require developing new norms and practices related to the ways to let the PNP grant varying levels of permission for tracking depending on the decision of the user about privacy.[55]

This will be challenging because there still is no clarity about what constitutes public versus private data. Is an individual's health care data really private? Changes in what constitutes private data are evolving rapidly. With significant co-investment in the creation of data how should we define the ownerships of an address book on FaceBook, travel itineraries on TripIt, or house data on Zillow? Ultimately "Web 2.0" and related applications (including online content) will create huge amounts of new public data without clear property rights—end users or companies can take advantage of it yet ownership is unclear. Organizations such as dataportability.org are a start, but are narrowly focused on social networking, not on the broader problem. In the summary chapter we will lay out reasons why this is a critical area for policy innovation for consumer and producers to take advantage of the innovations enabled by the inflection point.

High-End R&D: Leaving the Lab

The Cheap Revolution, modularity, and pervasive broadband networks open the potential for radical new users for ICT and radical new business models as ICT leaves the cloistered world of "the glass house." Today, leading research universities are marrying advanced ICT to conventional disciplines to adhere the power of silicon economics to more traditional research questions and challenges. For example, millions of remote sensors for medical, environmental, and other applications generate huge amounts of new data for research and management. The intersection of these huge data sets and associated technologies, combined with Cloud-style systems, means that huge data collection, monitoring, and analysis operations can routinely help guide environmental controls, monitor personal medical treatments, and more.[56] This creates new research opportunities, new research models, and ultimately new sets of ICT capabilities. All of this matters because basic R&D is central to the commercialization of ICT.

Most analysts overlook the importance of basic R&D for commercialization of ICT. Today, at the bleeding edge of research[57] in US universities, large-scale computation and new observational systems are redefining disciplines. Bioinformatics, for example, is transforming biology. At the same time, early prototype sensor systems help biologists study seabird nests and redwood groves.[58] Similarly, wireless sensor networks tied to local computers could monitor animal flocks and herds to provide early warnings of disease outbreaks while simultaneously producing huge new databases that could advance veterinary medicine.[59]

More ambitiously, consider medicine. Researchers imagine medicines with smart tags that can verify the authenticity of suppliers and distribution data if there is a recall. The same tags could interact when put side by side to warn of possible complications if the medicines are taken together.[60] They also could interact with monitoring devices inside patients that continuously transmit data that permit the creation of smart profiles of a patient's medical conditions that could in turn interact with prescription medications to monitor for complications or compliance. Or, these profiles might produce automatic alerts to see a doctor or cause the release of medicines implanted in the patient. Deploying powerful, inexpensive networked applications on this model could generate huge health-care savings.[61]

Such applications also will fuel new business models. Big pharmaceuticals are experimenting with offering "open-source" licenses for important research inputs that they develop. This allows them to (1) commoditize these aspects of the research and production system, (2) create a shared research community to leverage their expertise on these phases of the research task, and (3) focus on what they consider their critical advantages.[62]

New models for research and systems management also are in development. As the number of available real-time data observations for patient populations expands significantly, the medical research and care system will morph, propelling changes in the patterns of creating and testing drugs and medical devices. Patient tests will be run outside medical labs, allowing greater flexibility and removing many restrictions that hamper research. One major medical research challenge is to determine the extent of the relationship between genetic and environmental factors in the onset or absence of disease. Sensor tracking and monitoring systems will allow more precise recording of patients' behavior and environmental surroundings, expanding research and treatment options.

Similarly, the management of environmental problems intersecting with crop yields, air quality, running the electric grid, or climate change will evolve when evidence-based evaluation systems process billions of observations and provide real-time feedback to applications of commercial and social value.[63] At present, even the best climate models are too imprecise to allow a large state such as California to plan with any granularity about water management issues when considering changing weather patterns.[64]

The cost and complexity of many state-of-the-art research facilities raises another fundamental challenge for science. The capabilities and costs of research and design tools for products created by computational chemistry and nano-level materials sciences are on the rise, requiring more cost sharing and large communities of virtual users. The data storage and processing needed to produce these systems demands immense quantities of bandwidth and complicated software tools. For instance, the collaborative visualization systems that link researchers and data in supercomputer systems can require half a terabyte of data on the network. The fields of advanced visualization and bioinformatics are using networked supercomputing to allow researchers to walk through "virtual" gene strands to visualize research possibilities in new ways. Biotech firms are scrambling to be linked to these research tools. (Figures 3.4 and 3.5 illustrated the growth in network traffic as major research facilities were networked together.) A few commercial users (e.g., oil companies that model possible exploration sites) already are populating this territory. New collaborative computing facilities likely will emerge from grassroots organizations, much as the search for extraterrestrial intelligence (SETI) was an early application of grid computing. These may tackle major modeling challenges, such as improvements in how to design sustainable buildings and vehicles.

New research tools do not guarantee effective innovation. It takes changes in the organizations of markets and institutions (both commercial and non-commercial) to tap these capabilities. It requires translational organizations to create network links among research projects and between researchers and potential innovators in business and government.[65] The point is: prospects for data and computationally intense innovation performed collaboratively and globally are emerging at the inflection point.

Today's high-end labs will inform future commercial applications. This was true in the past and is probably still accurate. This signals a move toward a world of diverse terminals (some powerful, some dumb, and almost all incredibly small and cheap relative to their function). These terminals will rely on ubiquitous networks to capture and deliver data in new and startling ways. Moving data from the natural world into the ICT fold will accelerate this process and will create new applications and new uses around this data. In view of the specialized nature of many of these applications, a blossoming of specialized devices and information services providers is inevitable. Moreover, the low cost of distribution and the presence of sophisticated global supply chains to design and deliver products will result in a world that resembles Silicon Valley more than the traditional pharmaceutical market where scientists in biotech rely on "big pharma" to take new products and compounds to market.

Stumbling Blocks along the Road to a Digital Paradise

This analysis of the implications at the inflection point concludes with a brief discussion of likely policy controversies. We begin with long-standing concerns about competition and innovation, and then turn to transactional inefficiencies that may undermine the inflection point's promise.

With the initial introduction and spread of competition, the main worry was that dominant firms—traditional telecoms or the victors of winner-take-all competitions for semiconductor and software platform superiority—would be only marginally responsive to consumers, providing expensive services, slow innovation, and reduced future competition. These concerns still echo in policy-making circles. Although increasing modularity should limit these risks, difficult issues remain. Even with the beginning of competitively provided broadband, some issues related to network infrastructure remain.

To paraphrase Bill Clinton's 1992 campaign: "It's the bandwidth, stupid!" No country has resolved fully the broadband issue and the availability of ample networked broadband is indispensable to fulfilling the inflection point's potential. Despite improvements in wireless networking, high-end data flows are a long way from being ubiquitous. Future prosperity depends on the provision of ample network capacity, seamless inter-networking, efficient pricing, and flexible responses to the many sides of the networked ICT platform.

The contrast between rich and poor countries on networking is deeply disturbing. Mobile networks and competition are helping solve connectivity problems in regard to voice and narrowband networking, but the provision of true broadband and ultra-broadband, even at the backbone level, remains a challenge for bridging the digital divide.[66] Figure 4.3 shows that international traffic across the Atlantic and Pacific still dominate, The data for Latin America and the paltry flows involving Africa are out of date, but only slightly.

In wealthier countries the problems are less dramatic, but they are real. The roadblock is that so far in the United States the spread of broadband for consumers and small and medium-size businesses is deplorable. As of mid 2007, the US had fallen from the top of the international rankings for broadband ubiquity and speed to number 14.

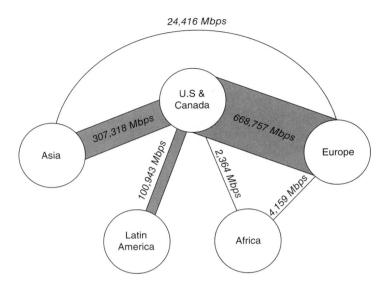

Figure 4.3
Backbone fiber connectivity. Source: Primetrica, Inc.

Still, major customers usually have the bargaining leverage to secure whatever network facilities they need. But even in the United States the number of huge customers is quite small. For example, one regional Bell considered only its largest 400 customers—those that spent more than $2 million annually—as top-tier customers. In 2004, fewer than 10,000 of that company's customers spent more than $100,000.[67] Although smaller customers can gain from their presence in large office buildings or corporate parks, the availability of big broadband rapidly drops off below the Fortune 500, the largest urban office buildings, and the major research universities.[68] Indeed, competition even for office buildings is weaker than commonly assumed. In its approval of the AT&T-BellSouth merger, the FCC discovered that AT&T only provided its own competitive broadband facilities to 317 office buildings in BellSouth territory. Only 31 office buildings in BellSouth territory had AT&T as the exclusive provider of fiber access facilities.[69]

There is one mitigating factor. US consumer broadband is slow, expensive, and less ubiquitous than the world's leaders, but the US is ahead of most countries in building out its competitive broadband infrastructure. (Most countries rely primarily on regulators to require network sharing by the dominant carrier.) Although it still designs its residential plant for much slower speeds than it is capable of providing, cable television now is a real rival to the local phone companies and it aggressively markets broadband to small business.[70] Moreover, the western US in particular has huge municipal fiber capacity that is waiting to be unlocked. And the US may manage to deploy wireless broadband more extensively than others. Of course, poor regulatory choices in the US and elsewhere could prevent progress toward the future pictured here.[71] We support regulatory reform related to pricing and supply that eliminates or at least minimizes the need for future regulation.

A second issue involves networking as competition increases. The greater centrality of networked ICT allows for new twists on reciprocal compensation. A fair and reasonable system is needed to allow networks to compensate each other for exchanging traffic.

A third issue arises because some parts of the ICT network infrastructure may create competition problems not identified in second-era policies. It always is tempting to apply guidelines that succeeded at an earlier technological stage and recycle them in competition policy. Evidently, EU, Japanese, and Korean competition authorities are determined to fight the type of leveraging of platforms that they associated with the second ICT era and the influence of Intel and Microsoft. This emphasis could be ill conceived at the inflection point. This pertains to parts of the ICT infrastructure that change more slowly for a variety of reasons, including slower turnover in hardware.

IBM's strategy of using Grid-style computing to achieve more ambitious software solutions involving larger databases (e.g., to reinvent business processes) was discussed earlier. Many European firms have similar plans. These solution packages represent forms of vertical integration extending from enterprise data to end services. The large data centers and their supporting infrastructure are renewed constantly, but not at the vociferous rate of consumer items. Moreover, many solutions require complex consensus decisions among many independent stakeholders to design and modify the application.[72] Thus, these integrated solutions may have greater staying power for vendors, but their specificity makes them unsuitable for creating general platforms.[73] This is true because often the solution is embedded in physical elements (smart transportation systems, GPS systems) and because there are political processes whose complexities make it hard to reopen competitive alternatives for these complex systems.

The complex system applications that need the consent of many stakeholders permit strategic games and policy choices that could raise significant obstacles. The challenge for innovation and consumer welfare could be that legacy firms lock-in their customers. For example, if independent actors control many decision points, the implementation of applications such as setting road standards could grind to a halt. Meanwhile, large corporate users are seeking ways to reduce lock-in by insisting on interoperability. Here, the "white hats" and "black hats" are not obvious to those assessing competition issues.[74]

A fourth set of issues relates to difficulties that arise from unlocking modularity in the content market. As modularity proceeds, ICT infrastructure issues take different twists, but they still resemble the debates of the 1990s. In the late 1980s the US cable industry locked up control of significant television programming content. To create a competitive broadcast infrastructure, the FCC finally ordered the cable industry to make its programming available to satellite broadcasters on non-discriminatory terms. Similarly, in 2006 the British regulator, Ofcom, began investigating concerns that Sky TV's control over sports programming could block growth of the cable infrastructure.[75] Analogously, as we noted earlier, although iTunes does not have exclusive licensing rights to the original music, iTunes retains the exclusive right to interoperate with the music it sells. Still, there may be nothing in music rights that has as much market impact as control of the rights to the two or three major national sports. Of course, keeping control of content also is more difficult in a modular digital age.

Traditional national content policies will clash with global digital content. Joost exemplifies important questions that highlight potential obstacles to innovation: Will regulators allow television content to leak easily over national borders? Will divided broadcast and regulatory authorities in various countries agree on sensible competition rules, or will they try to set quotas on foreign broadcast via the Web? Will content providers possess the business sense and legal and policy tools to craft new options for licensing and monitoring the use of their content?

A fifth large risk involves transactional inefficiencies. The inflection point allows wider sharing, mixing, and matching of all digital information and content. But current ownership and exchange procedures make it difficult for mutually beneficial exchanges. Despite major debates over copyright reform, copyrights will remain an important factor in the marketplace.[76] Thus, it is important to consider the transactional difficulties tied to these rights. The logic of modularity means that digital rights must be available on an efficiently traded basis. Today, as content sites repeatedly complain, it is difficult to figure out who holds rights and how to license them efficiently. This issue goes beyond who wants what and what is it worth to them. What matters is the ability to execute transactions more easily, thus allowing more efficient trades and contracts.

Content extends beyond the traditional commercial media and databases venues. At the inflection point, a significant form of content is information created by, and about, the individual user. YouTube highlights the scale of individuals' generation of content and raises questions about how much control over their own content individuals will demand in the future. But, departing from the usual treatment of privacy as a form of civil liberty, data about individuals, including height, weight, and buying preferences, is valuable content for the organization of the Web world. The question that repeatedly arises is: How much information will any person give up about herself and under what conditions?[77]

Some people like to shop in the neighborhood store for the communal social experience. Others prefer less personal stores on the mall to achieve some measure of privacy (not just price or variety). A similar set of tradeoffs can exist at the inflection point. The bottom line is: What does a person receive in return for yielding their information? The inflection point opens

Table 4.3
The path to modularization.

Modularity and the Cheap Revolution
Microelectronics price/performance
Innovations in fiber optic and wireless bandwidth
Changes in software design and costs
Digital media content

Three Alternative Metaphors at the Inflection Point
Information Utility Metaphor
Systems Integration Metaphor
High-End Fashion Industry Metaphor
  iPod as "poster child"
  Convergence and broadband will restructure service and content
  Emergence of "Personal Network Platform"
  Synthesis of new ICT applications reinforcing new models of innovation

Potential Stumbling Blocks
Bandwidth
Compensation for exchanging traffic
New competition problems
Content market problems
Transactional inefficiencies

---

the way to transactional management of privacy issues, but policy may ignore this potential.

Conclusions

Table 4.3 outlines the argument about the path to modularization presented in chapters 3 and 4. It summarizes the main drivers of the Cheap Revolution that is producing ICT modularity. It recalls three metaphors that might be used to represent the new modular reality, including our favored metaphor: that of the high-fashion industry. It recognizes that the path to modularity is strewn with stumbling blocks. Five of the stumbling blocks that were considered are noted. This table lays the groundwork for chapter 5.

5 The Political Economy of the Inflection Point

If the networked ICT industry is at an inflection point that challenges all major segments of this market, then it should be reflected in the political economy of market governance. Here we examine the evidence.

In this chapter we probe two dimensions of the political economy at the inflection point. We begin by arguing that the United States is and likely will remain for some time the pivot of this inflection point. (Although its agenda cannot determine global change, the US is likely to be the single largest influence on the global policy agenda.) Then we turn to the political economy of three major issues looming at this inflection point.

In chapter 4 we suggested that broadband is significant at the inflection point, which is prompting a major market-governance challenge. The debate over broadband competition policy and wireless networking in the United States reflects the politics of market entry today. The political agenda of Republicans tapped into the long-standing policy propensities built into the US political structure in a way that, after 2000, tilted the focus on broadband policy toward wireless. The ensuing debate over spectrum policy soon reflected the emerging impact of ICT modularity and smart terminals. New thinking about network use and pricing (multi-sided platform economics) further changed the assumptions for feasible entry. Moreover, all sides of the spectrum debate implicitly assumed that the vertical integration of networks was declining.

A second flash point for policy is the set of new interconnection challenges posed by the modularity of ICT. The power of market leverage from traditional platforms is declining just as the rise of the Personal Network Platform provides an incentive to mix and match content and network functionalities in novel ways. This led to the debate over network neutrality and a fragmentation of the traditional IT coalition powerfully influenced interconnection policies. New policy coalitions arose over network neutrality. One side argued that existing competition rules make creative combinations of networks and content easy to transact. Others held that customization of network functionality required much more attention. This debate does not fit easily within the traditional political alliances on ICT. The terms of the debate are clarified by briefly comparing it to the Japanese and EU debates over competition involving network neutrality and information platforms.

A third challenge involves broadcast media and other forms of content. The inflection point changes the economics of production of content and also erodes market segmentation by geography or service (as in Internet transmission of broadcast programming). This provoked debates over broadcast and intellectual property policies that became the basis for major political clashes. But US political institutions channel these debates less into topics of content quotas than into issues over pricing and ownership of content. Again, the cleavages among stakeholders are volatile. Rupert Murdoch's News Corporation controls MySpace and also threatens to sue YouTube. NBC and the *Wall Street Journal* launch Hulu to provide free television shows, movies, and clips from them as a competitor to YouTube. CBS experiments with more permissive content licensing, and MTV (with more "YouTube-type" fare) plays hardball. Electoral politics lead both political parties to shy away from policies shifting away from IPR that favors traditional content owners.

As was discussed in chapter 3, related to content is the emergence of online advertising networks as a new economic engine underpinning both Web-based software and online content markets (including user-generated content (UGC). Google's Adsense and other ad networks "match" advertisers with websites to deliver targeted ads to consumers as they browse the Web. In addition some publishers sell their own ads instead of relying on a network to source ads). These ad networks are becoming another focal point for governance.

Overall, this chapter shows that a sea change in market governance is again at hand. Precise stakeholder interests and risks are in flux. The winning formula for political leaders still is shrouded in shadow. The full implications for the global market and its governance are murky. However, some areas where politics and good policy can be reconciled are coming into better focus. The United States is our initial focus to keep the analysis manageable.

The Global Market Context: The United States as Agenda Setter

Transition points do not signal a single outcome. A space for change opens and the equilibrium within the space could take several forms. The ultimate equilibrium usually is set by the intersection of business strategy, technology potential, and public policies that influence market priorities and choices. Non-governmental organizations (NGOs), trade unions, and other interests sometimes tip the balance. Since 1945 the US market has been the most consistent agenda setter for the global market. Its policy choices shaped everyone else's strategic choices. This is not a uniform story; the challenge of Japan in the 1980s in IT and network hardware, the lead of Europe in mobile networking in 1990s, and the growth of mobile content markets all were important innovations that began outside the US market. Still, overall, on the economic, trade, and ICT issues that are of concern here the US was the dominant force.

We first argue that if the United States acts vigorously on the policy front, it can maintain its leadership position until about 2025. We are not predicting that the world will look the same then. Substantial policy missteps could markedly alter market paths. But especially before 2020 a combination of inertia and continuing American dominance in many arenas should guarantee that the US remains the pivot of the inflection point.

This view rests on five premises. First, the US has a large lead in its deployed ICT stock that is extremely difficult for other countries to overcome. This creates meaningful advantages in the ability of US buyers to deploy complex innovations, including a legacy of sophisticated users and buyers across the economy that have both the experience and the cumulative infrastructure investment to innovate rapidly and massively. Second, the US has the largest investment base and flows in the critical areas for innovation—national R&D spending, capitalization of the high tech industry, and private venture capital expenditure in IT and telecom. Third, the US will remain the leader for the foreseeable future in software, networked digital applications, high-value-added commercial content, and high end IT computing systems and solutions. Fourth, the US will continue to be among the top three global markets across the full range of ICT markets, from networking to software to services. In view of the breadth of the US position, the relative US position in any specific market segment (such as the world telecom service market or particular equipment markets) is less relevant than commonly claimed. Moreover, in view of the still sometimes fragmented nature of the "single" European market and the complexities tied to the less-than-transparent Chinese technology market, the effective market power of the US often is greater than the raw numbers suggest. The US is a single giant market that operates under relatively transparent rules and with a market framework that involves flexible capital and labor resources.[1] Fifth, the US is the leading producer of high value-added content (movies, television, music, video games), a critical element at present. Further, US legal decisions related to content (DRM, IPR, sharing, and monetization issues) will set the stage for any global arrangements in this arena. Intersecting with these market segments are the market institutions and policy choices that shape their crystallization.

Two types of innovation drive "technological winners" in contemporary ICT markets. It helps to distinguish between "upstream innovation" involving raw technical advances and "downstream innovation" that translates technical advances into valuable products and services.[2] Early and continuing US leadership forced competition and entry in all networked ICT segments creating a deep advantage in downstream innovation that fuels upstream innovation. Value-added services and intense competition in terminals primed new entrepreneurs to provide networked-based Internet services once commercialization of the Internet began in the early 1990s. This spurred an earlier IP-based Internet services explosion in the US than elsewhere. The presence of cutting-edge customers and broader PC deployment, first at work and then at home, also mattered. The over-building of fiber-optic backbones and the upgrade of cable television networks then created rival access to households by independent network infrastructures.

Overall, broad deployment of ICT capital stock built competitive telecom services infrastructure. Large amounts of venture capital also provided deep investment in network-based services and business models. As these matured and evolved through the "dot com" bust and now the "Web 2.0"/Software as a Service (SaaS) phase, the US continues at the leading edge for innovative network-based consumer-driven applications. But stand-alone businesses resting on competitive network infrastructure would have been impossible without portals and online bookstores in this second era.

The main US political economy goal was to foster network competition to foster IT innovation. This competition promoted lower networking prices for large businesses and middle-class consumers. When the regional Bells proposed that Internet pricing be treated like phone service pricing, US regulators rejected the idea.[3] This pricing stimulated competition and innovation across consumer-focused network services and applications. This created an early advantage in innovation at "the edge" of the network for the US that continues.

These policy choices and subsequent market evolution helped the United States remain the global market linchpin. Among the major advantages of the US is its dominance of the market for network-based applications and services, particularly in the consumer space and its leadership in melding business and consumer spaces into a seamless personal space on the Web.

Arguments that US Leadership Is Declining

Three distinct arguments suggest why the United States may not continue as the pivot point in the world market. In our view, two of them overlook the fundamental market changes created by the current inflection point, and one of them raises substantive policy choices for the US.

The first argument for decreasing US importance in world markets revolves around China. The increasing numbers of Chinese engineers, the emergence of Chinese firms as global leaders, and the sizzling Chinese domestic market are cited as evidence that China is assuming a global leadership position. Central to this argument is the ability of China to parlay the size of its domestic market (particularly investment in the domestic ICT infrastructure) into scale economies on the production side and the ability to leverage homegrown standards (e.g., TD-SCDMA) into leadership positions in adjacent market areas (e.g., handsets and applications).[4]

This reasoning assumes that China can develop a shrewd plan to implement this strategy. For familiar political reasons including corruption, huge labor displacement, changing demographics as the pool of younger rural workers available to industry shrinks, skyrocketing demand for natural resources, and environmental and health crises, China's continued economic boom is not a sure thing.[5] Even assuming sound strategy, the increasing modularity of ICT means that leveraging infrastructure standards into adjacent markets is getting more difficult. In a walled garden world, owning the network and the network standards opens the potential for building winning positions in applications and content. But this is a strategy with declining potential. If modularity increasingly rewards creative combinations, home grown standards and the size of local equipment markets cannot be easily leveraged to other markets.

The second argument that suggests the erosion of the US position stems from the continuing decline of US spending in major ICT market segments. We think these stories are overblown. Table 5.1 shows the Organization for Economic Cooperation and Development's 2000 to 2005 ICT market expenditures and forecast for the consolidated world ICT market through 2008. It is striking that the lowest share for the OECD is about 71 percent for hardware and the rest is comfortably in the upper 80 percent range.

Table 5.1
OECD ICT market expenditures 2000–2008 (millions of US dollars). Source: OECD Communications Outlook 2007, citing World Information Technology and Services Alliance. (Data for 2006–2008 forecast. CAGR: compound annual growth rate.)

	2000	2001	2002	2003	2004	2005	2006	2007	2008	CAGR 2000–2005	CAGR 2000–2008
Hardware											
Brazil	6,263	6,404	7,031	9,905	12,407	15,946	17,316	17,454	17,861	20.6	14.0
China	12,507	16,639	20,357	27,027	39,057	47,927	57,813	68,303	81,739	30.8	26.4
India	2,257	2,764	3,457	5,013	7,204	10,264	13,630	17,910	23,938	35.4	34.3
Russia	1,816	2,107	2,345	2,881	3,900	4,852	5,574	6,078	6,650	21.7	17.6
South Africa	1,661	1,707	1,698	2,503	3,457	4,024	4,412	4,646	5,150	19.4	15.2
OECD	398,488	325,333	302,735	325,390	360,929	377,547	402,346	433,459	459,076	−1.1	1.8
World	440,912	374,883	359,311	396,603	455,255	493,164	537,523	588,246	639,756	2.3	4.8
Software											
Brazil	1,602	1,698	1,787	2,469	2,877	3,566	3,828	3,803	3,785	17.4	11.3
China	1,085	1,658	2,253	3,344	5,295	7,940	11,376	16,328	23,002	48.9	46.5
India	358	456	588	948	1,350	1,908	2,519	3,336	4,378	39.8	36.8
Russia	343	395	450	570	742	923	1,056	1,182	1,313	21.9	18.3
South Africa	627	724	800	1,328	1,965	2,369	2,781	3,159	3,716	30.4	24.9
OECD	169,439	177,463	182,760	211,061	241,381	261,653	283,672	313,539	346,173	9.1	9.3
World	178,086	187,792	194,634	226,734	262,304	288,807	317,567	356,211	400,295	10.2	10.7

Table 5.1
(continued)

	2000	2001	2002	2003	2004	2005	2006	2007	2008	CAGR 2000–2005	CAGR 2000–2008
Services											
Brazil	4,937	4,792	5,101	7,353	9,040	11911	13,530	14,238	15,011	19.3	14.9
China	851	1,389	2,155	3,591	6,203	10,006	15,539	24,081	36,721	63.7	60.1
India	1,120	1,386	1,787	2,859	3,876	5,243	6,607	8,356	10,465	36.2	32.2
Russia	891	979	1,158	1,537	2,099	2,747	3,299	3,881	4,529	25.3	22.5
South Africa	1,293	1,351	1,486	2,440	3,632	4,408	5,206	5,951	7,046	27.8	23.6
OECD	453,777	462,018	466,182	525,938	587,996	621,625	661,820	729,732	795,838	6.5	7.3
World	472,814	482,679	489,766	557,614	630,025	676,656	730,407	815,394	904,296	7.4	8.4
Communications											
Brazil	20,609	17,691	17,757	21,491	24,006	30,642	33,996	34,240	34,748	8.3	6.7
China	29,917	32,129	37,612	41,437	47,102	51,759	57,586	63,668	70,138	11.6	11.2
India	12,841	12,239	14,166	16,873	23,734	29,023	32,549	35,978	39,864	17.7	15.2
Russia	6,064	7,508	9,134	11,566	14,798	18,806	21,695	24,017	26,381	25.4	20.2
South Africa	6,896	5,845	5,772	8,947	11,709	12,825	13,073	12,792	12,987	13.2	8.2
OECD	995,737	898,249	955,545	1,052,269	1,163,805	1,221,699	1,258,579	1,345,052	1,424,302	4.2	4.6
World	1,167,377	1,066,508	1,139,537	1,263,752	1,408,076	1,504,906	1,569,731	1,680,770	1,786,605	5.2	5.5

Table 5.1
(continued)

	2000	2001	2002	2003	2004	2005	2006	2007	2008	CAGR 2000–2005	CAGR 2000–2008
Total ICT											
Brazil	33,410	30,585	31,675	41,217	48,330	62,065	68,670	69,734	71,405	13.2	10.0
China	44,359	51,815	62,376	75,400	97,658	117,632	142,313	172,380	211,599	21.5	21.6
India	16,575	16,844	19,997	25,692	36,164	46,438	55,304	65,580	78,644	22.9	21.5
Russia	9,114	10,989	13,088	16,554	21,539	27,327	31,624	35,158	38,872	24.6	19.9
South Africa	10,477	9,627	9,756	15,217	20,763	23,625	25,471	26,549	28,899	17.7	13.5
OECD	2,017,442	1,863,062	1,907,222	2,114,657	2,354,110	2,482,523	2,606,417	2,821,782	3,025,389	4.2	5.2
World	2,259,190	2,111,861	2,183,248	2,444,703	2,755,660	2,963,532	3,155,228	3,440,621	3,730,952	5.6	6.5

The US is the largest player in world ICT across the board. It ranks between first and third in world standings for most market categories. Inferring leadership for hardware is trickier because of hardware's global production model. The largest segment of the market is communications. The 2005 OECD communications services data placed total revenues at $1.22 trillion, about 39 percent of which was from mobile. The US accounted for about one-third of the OECD market and, perhaps surprisingly, was the largest revenue market for mobile in the OECD. Together, the US and Japan constitute 47 percent of the OECD mobile market.[6] The US also remains the dominant ICT market overall with between 30 and 40 percent of the $3 trillion services and equipment market, but European IT spending is approaching US levels.[7]

Table 5.2[8] focuses our attention on global computer markets. Two things are particularly notable from the data. First, computer services represent more than 45 percent of the total market in 2005—more than 1.5 times hardware and more than twice total software spending. This likely does not include "software as a services" data in a separate category, which

Table 5.2

The global computer market in 2000 and in 2005. Based on data from *Digital Planet 2004: The Global Information Economy* (for 2000) and *Digital Planet 2006: The Global Information Economy* (for 2005), published by World Information Technology and Services Alliance. CAGR: compound annual growth rate.

	2000		2005		
	Million $US	Share of total	Million $US	Share of total	CAGR, 2000–2005
Total computer spending	1,091,812.7		1,458,626.1		5.96%
Hardware	440,912.4	40.38%	493,164.1	33.81%	2.27%
Software	178,086.1	16.31%	288,806.5	19.80%	10.15%
Services	472,814.2	43.31%	676,655.5	46.39%	7.43%
Geographic breakdown					
North America	521,333.1	47.75%	603,333.6	41.36%	2.96%
Latin America	22,107.7	2.02%	46,795.3	3.21%	16.18%
Europe	305,321.7	27.96%	471,194.3	32.30%	9.07%
Asia, Pacific	232,701.1	21.31%	312,010.0	21.39%	6.04%
Middle East, Africa	10,349.1	0.95%	25,292.9	1.73%	19.57%
United States	492,203.0	45.08%	557,121.6	38.19%	2.51%
Japan	173,284.2	15.87%	149,897.7	10.28%	−2.86%

probably means that overall "services" are far above 50 percent of the total market today. The second major conclusion drawn from the data is that although Europe is growing faster, the US still dwarfs all other geographic regions in total ICT spending (more than 40 percent of the total in 2005).

In short, although the United States may grow less quickly relative to other market centers, it remains the dominant market across the full ICT landscape. Although the EU (with 27 member states in 2008) now exceeds the American market in overall size, it is a less perfectly integrated market. Still, its magnitude means that it is the logical starting point for US international policy negotiations about ICT.

Other leadership dimensions are not tied to market revenues. For instance, US leadership on research and development expenditures remains secure compared to China and the European Union. The only significant competitor in the scale of effort is Japan, which spends a larger share of its GDP on R&D, although not enough to overcome the lead imparted by a US economy that is double its size.[9] Moreover, the market-size figures cited so far miss the importance of the buyer landscape, particularly the installed ICT capital stock across the US economy. In this respect the US is widening its lead over Europe in the IT stock. (US growth was almost double the IT investment per hour worked than Europe in 2005). This stock is especially meaningful because leading-edge buyers can quickly and nimbly deploy incremental ICT infrastructure for competitive purposes. This is a function of the flexible and competitive US product and labor markets and is reinforced by the deep experience of American multinational firms.[10] These advantages are coupled with across-the-board strengths in the size and depth of the high tech sector that are documented in table 5.3. In addition, global investment patterns for venture capital in ICT are shown in table 5.4. More than 70 percent of these venture capital investments occur in the US.

Overall, the United States remains the leading market for a wide swath of ICT solutions, which advantages local US firms. An example is the US strength in both the enterprise and the consumer Internet services market (search engines, IM, and e-commerce). Table 5.5 shows this leadership in Websites. JETRO, the Japanese trade organization, estimates the US e-commerce market to be almost twice the size of Japan's.[11] A related strand of US leadership stems from the advertising data presented in chapter 4—which showed the US market accounting for more than 50 percent of total digital advertising spending in every digital category. If the Personal Network Platform emerges before 2020, US leadership in the enterprise

Table 5.3

IT and telecom venture capital investments, 2002–2006. Sources: *Venture Expert*, *Indian Venture Capital Journal, Asian Venture Capital Journal.*

	2002	2003	2004	2005	2006	5-year average
US	72.1%	74.1%	76.3%	75.4%	72.3%	74.1%
EU	15.7%	11.6%	11.5%	12.7%	12.6%	12.8%
Israel	3.9%	4.3%	5.3%	4.9%	4.9%	4.7%
China	0.7%	5.5%	2.8%	2.8%	5.2%	3.4%
India	1.6%	0.2%	0.3%	0.6%	1.1%	0.8%
Japan	0.5%	0.8%	0.4%	0.4%	1.0%	0.6%
Other	5.6%	3.5%	3.4%	3.2%	2.7%	3.7%
Total ($billion)	24.73	19.25	21.56	21.47	25.32	22.46

Table 5.4

Global tech company market capitalization as of December 31, 2005. Source: Morgan Stanley Global Internet Trends.

	% total market value	Market value (billions)	Year-to-year change
North America	63	$2,455	−1%
Japan	17	$665	3%
Asia	11	$421	39%
Europe	9	$361	−5%
Total	100	$3,902	3%

market and the Web application market will be guaranteed. The increasing importance of broadcast and copyrighted content for "individual-based platforms and services" also reinforces US leadership. In addition, as content and broadcast converges with telephony and IT, the centrality of the US content industry and associated intellectual property issues becomes more prominent in the global landscape.[12]

The third argument against US leadership rests on the current deployment and trajectory of both wireline and wireless broadband networks in the US relative to elsewhere. This is not an argument about big fiber backbone and the ultra-broadband where US dominance remains. The argument holds that since the US lags in broadband network build-out to homes and small and medium enterprises (SMEs), its space for innovative applications and value-added services on the network will decline. Over

Table 5.5
Top ten online properties worldwide (ranked by worldwide unique visitors age 15+, excluding traffic from public computers such as Internet cafes and access from mobile phones). Sources: comScore World Metrix, June 2006 and May 2007.

June 2006			May 2007	
Rank	Property	Thousands of visitors	Property	Thousands of visitors
1	Microsoft sites	499,540	Google sites	527,572
2	Yahoo sites	480,933	Microsoft sites	520,238
3	Google sites	453,963	Yahoo sites	467,642
4	eBay	256,653	Time Warner Network	266,890
5	Time Warner Network	219,868	eBay	248,006
6	Amazon sites	129,320	Wikipedia sites	208,906
7	Wikipedia sites	127,982	Fox Interactive Media	147,760
8	Ask Network	111,864	Amazon sites	136,655
9	Adobe sites	95,831	CNET Networks	119,865
10	Apple Inc.	92,211	Apple Inc.	115,262
Worldwide total		712,976		766,188

time this means that more cutting edge users and buyers will emerge outside the US. Although the situation is not clear cut, it is an appropriate area for US concern and will be addressed later.

Consumer and small enterprise broadband has evolved with leadership by Asia since the late 1990s, followed by Northern Europe, and trailed by the United States. OECD statistics show that at the end of 2006 the US ranked fifteenth among OECD countries in broadband penetration. The results of a broader survey ranked US household broadband penetration at 24th at the close of March 2007, up from 25th a quarter earlier.[13] (For an overview of broadband penetration across the OECD, see figures 2.1 and 2.2.) Moreover, broadband systems in these countries often have much higher speeds than in the US at lower prices. (We return to the reasons later in this chapter.) Nonetheless, at the end of 2006 the US had "the largest total number of broadband subscribers in the OECD at 58.1 million. US broadband subscribers now represent 29% of all broadband connections in the OECD."[14] Moreover, the US had gone further than most in creating a competitive national infrastructure for broadband through cable modems.

Another point of potential weakness is US dominance of the content industry. The growth of new content markets (e.g., gaming) and the growth of "long-tail" markets means that this leadership may slip faster than in other market segments. This risk increases if slow and expensive consumer broadband inhibits the growth of new content applications in the United States. An offsetting strength is American leadership on business content that could merge with consumer content as the Personal Network Platform emerges.

A similar story of the United States lagging has developed for mobile networks. In 2003 global mobile connections overtook fixed connections. About 1.4 billion devices were in use and 500 million new units were sold each year.[15] At the end of 2007 the number of cellular subscribers worldwide reached 3.1 billion. The worldwide mobile industry is expected to be worth more than a $1 trillion at the end of 2008. By 2012 the number of subscribers is expected to reach 5 billion, the vast majority of which will not be Americans. [16] Moreover, the traffic on mobile networks follows different patterns than wired traffic. Non-voice applications (especially SMS) took off on low bandwidth networks much more decisively in Asia, and the EU also leads the US on this count.[17] Vodafone reports that non-voice (data) revenues averages 17 percent of total revenue across its global holdings, but the US is only at 8.9 percent.[18] In addition, the US has lagged in experimenting with m-commerce compared to other countries and regions.

There are three complicating factors on mobile. First, after the EU-27, which is not yet a fully integrated market, the US remains the largest industrial market for mobile and has more room for growth than most.[19] Second, US price levels are among the lowest (about $\frac{1}{4}$ the EU average), and so the minutes of use per subscriber are among the highest (about twice EU levels).[20] In view of the pricing pressures at the inflection point this is a more realistic pricing position. Third, 3G and other technologies are opening the way to broadband wireless networks. By early 2008 almost 300 million subscribers connected using a 3G technology.[21] Korea and Japan have led the world in this deployment, but the US is competitive with all other major countries. Enormous amounts of experimentation are in progress in the US with other forms of wireless broadband systems. Moreover, as wireless becomes an extension of the Web, US influence increases because the salience of Web expertise rises for successful mobility ventures.[22]

In short, being pivotal to the dynamics of the world market does not mean being number one in all market segments. Being number one takes strength across the board, global dominance in a number of segments, and a strong ecosystem of innovation. The US still fits this profile although its relative standing inevitably will change. But the inflection point's dynamics will be set off the momentum from current configurations of the marketplace. The activities and preferences of the EU, Japan, Korea, and increasingly China all play important roles. However, if the US exercises policy leadership, it almost certainly will remain the most important player shaping the global agenda as it adjusts to the inflection point. To understand this process, we next turn to a deeper examination of the political economy of initial American choices in response to modularity at the inflection point.

Policy Issues and the Inflection Point

The Political Economy of Entry and Spectrum Policy

When the Republicans captured the presidency in 2000, they controlled both the executive and legislative branches of government. This reduced the normal checks on policy imposed by divided powers between Congress and the Executive Branch. Although insufficient to overcome the normal obstacles to major new legislation because of a closely split Senate, it increased the Republicans' ability to exert coordinated pressure on the FCC and the Executive Branch to install leadership with more conservative views on economic intervention in ICT. Still, the FCC's considerable autonomy meant that wholesale policy reversals came slowly, especially because the FCC had to create a public record to justify policy changes that would stand up in court challenges. Furthermore, elements of the corporate competition coalition still strongly supported increased network competition, especially the provision of new broadband wired and wireless networks.

Republican policy makers set out to demonstrate that competition among network infrastructures was vigorous enough to allow regulatory relief for the Bells. They also needed a response that addressed a potential political embarrassment—the US deployment of broadband began to lag other major countries in 2000.

The new synthesis reflected the general Republican alignment with the Bells, conservative distrust of extensive government market supervision, and the increasing unrest among economic theorists about the efficiency of interconnection rules crafted by the Democratic FCC that many other countries subsequently emulated. Economists worried about regulatory requirements to "unbundle" the functional elements of a dominant carrier's network and make it available on cost-based terms to competitors. Whatever the theoretical merits of the idea, there was a rising tide of opinion that this approach was overly regulatory especially in light of the US competitive circumstances.[23] Moreover, in view of the similarity of telecom and IT as platforms, competition policy on IT platforms also was skeptically received. Limited remedies in the Microsoft case were one example of this thinking.[24]

In the new political environment the shift in broadband policy had three main justifications. The first was the growth of competition in backbone fiber-optic networks for long-distance and the major metropolitan business centers.[25] Predictably, prices fell for long-distance and large business data customers. Second, in the two-thirds of US households where cable connections were available, cable television made a strong entry into telephone and broadband services for households and, to some extent, SMEs.[26] Third, mobile telephony emerged as a credible substitute for voice services, and the rise of VoIP services could arbitrage much of the power over pricing and service options for voice services.[27]

Policy makers then addressed some conspicuous remaining difficulties for proponents of weakening the Bells' network unbundling obligations. (Unbundling was the specific policy package adopted after the 1996 Telecommunications Act that implemented the long-standing norm of network sharing.) In the backbone fiber market, even for business services, the means and costs of originating and terminating traffic remained a barrier to entry controlled by the local Bell operator. The FCC and the Department of Justice ruled that large mergers of Verizon with MCI and SBC with AT&T and BellSouth (now renamed AT&T as a group) did not harm competition, but these combinations did not improve the options available to consumers. In addition, the broadband market for SMEs and households was, at best, a duopoly where economic theory predicted that there was a strong possibility for suboptimal competition.

ICT is a high-profile industry that serves as a marker of national technology prospects. Predictably, technology policy draws intense lobbying efforts and keen press scrutiny. Retreating from unbundling did not translate into a positive political message on broadband development issues. The Republicans needed a new formula with their own secret sauce to brand their efforts. In response, the FCC identified the potential opened by modular elements of the inflection point. Specifically, technological innovation could accelerate the deployment of new broadband wireless networks.[28] The FCC's pioneering work on introducing "spectrum flexibility" through 2004 dramatized this approach.

The idea was to promote more efficient allocation and assignment of spectrum to prompt innovation in wireless broadband networking. One goal was to increase available spectrum for all wireless services. This often required engaging in complicated and controversial plans to reallocate existing spectrum and move its current users to other bands. Intense effort went into finding more spectrum for unlicensed services so that new technologies including WiFi, WiMax, and low powered "smart terminals" could be leveraged into "bottom up" broadband networks.[29] A second goal was to release more spectrum for use and allow the free resale of spectrum to stimulate more flexible use of licensed spectrum. Then, market forces might redeploy spectrum, choose freely among technologies, and select services to be provided. For example, spectrum "band managers" might emerge that would treat large bands of spectrum like a commercial mall built by a developer who tries to lease it to achieve an optimal mix of stores. Third, this policy facilitated a political agreement to let licensees more freely monetize their holdings. Permitting the resale and recombination of valuable spectrum controlled by incumbents created incentives for more efficient spectrum use.

The promise of wireless broadband was a powerful rationale for allowing the FCC to relax regulation of the Bells' new broadband networks.[30] To spur more rapid investment, the FCC exempted the Bells from network-sharing obligations for fiber broadband networks. (This was parallel to the exemption for broadband use by the cable television networks.) The Bells promised that this mix would stimulate broadband deployment in rural areas because they would be able to earn higher returns on their new investments.

The political economy of this policy sequence reinforced the politics of the Republican majority. By 2001, most competitive local-exchange carriers had collapsed, eliminating a major rallying force against policy change. The corporate competition coalition based on the information industry and large users remained potent. Nonetheless, the inflection point induced a realignment of their interests in three ways.

First, as was previously noted, a recurring propensity of US political economy is to create compromises built around encouraging new technologies and entrants. The new spectrum policy followed in the tradition of market openings of the railroad expansion and westward farmsteads. The changing economics of ICT production eased new entry into specialized technology ventures for wireless networking. New ideas about wireless could more easily and cheaply be matched to production capabilities. Moreover, since network applications could substitute for each other, gaining entry into wireless data was equivalent to gaining a vantage point in voice and multi-media. So business plans could dream of large end service markets served by a hybrid mixture of networks and technologies. The new spectrum policy also rallied support from equipment vendors intrigued by cross-entry from the wired to the wireless markets.[31] This attracted Cisco and Intel, which invested heavily in new wireless technology. Wireless also attracted big software and computer companies that wanted to increase competitive pressure on the major network operators to deploy faster networks.

Politically, this technological version of "supply-side" economics argued that lightening government control would stimulate growth and investment. This played to the Republican "brand" in national politics. Network-sharing policy required detailed government choices to redistribute advantages in the telecom market. Spectrum policy's similarity to opening new territory for expansion of the network appealed more to Republicans than the redistribution of advantages among established enterprises. Spectrum policy reform also attracted "geeks," who were important in ICT discussions. At the time, major players in spectrum policy reveled in the do-it-yourself entrepreneurial energy sparked by the idea of deploying unlicensed networks guided by technology enthusiasts. (By 2004, some of these same technology entrepreneurs, disheartened by the absence of alternative networks, began advocating for network neutrality rules.)

A second subtle advantage of spectrum policy was that it provided some help on the thorny issue of pricing policy in ICT networks. Pricing controls of various flavors are difficult to completely avoid in conventional phone services on traditional networks. Spectrum policy promised to produce "winners" outside these traditional boundaries. Thus, new networks might develop with fewer constraints imposed by legacy pricing and cross-subsidy policies than their predecessors. For example, it was predictable that VoIP delivered over the wired network ran into stakeholder demands for "parity" in the treatment of VoIP in universal service subsidies. They complained that municipal WiFi networks sponsored by companies hoping to generate search traffic and revenues offered free voice, which would further undermine pricing and subsidy regulations.[32] (In truth, Google and its searchers already must pay for bandwidth. Nothing is really free.) Expanding this wedge, the FCC ruled in March 2007 that broadband wireless access to the Internet was an information service.[33]

Third, as spectrum policy moved to the forefront, many ICT industry leaders and large corporate users pulled back their support for a strong set of network-sharing rules. This went beyond tacit or explicit acquiescence to the roll back of interconnection rules that were originally spurred by the 1996 act. It surfaced when they hedged their bets on the debate over "network neutrality" rules that proposed to require pricing rules for data services. (The political economy of net neutrality is discussed shortly.)

The spectrum policy initiative rested on several aspects of modularity at the inflection point—smart terminals, multi-band and multi-protocol options for networking, the ravenous demand for bandwidth, and the possibility that convergence would fuel expectations of a larger addressable market for any new network. It was a Republican supply-side spin on the long-standing propensity in the US for policies favoring easier market entry. It did not, however, resolve the issues about the growth of broadband networks in the US. Two examples illustrate the issues.

First, a bitter debate rages between advocates of strengthening property rights for spectrum holders which favor auctions, rights of resale, and the ability to aggregate spectrum and the proponents of a "commons" approach to spectrum and wireless networks. The former suggests that profit incentives will lead to greater investments and innovation. The latter group emphasizes the innovative potential of bottom-up building of networks on unlicensed bands or "white space" and guard bands for licensed spectrum.[34] Two points that demonstrate the power of the inflection point are relevant here. (1) Both camps stress the importance of modularity and smart terminals. They differ over the incentive and control system for innovation. (2) Both groups envision a market where the control by vertically integrated carriers is declining. Indeed, advocates of commons approaches sometimes assert that this is their goal. Although its position is more ambiguous, the property rights movement envisions carriers in a larger, more complex ownership and technology universe. If carriers dominate, they may one day resemble managers of a spectrum "supply chain" more than an encapsulated, vertically integrated supplier. Both perspectives reflect the underpinnings of the inflection point, but they spring from different views of American political economy. The commons movement wraps its claims in an historical analogy to the political economy of the Internet's foundations. In particular, they analogize the use of regulation to support a new networking approach, the Internet. For wireless the most fervent voices in the commons movement want to assign, or condition the use of, spectrum to foster unlicensed uses such as WiFi. They favor setting high performance standards for the equipment that deploys and uses the network to avoid interference while agilely using the spectrum.[35] Government forfeits rents it might have gained by auctioning spectrum, but may unleash innovation and experimentation that creates major benefits. As we have already noted, advocates of spectrum auctions persuaded governments to reform command and control licensing systems by making them money. This proposal falls short on that count; it creates potential winners, but not definite winners. In other words a tough political decision does not immediately create highly committed and organized winners that will promptly defend and endorse the decision. In contrast, licensing quickly creates such winners. Moreover, the other key to the success of the Internet was the emergence of e-commerce. As the Web and e-commerce burst into prominence without any dominant firm in control, the government kept its hands off and chose not to regulate it.[36] The US only had to stand aside and allow the Web to develop almost untouched, a relatively easy task in a political system susceptible to legislative deadlock.

The second unresolved issue is the adequacy of build-out of wired networks. There are doubts that wireless will provide sufficient and adequate infrastructure for ultra-broadband connectivity to residential and small- and medium-size businesses. So the technology community worries whether wired broadband has sufficient capacity, technical flexibility for applications, and quality of service. The re-introduction of unbundling, whatever its substantive merits, seems unlikely at the inflection point, because it is a policy reversal that is difficult to achieve when the competition coalition has grown deeply divided. The question, as a matter of policy and politics, is whether one or both of the major American political parties will try to claim credit by crafting a tax incentive to help build out new networks. Incentives always are attractive for politicians because they are less visible as direct budget expenditures.[37]

Network Neutrality

Net neutrality emerged as the flash point in a heated debate about how to promote innovation through networked ICT policy. This controversy revolved around how network infrastructure and services should intersect with Web services and terminals. We examine it mainly in the context of the US political economy, but also briefly probe the reasons that the debate looks so different in Europe and Japan.

In its purest form, the logic of net-neutrality proposals rested on two ideas. First, price controls on networked data transmission should create a single non-discriminatory price for data transmission for information services at a particular bandwidth. So some form of flat-rate pricing should guarantee that high-volume users are not charged more than low-volume users at any specific network speed. Second, except where legal requirements exist, networks should not block or delay access to websites and their content. Non-discrimination rules regarding content and value-added services should be enforced. Network enhancements, such as network caching services, should be freely accessible to users.

The logic on pricing springs from the political economy of the early history of computer networking and the Internet when leverage was strong and modularity more limited. At the time there was enormous suspicion of vertical leveraging by incumbent telecom carriers. Also, flat-rate pricing for data transmission for information services when dealing with dominant carriers was a hallmark of FCC policy. So any retreat by this policy's traditional backers in the corporate competition coalition is noteworthy. Such reversals occurred in parts of the ICT industry for two reasons.

First, after the "dot com" bubble burst in 2000, hardware suppliers and other ICT producers wanted to revive the market for infrastructure from the doldrums. The Bells and some of their largest customers felt they too would benefit. Expanding broadband build-out also could increase demand for upgraded electronics and software, aiding companies that produced them. In some respects a two-tier network already existed, insofar as Akamai (a leading Web application acceleration and performance management firm) and other companies expedited traffic for large Web portals. Generalizing the precedent seemed a positive, incremental step to these ICT companies. Moreover, prioritizing and inspecting traffic (for security reasons) were important tools for building new equipment markets working from the router out through the rest of the network. Cisco, for example, is buying into service application companies that feature traffic prioritization and security schemes based on capabilities installed in Cisco routers.[38]

Second, many large users and ICT suppliers no longer believed that control of the network infrastructure provided carriers with much leverage over network applications or pricing. Their hunch was reinforced by economic studies on pricing logic that suggested that price controls on broadband (what net neutrality imposes) might perversely create a significant incentive for the carriers to discriminate upstream or downstream.[39] Carriers pleaded that their primary goal was to maximize the customers' experience by managing their networks to bolster their performance and make certain their networks were secure in the face of staggering growth in Internet traffic, especially of video traffic that threatened to jam networks.[40] However, when Comcast was found to be secretly filtering and degrading P2P traffic for those using BitTorrent (a bandwidth-gobbling video file-sharing program), it demonstrated that often-raised concerns about net neutrality were justified.[41] This uproar grew when Comcast secretly packed an FCC hearing on the matter at Harvard by hiring people to take places that might otherwise have gone to net-neutrality activists.[42] In August 2008 the FCC sanctioned Comcast for its actions.

At the same time, a new tier of companies in the Web services market that concentrated on the mass consumer market for ICT (e.g., Google and eBay) became politically active. These newcomers were unlike the equipment companies and firms that traditionally focused on larger users. They are the leading edge of a new political economy coalition shaped by the economic engine that drives much of Web-based innovation. In short, ad syndication of the kind offered by Google and Yahoo is critical because it fuels a new economic engine for innovation built on top of the existing Internet standards-based infrastructure. Simultaneously, a wide variety of content producers and content owners now are deeply tied to an ICT infrastructure that rests on ubiquitous access to services and bandwidth that requires a heterogeneous, modular infrastructure. This alters the political calculus for any change that would disrupt the growth of the nascent marketplace that rests on these ICT foundations.[43]

Some players in the Web-based coalition continue to worry that differential broadband pricing for high and low bandwidth residential users within a bandwidth tier (e.g., 1 megabit per second) could hamper mass-market growth.[44] Others feared that some services (for example, music on demand) would be offered with quality of service and price packages that would be made available to some customers (perhaps users of a network provider's Web platform), but not to others.[45]

As large consumers with huge bargaining power, major software firms were less concerned about the precise price point for bandwidth than about the combination of price and functional discrimination. They feared having to wait for "permission to innovate" for new service packages because that could give carriers leverage over the modular redeployment of network capabilities. Lengthy negotiations over prices or functionality with networking could weaken business cases that require swift action, huge amounts of flexible bandwidth, and remote data storage.

The complaints of Web firms reflected the pinnacle of self-interest and innovation at the inflection point. Many of the Web companies foresee a Lego-like networked ICT infrastructure that is constructed from inexpensive standardized capabilities that can be mixed and matched. In short, net neutrality is a government program to promote modularity.

The mass consumer software companies found allies in the traditional Internet research community that saw flat-rate pricing as a spur to technological innovation. In an imperfectly competitive world, researchers believed that large carriers would prefer to charge different prices rather than figure out how to build network capacity cheaply and make profits charging flat rates. These researchers also suspected that networks would discourage value-added functions that allowed network users to innovatively manipulate protocols and services. They favored simple and cheap solutions to increase bandwidth over elaborate schemes to prioritize narrower bandwidth.[46] Many advocates for consumer interests echoed these fears.

The software and research community won allies among Democratic political leaders who were wary of the Bells. The Democrats also sought a wedge issue that appealed to the technological community and reaffirmed their efforts to build allies with consumer action groups. So in 2006 the two Democrats on the FCC forced ATT to pledge to maintain net neutrality for at least 2 years as a condition for approval of its merger with Bell-South.[47] When the Democrats regained control of Congress in January 2007, their committee chairs promptly reintroduced legislation in support of net neutrality. However, since the US system is stacked against ambitious legislation on hotly contested issues, legislative deadlock on telecom issues remains likely.[48]

The remaining common ground was at least as intriguing as the new divisions among segments of the old corporate competition coalition. Agreement remained on rules governing network functionality. Three issues, corresponding to upstream, downstream, and horizontal leverage questions, reflect a combination of old and new. All of the rules facilitated modularity, but, except for disadvantaging traditional telecom carriers, did not tilt advantage to a particular strategy building on modularity.

First, all corporate competition coalition segments want to reaffirm modularity as a basic principle. They want to guarantee the right of users to choose the appliance and devices they attach to the network. This right is essential to innovation led by intelligence at the edge of the network.[49] This principle, in effect, bans upstream discrimination on terminal equipment.[50]

The other two issues, downstream and horizontal leveraging, involve what might be called rights of "value-added interconnection." Downstream, the coalition seeks clear rules that forbid discrimination against interconnection to content or websites.[51] Most innovatively, concern over horizontal leverage arises in terms of "next-generation interconnection" among networks and service applications. It focuses on the terms on which two networks connect and exchange traffic fundamentals (a form of interconnection that is usually called "peering"). Inter-networking relies on the rights for "peering." The coalition wants major networks to prevent discriminatory peering, especially on quality of service and security. They also want to prevent discrimination against value-added services (e.g., network caching services for e-commerce firms) using proprietary software architectures or VoIP. This recognizes that the general network architecture and capacity is, as always, a step behind on innovation because customization is critical to customers.[52]

The December 2006 merger of BellSouth and AT&T was sealed by a voluntary corporate pledge to embrace these network peering principles and a commitment to provide a $19.95 per month broadband service for 30 months.[53] This concession suggested three things. First, the bargain allowed the Democratic FCC commissioners to keep alive the peering issues until after the next election when Democrats might win control of the White House and Congress, and permanently change policy. Second, AT&T implicitly admitted that its network build-out and revamped billing system would not be ready until 2008 or 2009. Third, the principles were so general that AT&T did not yet have to commit to firm positions about next-generation issues. These peering issues go to the heart of network management and value added. So consensus at this level of generality does not constitute a hard test of what they really mean.[54]

The evolution of corporate coalition positions in regard to mobile wireless carriers was more convoluted. For example, Google and Yahoo initially courted these carriers in order to be preferred portals or advertising partners. Later, consumer Web companies challenged the wireless carriers by advocating changes in spectrum policy to get more new devices into the marketplace to fuel demand for their services. This became a challenge to wireless carriers in regard to net neutrality for their networks.[55] The prospect of multi-band, multi-protocol networks, part of modularity at the inflection point, gave the Web firms greater confidence when challenging the carriers.

The first challenge to wireless policy was the effort by Skype (now owned by eBay) to open the mobile market by demanding freedom of attachment of consumer devices to the wireless networks.[56] Telecom handset suppliers may eventually align with Skype because modularity increases competitive pressure on these equipment suppliers. For their part the carriers are experimenting with upgrading the role of original design manufacturers (ODMs) to more tightly control branding linked to their networks. They plan to take greater control over design and innovation, thereby reducing the value of branded handset suppliers.[57]

The Carterfone analogy went to the core of the US politics of open entry. It intrigued Democrats seeking a distinctive position on ICT largely at the expense of the Bells' wireless carriers and eventually persuaded some Republicans. But the broader issue of net neutrality for wireless remained unresolved in 2008. Still, the early policy struggles suggested how political entrepreneurship might be married to commercial advocacy to create policy "work-arounds."

One suggestive example of how the political economy of the inflection point could unfold was the ultimately unsuccessful bid by Frontline Wireless, a company with a bipartisan team of Republican and Democratic leaders in telecom and IT policy.[58] Frontline responded to the FCC proceeding to set the rules for auctioning in the 700-MHz band (the television spectrum to be relinquished when the US switches over to all-digital television in February 2009). It proposed that the FCC auction the public safety spectrum to a private network to meet the FCC's goal of building a national public safety network in that band. The private network would have 10 MHz for its own commercial use and 12 MHz to serve the public safety community. Frontline dreamed of building an open standard network with 4G capabilities (uploads of 50 megabits per second and downloads of 100 megabits per second) that would have served public safety and private users. It proposed that any licensee would be required to offer its network capacity on a wholesale basis to all takers.[59]

This proposal sought to leverage modularity and open standards to fashion a new business model for broadband. It promised spectrum revenues to the government and a subsidized network for the public safety community. It also embraced network neutrality by creating a broadband network to provide resale capacity, open standards, and freedom to select terminal equipment. But, to appeal to Republicans, it did not force existing carriers to accept these policies. Eventually the FCC set aside spectrum for auction for a network requiring commitments similar to the Frontline proposal. The FCC rules, however, had some liabilities from the viewpoint of ventures such as Frontline. For example, the FCC rules required the winner of this spectrum to reach agreement with the public safety community on implementation after putting its auction bid (perhaps one billion dollars) on deposit. It was possible for the public safety community to demand additional expensive features and argue to the FCC that the failure to provide them meant that the bidder should forfeit the auction bid as a penalty. This kind of commercial risk (unexpected costs of build-out or forfeiture) discouraged financial investors.[60]

If Frontline had succeeded it would have provided a different form of competitive discipline for incumbent carriers and a new way to fund public infrastructure. From our perspective this sequence shows how modularity enables new approaches to networking and policy compromises that promote diversity of business approaches rather than detailed regulations of the conduct of all licensees. However, simply the potential for new models is not enough. It still takes crafting adroit political compromises for policy to enable them.[61]

Meanwhile, Google entered the debate over how to license the 700-MHz spectrum.[62] It proposed that the auction set aside about a third of the spectrum for licensees that agreed to resell capacity on a wholesale basis and to allow terminals and software packages that would not harm the network to freely attach to it. (Google promised to issue specifications for anyone who wished to produce "Google mobile terminals," which eventually became Google's "Android" blueprint for mobile networks.) If the FCC would agree to these rules for all bidders on these licenses, Google pledged, it would bid more than $4 billion. (Google objected to bidding against networks that might pay a premium to keep spectrum out of the hands of innovative newcomers.)

Predictably, the carriers complained that Google's conditions would favor one business plan over others. They argued that auctions ought to make money for the government and also yield information to market participants to help them to rationally value the radio resource. The auction should not specify a business plan.

The ultimate FCC bidding rules split the difference. It granted consumers freedom to select their terminals and software, but network resale was not required. In the 2008 auctions, Google reportedly fulfilled its bidding pledge and then quickly withdrew from the auction, leaving incumbent carriers with the licenses but an obligation to embrace open terminals and user software choices.

The 700-MHz debate revealed other policy tensions at the inflection point. In the 1990s it was assumed that if enough strong competitors would allow the government could to step back from detailed regulation. The US mobile wireless market boasts at least four national competitors (Verizon, AT&T, T-Mobile, and Sprint-Nextel) and several regional and local entrants. Yet the software coalition and many users concluded that these firms still impede innovation by running walled gardens. As expected, many economists responded that competition would eventually force the carriers to change.

What explains these divergent views? Was it typical self-serving posturing by firms seeking a better deal as users or a piece of the supply-side action? Obviously self-interest was involved, but more fundamentally a deep chasm emerged. On one side were large firms whose business practices and "corporate culture" sprouted from the world of regulation. Opposing them were firms that emerged from intensely competitive, rapidly changing markets where government played only a marginal role in pricing, entry, or detailed regulation of conduct. Whatever the market incentives, industries often respond in ways shaped more by their previous market environments than by present market conditions. They may put a higher premium on foreclosing future competition than standard economic models suggest.[63]

Other factors may induce strategies not predicted by standard competition models. For example, many of the pricing eccentricities rooted in the monopoly telecom system still linger. Their complete reform is unlikely. Contemporary economics argues that temptations for anti-competitive behavior arise from perverse incentives created by regulated prices. Those with potential market power are blocked from framing profitable, efficient schemes to share the use of their networks. So they choose schemes that are permissible but not conducive to maximizing economic welfare for society.[64]

Even without pricing disincentives, the Bells and the cable television network operators (as effective duopolists) may be in a strategic game of mutual forbearance to avoid stumbling into an "arms race" with unpredictable results. Even the wireless broadband market has lost some of its disruptive potential as Verizon and AT&T built much larger spectrum holdings than their rivals. These concerns are at the core of this political economy debate—parts of the ICT industry are deeply suspicious that the carriers will not change enough in a timely way.

Network neutrality also spills over to the inflection point's innovation model. The high-end innovation in the Grid is following the traditional US commitment to technology neutrality on network development. Economic policy scholars still see picking winners as politically difficult and intellectually suspect. Still, these new uses of wired and wireless networking for novel vertical and horizontal applications will require considerable care in regard to quality of service, security, and privacy. They also will involve huge flows of traffic and generate new tools for managing large-scale applications of networked ICT that will be beyond the proprietary control of any group.[65]

Continued strong support for national R&D policies that are deploying experimental ultra-broadband networks and work on massive radio sensors deployment will continue to be important. The US R&D expenditures on communication and information technology are considerably above those of the EU.[66] However, Bill Gates and others worry that "federal research spending is not keeping pace with our nation's needs." He noted to "the Task Force on the Future of American Innovation" that "[a]s a share of GDP, the US federal investment in both physical sciences and engineering research has decreased by half since 1970. In inflation-adjusted dollars, federal funding for physical sciences research has been flat for two decades." This stagnation in spending comes at a time when China and the EU are increasing their public investments in R&D.[67]

Net Neutrality in Japan and in the European Union

Technological shifts pose a challenge to political and economic interests that may lead to policy changes. But technology does not dictate the response. Political and market institutions and legacies shape the path of transformation. We briefly sketch the major differences among the United States, Japan, and the European Union on net neutrality in order to rein-force this point.

Throughout the 1990s Japan lagged behind the United States in Internet adoption because of the continuing effects of a political bargain underlying NTT's market dominance. Even though Japan allowed competitive telecom carriers for long-distance and local telecom services (plus data networking) in the same time frame as the US, it never permitted open entry. Moreover, the government strictly managed a complex price and service system. As a result, prices remained high in Japan and Internet connectivity took off slowly. Only NTT, the former monopolist, and the Japanese equipment industry that supplied its unique network standards earned huge profits.

Japan's decade-long economic downturn and accompanying political reforms began to rebalance the policy game. In the late 1990s, the Japanese government ministry charged with telecom policy pushed for the breakup of NTT into two local service companies (NTT East and NTT West) and a national NTT Long Distance company. (There was a single holding company for the units, but structural separation of accounts.) The Ministry also advocated US-style interconnection and unbundling policy in 2000 as a way to accelerate broadband connectivity to the home and stimulate new services from Japanese information services industry. Further, it suggested that broadband competition would open the door to Japanese electronics firms reorganizing their strategies around global standards favored by new entrants.[68]

Unbundling achieved its purpose. The dramatic rise of Softbank/Yahoo and eAccess symbolized the ensuing race to lower DSL prices and pump up DSL speeds. In 2006 the price in Japan for ADSL was one-seventh (per 100 KB/s of capacity) that of the US, and the average speed was more than 10 times higher.[69] The new competitors relied on the interconnection regime's inexpensive pricing of network capabilities and on the retail pricing umbrella provided by NTT's reluctance to make big price cuts.

In response to government prodding NTT adopted the world's most aggressive plans for fiber to the home. (In 2007 there were roughly 14 million ADSL subscribers, 10 million fiber to the home subscribers, and 4 million cable modem subscribers.[70]) With ADSL providing more than 50 megabits per second at low prices the short-term economics of the NTT fiber build-out is highly uncertain. But this approach provides NTT with its best chance to escape unbundling and create differentiation on service capabilities. However, the government is concerned that NTT could try to use its dominant control of the fiber infrastructure to push Japanese IT service and equipment makers into an architecture that would not serve Japan well in world markets. So it seeks unbundling for fiber to the home for NTT East and NTT West and the creation of rules that resemble American value-added interconnection concepts.[71]

The third major player is Europe. Like the United States, the EU-27 requires a complex system of governance with strong elements of federalism. The legacy of regulatory nationalism and the continuing powers of the national regulatory authorities made the transition to competition complicated.[72] Unlike the US, a strong nascent alternative to ADSL in the cable television network was absent in most EU countries.[73] In addition, over-building of fiber for larger establishments was less common in the EU than in the US. This was the case because in most of Europe actions against market dominance by old state enterprises (many of which still had partial government ownership) was slower to materialize. The telecom boom and bust of the US in the late 1990s did not transform European infrastructure to the same degree.

The EU adopted a technology neutral and comprehensive approach to services in its 2003 directive on Electronic Communication Services. As the EU clarified the elements to be used in the analysis of risks from significant market power by a carrier, and its remedies, many EU members adopted extensive unbundling rules for dominant carriers. This spurred rapid deployment of inexpensive ADSL for consumers in most major markets and significantly curtailed the risk of anti-competitive behavior at the wholesale market level for either smaller rival carriers or ISPs independent of the dominant carrier. A debate remains in the EU on the risks of non-price discrimination by carriers with significant market power. This may lead to more use of imposing structural separation of the wholesale network and the retail services. Still, unbundling has defused much of the controversy over net neutrality in Europe at the EU level.[74]

There are two reasons that a version of net neutrality may reappear on the EU screen. First, extensive variation at the national level in broadband competition may keep the issue alive. Second, the EU's mission in telecom is rooted explicitly in its mandate to strengthen EU market integration in order to advance EU competitiveness in world ICT markets.[75] The continuing weaknesses of European ICT may trigger broader reconsideration of policies for value-added interconnection. However, the EU may conclude that the risk to net neutrality is more on the information side of the ICT infrastructure.[76] The EU's worry is that suppliers of dominant platforms on the information side of the infrastructure can leverage the market for networked services (such as media players) or the intersection of ICT capabilities. This concern goes directly to fears of EU suppliers about their global competitive position, as discussed in the next chapter.

Content and Media

Content, a third issue, is an expanding fault line for policy and politics. Broadcast regulation and programming is one phase. Copyright management is the other.[77] Unlike most of Europe, US broadcasting and multimedia policies do not face the double burdens of divided regulatory authorities and explicit cultural protection policies. Although US spectrum policy requires coordination between the FCC and the Executive Branch on spectrum used by government agencies, there is no split between telecommunications and broadcast authorities to hinder the development of spectrum and competition policies. This unified regulatory authority permits coherence in the treatment of multi-media and traditional movie and broadcast content on broadband networks.[78] The British also are well organized for this task. Moreover, the FCC has no mandate to protect American culture.[79] Even though it debates the merits of policies to encourage children's programming, public decency, and news programs on television and radio, the FCC is indifferent to the source of programming (or languages).[80] This reflects the international dominance of English-language programming as well as the economics of 100-channel broadcast systems that provide all forms of niche programming.[81]

The ability to inspect packets on the new IP networks makes it plausible for governments to promote media content they support and restrict media content that they find objectionable. Policy discrimination comes in different flavors. For instance, stated US broadcast policy eschews cultural protection.[82] No US president would declare, as the president of France has, that the government must subsidize a national search engine to protect its national culture.[83] But US lawmakers opted to limit Internet gambling and restrict pornography on mobile and Internet Protocol television (IPTV).[84] Countries also differ over whether and how to support public media. Although our main focus is on the build-out and operation of robust global networks (the conduit), the rise of modularity at the inflection point also raise important conflicts over the treatment of content. The issues noted here are but the tip of the iceberg.

Until about 2020, three policy decisions will especially influence how modularity plays out in the content market: intellectual property rights (IPR) decisions will influence the mix and match capabilities for content, rules governing ad networks will be critical because these revenues fuel many new business models, and the rules governing how one can mix personal data with commercial sites will set a path for the Personal Network Platform.

The most publicized content issue at the inflection point concerns intellectual property rights. The economics and technology of the inflection point make oversight of content difficult and instability more likely. As we noted in previous chapters, illegally copied content is becoming a convenient close substitute for copyrighted material. The options for producers of copyrighted material are to substantially change pricing schemes, reduce the availability and dissemination of material, or move to an entirely different revenue stream.[85] Online user communities now provide huge amounts of original music and programming. For example, a significant amount of the content on "user community" networks involves elements of "remixing" fragments of content that already is copyright protected. Perhaps most tellingly, well-known producers and artists are creating music that builds on remixing and often intentionally probes the limits of copyright.[86] The immense consequences of such "horizontal networking" for innovation and creative use of content are only now becoming clearer.

In the United States it is a challenge to find a political formula that allows for easy clearance of digital rights, reasonable fair use, and efficient charging and disbursement of fees for uses of copyright. The politics of networked ICT limit the solution set. The entertainment industry mounts skillful, high-profile campaigns to argue for copyright protection. Republicans will not go against their brand by aligning with IPR critics. Democrats listen to consumer groups that equate traditional copyright with anti-consumer tendencies, but no Democrat can win the presidency without carrying New York and California, the two largest content-creating states. And there are large numbers of congressional Democrats from states and districts with high tech aspirations that support strong IPR. So critics of the existing copyright system confront stiff political constraints. However, wrangling by content owners over such sites as YouTube and Hulu (owned by two large content companies, NBC and the *Wall Street Journal*) suggests that bargaining within the private sector will lead to significant changes. Smaller stakeholders can abet this ferment through legal and political challenges.

Implementing solutions, including DRM schemes, will be difficult even if there is an agreement on the underlying bargain. For example, the great diversity of the US media industry produced a major and difficult-to-manage tangle of intellectual property.[87] Moreover, practitioners in the IPR field note that copyrights are domestically granted, often are interlocking (involving more than one IPR claim), and are not easily uncovered. Yet they have global implications. There are significant challenges to enforcing rights over diverse national jurisdictions even without the challenge of digital copying, sharing, and remixing. So DRM schemes face enormous difficulties even if hackers could not break the control software. On roaming global phones that also download music and video there will be many questions on how to sort out licensing rights on the digital content because many licenses are currently limited to specific geographic regions. And even if a DRM system can sort out these challenges there is the issue of whether or not the management system for the DRM might not open the way to collusion among content providers in ways that violate competition laws.[88] Achieving balance, cooperation, and accountability for content may be one of the hardest challenges at the inflection point.

Although IPR for content gets the spotlight in the blogging world, ad networks are going to be important for governance because they are characterized by economies of scale and scope. Larger ad networks can capture more data about users behavior. This can translate into a greater ability to target ads effectively, making it more attractive to advertisers. This possibility raises governance questions about competition in the online ad market, because the potential for anti-competitive behavior may increase as the market consolidates around a small number of large ad networks.

The importance of scale and scope (measured by the size of a publisher network) was reflected in Microsoft's early-2008 bid for Yahoo. In 2007 Google's online advertising revenues grew by 44 percent, versus 15 percent for Yahoo, Microsoft, and AOL.[89] However, the same data shows that a combined Microsoft-Yahoo would be the third largest online ad provider (by revenue) after Google and News Corp. As Microsoft CEO Steve Ballmer remarked in March 2008, online advertising, already a "big thing," is poised to be the next "super-big thing."[90]

From the perspective of political economy, Microsoft's bid for Yahoo shows how coalitions are shifting as IT, media, advertising and all things "online" (e-commerce, software, social networking, etc.) blur together in a rapidly changing market landscape. The dispute will be over how to share the returns from information. Already, some newspaper publishers are pushing back against horizontal search engines that allow users to reach their content without going through their news portal. As we noted in chapter 4, vertical search engines, often tied to specific producers of information applications, will contend more strongly with the search giants Yahoo and Google.

Although the size of the traditional media market makes it the obvious starting point for a discussion of content, it is only the start. The inflection point is closely linked to the new ability to organize data inexpensively and powerfully for totally new applications. The best policy bargains for content may look different than for data. The potential of "Web 2.0" may be that data becomes the "Next Intel Inside." Races to win control of lucrative database content such as location or product identifiers are likely.[91] As the Personal Network Platform takes off, people will co-invest with Web service firms in building personal profiles of data that are of mutual interest—such as health data profiles or detailed documentations of investments in upgrading their homes (to improve credibility when selling the house). Who owns this data? Is the analogy to "number portability" in competitive telephone markets? Or is it, like many forms of insurance data, locked with the insurer? This issue goes beyond the boundaries of traditional privacy debates because users may have voluntarily disclosed their information-to-information application providers. The question is: Who owns the information?

II   A Theoretical Interlude

6   Theory before Policy

We theorize because a good theory can look across markets and countries to find common causal dynamics about how politics and policy shaping global and national markets. Our story is one of political economy. The preferences of the powerful across the globe, informed by their domestic political economies, the dynamics of negotiation, and the need to build support for proposed global actions ensure deeply political alternatives dominate governance.

Global market governance—whether by informal or formal agreements and institutions—is important because choices about the design of market governance influence the winners and losers and the innovation and efficiency in the global ICT market. These market-governance arrangements provide countries with collective capabilities including information, the facilitation of bargaining, and dispute resolution.

International institutions often make and administer rules for the marketplace including technical cooperation on standards and competition rules. Sometimes they provide global services. (For example, Intelsat provided global satellite services from the 1960s through the 1990s.) A significant choice in market governance is the decision about which powers to delegate to what formal (international organizations) or informal institutions (non-governmental organizations) because the choice of the agent implies an agenda for future bargaining and action. Changing global governance may require shifting the lead institution.

Imagine a typical, if stylized, dynamic for changing governance. Initially, changes at the technological frontier induce stakeholders to reconsider their market interests. If major changes in the leading powers' domestic market policies and political economies emerge, it disrupts the equilibrium of existing global market-governance arrangements. There are two disruptive paths. First, traditional diplomacy has to change. For example, the United States' move to a more competitive networked ICT model in the

1980s led the US to become a strong advocate for reorganizing the global governance of ICT markets. Second, the expectations of major stakeholders in important countries shifts. The breakup of AT&T and the United States' embrace of the emerging Internet prompted companies and expert ICT communities in other countries to consider more urgently whether the old arrangements were sustainable. They began to champion change in their own domestic markets and became more favorable to global change. However, the processes of strategic bargaining and the set of governance options for organizing world markets strongly influenced how the potential for change translated into a governance choice. The case studies in chapters 7–9 on competition and trade rules, organization of the global wireless infrastructure, and Internet governance show the potential for innovation and the compromises needed to accommodate global political economic realities.

Explaining Changes in Market Governance

Why do market-governance systems change in certain directions? Numerous explanations exist in scholarly writings on political economy. The four most pervasive are variants on power, technological determinism, ideas, and domestic politics. Let us briefly review how these explanations pervade people's thinking and then explain the problems with each of these four approaches that lead us to a different synthesis.

Power

The power explanation for market governance focuses on the distribution of global power. International outcomes often are described as the result of what the powerful seek for the good or ill of the world. But scholars tell a subtler story about when power may enhance global welfare. Two examples illustrate the dynamics. A dominant major power, or a small group of powers with closely aligned interests, may possess the incentive and ability to advance productive governance to achieve collective goods such as clean air. (The trouble with air-pollution control is that "free riders" do little but still breathe air made cleaner by others' donations.[1]) From this perspective, collective success depends on the involvement of a major power because its stake in the outcome is large enough to push it to decide to use its own resources or induce others to contribute. Similarly, suppose there is strong interest in a common approach (e.g., deciding which side of the road to drive on), but a paralyzing conflict (e.g., the costs of switching) prevents a common approach. A great power may ignore dissenters and push through an outcome that it prefers but also benefits others. Everyone can prosper because a great power finally pushes through a decision.[2]

The great power (or power club) has enormous influence because it usually sets the agenda for action. In any decision process, control of the agenda is a prime source of influence. In the global context, the powerful have a veto power that means that no alternative to the status quo can succeed without their consent. This has been dubbed "negative agenda power" in the study of legislatures.[3] In a technologically dynamic market this negative agenda power has special portent because the powerful can block efforts to respond to market innovation by "nipping and tucking" the traditional arrangements for market governance. Deadlock can force consideration of new governance alternatives.[4] Moreover, a great power has the ability to make side payments and manipulate linkages among diverse issues to reinforce its influence.

Both variants of the power story leave huge holes in explaining outcomes about global market governance. Power does not explain what the powerful seek—multilateral cooperation or a coercive empire, for example. Neither does power explain how the organization of decision making and action (market governance) shapes how preferences and influence are transformed into decisions. The United States may be the "indispensable power," but its track record on diplomacy is spotty. If power does not explain most of motive or the bulk of outcomes, other explanations are needed. For example, the decision process itself affects outcomes.[5]

Technology

Technological determinism, a favorite of the business and scientific community, is the polar opposite of a power explanation. This approach assumes that technology has a logic built into it that dictates the path forward. The microchip and data storage, in this view, should dominate any account of ICT governance change because they changed the logic of technology. The accounts of US market governance and Internet governance in chapter 9 should put this notion to rest.

Important shifts at the technology frontier alter the costs and benefits of all stakeholders concerning market competition and its governance. They make new forms of organization possible and invite entrepreneurship in all parts of society. Still, this line of thinking errs. To begin with, as scholars of economic growth and technology have shown, societies have turned against technologies.[6] In the 1980s, nuclear power plans were curtailed in many countries. More critically, the mix of technologies deployed and their use varies significantly across societies. Railroads and automobiles play different roles in different countries. Medical practices and drug dosing diverge across national boundaries. The mix of ICT technologies and their applications also vary. The technological system embodies a legal and market "code" in its deployment that shifts this mix.[7] For example, the path of technological innovation shifted when financial and legal reforms spurred venture capital markets and accelerated the decline of giant, vertically integrated companies.

Thus, large technological shifts pose major disruptive choices for society, but there is no one blueprint built into them. Analysts break this disruption into component pieces that can be more precisely matched against political and market dynamics.

Ideas

The role of ideas as an explanation of change has recurring appeal in the ICT community. It is a favorite of Hollywood—for example, the early *Star Trek* was a combination of a frontier Western and a testimony to the gospel that civilizing ideas could overcome human or extraterrestrial foibles.

Ideas might matter in several ways.[8] Stakeholder communities, expert and amateur, organize around predominant ideas about cause and effect, and about moral desirability. As these ideas evolve they suggest an agenda that can sharply redirect policy. Human rights organizations and the arms control community are prime examples.[9] In this perspective ideas are powerful forces that drive change. A narrower version holds that ideas organize information thereby permitting successful bargaining on collaboration by providing "focal points" for organizing strategic behavior. Thomas Schelling, a father of modern game theory, argues forcefully that the idea of "no first use" for nuclear weapons stabilized deterrence by guiding decision making by the nuclear powers.[10] The "end-to-end" connectivity principle for Internet architecture was similarly critical.

The limits of ideas as an explanation for policy arise from a different question: Which ideas matter and why do they shift over time? Ideas cannot be reduced to questions of the preferences of the powerful or the interests of economic actors. However, their policy role is powerfully shaped by their relationship with those with power and interests. As chapter 9 shows, the de facto selection by the US government of one engineering community over another made a huge difference because different wings of the IT community had opposing ideas about networking architectures.[11]

Domestic Politics

The fourth explanation is old-fashioned domestic politics. Typically, commentators remark on interest-group politics or bureaucratic politics.[12] The former looks for the influence of organized groups in shaping government decisions through lobbying, campaign donations, or political action with voters. The emphasis is on the privileged position of concentrated interests because they are easier to organize and have higher stakes in the outcomes as compared to the broad diffuse interests of consumers.[13] Policy is the result of the give and take among organized interests.

A different but often complementary notion is bureaucratic politics. This views government officials or non-profit leaders as career-promoting and power-enhancing entrepreneurs who strive to build their domains. Policies often reflect conflict or cooperation among these bureaucratic players. One version of bureaucratic politics, public choice theory (much beloved by many economists), argues that the march to expanded budgets, higher taxes, and more regulation is a good first-order approximation of the predictable outcome of the process.[14] When paired with interest-group theories, bureaucratic politics becomes an elaborate tale of an exchange of, usually legal, initiatives between bureaucratic agencies and interest groups with aligned interests.

These notions are appealing. Anyone with significant experience in Washington, Tokyo, or Paris will see some truth. Yet scholars point out deep flaws in their conception of politics and the role of political institutions. For example, in democracies top politicians seek elective office and effective control of their government.[15] They respond to the imperatives of the ballot box and worry about what voters will support and how to build a dominant legislative party. Political parties are the vehicles used by political leaders to build "brand names" that appeal to voters. This has implications that are not captured by interest-group politics. Even the dance of bureaucrats ultimately responds imperfectly to the design by political leadership.

In summary: The four predominant explanations reviewed here point to important elements of a workable theory, but they have individual failings and omit important arguments. An alternative synthesis is needed. That comes next.

The Independent Variable: Forces Changing Global Market Governance

Choosing theories comes down to picking between parsimony and elegance and accounting for fine variations in the variables that explain the detail in governance outcomes. Our approach is closer to engineering than physics. It is rooted in theory but meant to provide a blueprint for action that is more detailed than elegant. This synthesis builds on the explanations just reviewed.

What explains the choice of changes in governance? The argument, in brief, is that global market governance for ICT responds to political and economic forces of demand and supply. These changes always play out in an institutional and market landscape with established stakeholders. Thus, the choice of governance is never a green field design operation; it is a choice between the status quo and some alternative that is politically feasible. This section focuses on the demand side; the next section explores the supply side of the equation—the options for governance compared to the status quo.

On the demand side, a significant disruption in the domestic markets of the United States and other strong national markets inevitably precedes shifts in the important rules and institutions shaping world markets.[16] These disruptions usually arise from technological shifts that induce two changes—shifts in interdependence and reconsideration by all stakeholders about their governance interests. These catalytic upheavals are decisively shaped and filtered by domestic political and economic institutions. In response to domestic changes, powerful countries use diplomacy when seeking change, but they exercise even greater influence using two other routes. First, they forge new domestic arrangements that erode everyone's faith in the credibility of old global governance bargains. This sets off a search for alternatives. Second, they often block alternative international responses to market forces to advance global alternatives more attuned to their new domestic governance approaches.

If the powerful provoke change, what shapes their preferences? Domestic institutions matter and respond to the broad impulses shaping society. Their leaders try to shape strategic alternatives around these forces. Thus, the critical role of technology in shaping ICT policy requires attention.

Technological Catalysts and Domestic Political Economy

Technology forces choices on the players in the global markets. It upsets the balance among interests and strategies of leading players by creating major opportunities and risks and challenges the prevailing intellectual model of the marketplace. In short, it raises the possibility of change, but it does not dictate a particular set of changes. As the cumulative degree of technological change explodes, market governance changes.

Significant shifts in the technology envelope can change global market interdependence dramatically.[17] (Markets differ in the degree and form of their interdependence, so not all markets have similar starting points for global governance.) Analysts usually focus on supply-side interdependence—that is, the integration of global production systems or the degree of price convergence due to more open markets and stiffer global competition. Our discussion of the process revolution is in line with these analyses. However, for a significant input, such as ICT, user interdependence is equally important and has had major consequences for the global ICT infrastructure. As we noted earlier, since the 1950s large corporate ICT users have experienced major transformations. In many respects financial institutions and multinational manufacturers became information analysis companies that deliver financial or engineering product information. As users, they needed less expensive but more powerful continental and global ICT infrastructures to tie together their global product operations. However, telecom companies consistently lagged behind their customers in recognizing the importance of these changes. As we document in chapter 7, this helps explain why the corporate competition coalition pushed for global "trade in services" rules.[18]

Technologically enabled shifts in the market force all to rethink their interests about their market strategies and government rules influencing markets. Entrenched incumbents may have to cope with pricing changes. Opportunities open for new entrants. Other stakeholders in market governance, such as well-organized groups of consumers or the research community, also recalculate their interests. As the interest-group thesis suggests, strongly motivated stakeholders have the interest and ability to mobilize in the political arena and the marketplace.[19]

Change extends beyond interest-group thinking. Significant changes in the technology envelope attracts the attention of political entrepreneurs in the major powers, including ambitious legislators, denizens of think tanks, and others searching for the next big policy idea. The political policy establishment then seeks ways to modify policy to advance the public interest or to improve their political positions.[20] Knowing the dance steps is a prerequisite for idea-based explanations to matter.

When major technology shifts gather momentum, the fluidity of labor markets and of venture capital fueled American capital markets and strongly influenced how technology innovation in the United States differs from technology innovation in Europe.[21] The arrangement of political institutions influences these market institutions. These variances in political and market institutions in large countries set a baseline for the case studies of market governance change.

The Role of Powerful Countries: Diffusion and Agenda Setting

So far this picture of change has finessed an important question: Who sets the agenda for governance change? Major countries dominate the agenda setting for international arrangements and control the bargaining resources to ensure implementation. They can coerce, provide incentives, or link issues through the formal processes of government diplomacy, through transnational networks that advocate change, or through market processes.

Crucially, a domestic shift in the market leader sends a credible signal to all countries that a shift in governance is likely. More than a diplomatic initiative, reorganizing the domestic market means that the market leader is serious. Moreover, if the United States heads along one path, it forces firms and interest groups elsewhere to reconsider their commercial options. Thus, when the US broke up AT&T, large British, French, and Japanese banks asked themselves if the new US networking environment would give their US rivals operational and cost advantages. The absence of significant Internet regulation sent another powerful signal. Policy and political entre-preneurs worldwide wondered how each dramatic shift in an important growth sector altered their options. In time, policies in each major market shifted in response.[22] The diffusion of reform among ICT market leaders eventually turned global trade negotiations into a coordination problem. At issue was how precisely to shift delegated authority to the WTO, but the major adjustment costs and risks involved in the change of governance were so difficult that they nearly sunk the WTO talks on liberalization.

Large mismatches between international and domestic market gover-nance create deep structural tensions that can eventually fray governance arrangements and raise questions about global market governance. Calcu-lations about the impact of the strategic market position of the leading market powers intersect with considerations of which arrangements are compatible with their domestic ICT governance. Inevitably, political and economic pressure on the global policy status quo increases.

Powerful countries have significant impact on the choices because they have strong influence over setting new agendas (at international institu-tions and when making unilateral changes of great international conse-quence) and on blocking incremental adjustments (negative agenda power) that may force larger alterations in governance. Deadlock at the Interna-tional Telecommunication Union over the reform of standards setting led to a dispersion of standards setting activities in ways that fragmented markets and changed innovation cycles. US preemptive action led to new non-governmental mechanisms, in the form of the Internet Corporation for Assigned Names and Numbers (ICANN) and the Internet Engineering Task Force (IETF), that put agenda setting in the hands of a technically sophisticated expert community with a common view of the future of networking.

Logically, international institutions could initiate a major shift in market governance at the international level. Smaller countries use international institutional efforts to advance initiatives that they cannot push alone. They use international institutions' voting rules to bolster their position and international meetings to publicize their cases among the voters of larger countries.[23] Smaller countries can exercise some collective market power because some policy reforms work better with, or even fail without, complementary international reforms. But initiatives on big ICT markets requiring the common agenda of many smaller players are more difficult to pull off.[24]

So far the analysis has focused on how to conceptualize the forces that drive change. This is the equivalent of speaking only about the demand side of a market. The supply options also matter for the final outcome. Market-governance arrangements are the supply side of the equation.

The Path of Change: The Intervening Variables

Disruption of the status quo and plans for change are important, but global governance emerges out of the accommodation of diverse preferences in a world market with decentralized national authorities. The costs of organizing and implementing governance strategies are an important feature shaping the overall governance equilibrium. Social scientists think of these factors that can mediate or transform the original path of change as intervening variables. It is convenient to conceive of them as the supply-side options for governance. We focus on two aspects of the supply side. One is the role of market governance. The other is the structure of decision making and delegation, including the ideas around which delegation is organized.

Market Governance

On one dimension, market governance organizes, enables, or mediates three classes of outcomes that render market coordination easier and thereby generate efficiency gains.[25] On another dimension, negotiators incorporate these outcomes in arrangements that scholars have dubbed "soft" or "hard" obligations, depending on how explicitly they are codified.

The first role of market governance is straightforward. Market governance can contribute to the facilitation of bargaining, decision making, and implementation of formal or informal agreements among international stakeholders. This is done in part by creating or endorsing arrangements that build consensus on the facts concerning a problem or help to mediate and settle disputes. To minimize their coordination costs, these institutions also gather information about compliance with rules and expected behavior.

Not all governance arrangements are efficient or desirable. They can become overly bureaucratic. Anyone who has endured an inter-governmental meeting has questioned coordination. Nonetheless, a shift in basic direction requires that the governments of the largest market centers agree on common principles to guide their collective undertakings. This rarely occurs unless they already have sorted their domestic choices and considered how international arrangements might help or hinder their prospects.[26] This means that the process of international discussion and bargaining is a time-consuming bottom-up process for three reasons. First, sharing information and making it credible to all parties is difficult. Voluntary consent requires credible information. Information is more believable when it is costly and verified.[27] This is why so much of governance is about structured sharing of information. Second, policy shifts rarely come out of the blue from the chief executive. Leaders proposing sweeping international changes may endorse ideas that would benefit all in the long term, but even the most benign change usually implies losses for some, adjustments for all, and relative winners and losers. It takes careful development of constituencies of sympathetic stakeholders and their mobilization to wield the political capital to work through the process.[28] Third, bargaining plus governance allows finer-grained choices about how much compliance to promises is needed for change to improve the status quo.[29]

The World Trade Organization's negotiating process typifies how governance can improve the information available to governments. The bargaining leading to the WTO telecom agreement collaterally created an informal network of information sharing among national communications authorities that influenced their policy views.[30] As we will show in chapter 7, the WTO also introduced innovations on how to schedule national commitments on market access and a mechanism for dispute resolution that allowed countries better tradeoffs on the timing and degree of implementation of commitments.

A second role of governance systems is to set and administer rules on technical coordination and market competition. By establishing a system of property rights, ownership and control of the global marketplace is shaped. Since the early 1980s the rules setting global technical standards often were in turmoil. Simultaneously, the global rules governing competition and property rights underwent a revolution.

Those not familiar with international rule setting often assume that international rules are like domestic legislation, which can run to more than 100 pages for large and complex matters. Such rules do exist in the international realm, but the modes for setting international rules are much more diverse. Many rules are more like "commandments"—relatively brief statements of basic principles and obligations that coordinate expectations but do not lay out the details of implementation.

Two important developments in international coordination were keenly honed by the experiences of bringing the EU member countries together. The EU undertook "harmonization" of some important national regulatory obligations—a few things that each member country had to do in regard to a market. These were worked out in detail. Countries were free to have other national rules for the market, so long as they did not clash with the harmonized obligations. At the same time, the European Union forged "mutual recognition agreements" for many product markets. These pacts laid out the functional requirements that, for example, defined a safe product and characteristics of a process that could enforce the certification. After certification of a product's safety by one EU member, others were required to accept it. (Mutual recognition agreements exist globally for many products, such as telecommunications terminal equipment.)

In a third role, governance can allow various actors and interest groups to create collective capabilities, including for the provision of global services. Early on international satellite communications was provided by Intelsat, an organization jointly owned by the government telephone authorities, which were intent on adapting the tradition of national monopolies to a new technology.[31] This hybrid organization, combining elements of an international organization and a corporation, dominated international satellite services for more than 30 years before a tortuous process of disputes and diplomacy opened the market and ultimately privatized Intelsat. In the late 1990s, ICANN again exemplified the international provision of infrastructure. Although non-governmental in nature, some international functionalities (including the World Wide Web

Consortium, which coordinates the development of standards for the software code that makes the Web possible) are effectively global supply services.

A second dimension of global governance is the degree to which it is "soft" or "hard."[32] There is a rough cost-benefit analysis of the merits of making obligations into agreements that are spelled out in formal agreements and embodied in inter-governmental institutions. The institutions for market governance include formal government agencies (e.g., the Federal Communications Commission and the International Telecommunication Union) and less formal collaborations or synchronization of expectations. For example, national regulators may expect and anticipate that foreign regulators will act in a predictable manner. The choices of how much to formalize cooperation and how much to set in formal international rules (as opposed to depending on informal coordination) are an important design element.[33] Non-governmental institutions also may be included as part of the governance structure. Some agreements, including detailed arrangements for the sharing of intellectual property and ICT standards setting, primarily are worked out in the private sector. There is no single formula for organizations. However, governments tend to keep a tighter leash on choices dealing directly with security or major distributional implications flowing directly from choices made in an international arrangement.

Delegation and Governance

Choices for decision making and implementation are central to bargains about policy choices. They influence judgments about the credibility of proposed solutions and expectations about the future agenda of collective action. The importance of these arrangements pushed academic analysts beyond their original understandings of bureaucratic politics.

Scholars have developed a deep understanding of the implications of decision making and membership rules. In working through major governance choices there often are major conflicts among stakeholders; institutions vary in their ability to resolve them. As the number of decision points (veto points) in a policy process increases, the process becomes more likely to maintain the status quo or produce a decision skewed to serve the needs of players with the strongest veto power.[34] The ITU and other international institutions employ unanimity rules in decision making, further increasing veto power, although ad hoc political and economic pressure may induce reluctant parties to acquiesce.[35] This made it difficult to resolve issues over IPR commitments when setting technical standards.

Some conflicts over decision making are addressed by membership rules or by altering the obligations of members.[36] Limiting the range of countries involved may produce a group with more intense and similar preferences, thereby easing, but not ending, coordination problems. Regional trade associations and security pacts such as NATO are examples. Or organizations may have extensive membership and intense rules concerning obligations, but allow for more limited participation of members in some negotiations. The WTO's telecom negotiations involved only a minority of its members and initially only those participants submitted market access commitments. Those that abstained acquired no new obligations as a result of the agreement. This made the negotiations tractable for those interested in the pact. However, owing to the WTO's "most favored nation" rule, countries that did make telecom commitments had to extend them to all WTO members, not just those in the telecom pact. This created a complex diplomatic calculus.

The design process of institutions can be broadly conceived as a series of decisions about the "delegation" of authority by "principals" to their "agents." The main idea is that it is inefficient for national governments (principals) to do everything themselves. Sometimes they must cede authority to specialized actors (agents) that have expertise, the ability to gather information, and the authority to shape agendas for action. Moreover, these agents sometimes receive limited powers to make decisions under carefully understood procedures for voting and review. They also may help to monitor and administer a global resource (such as Internet domain names) or to resolve disputes. By granting authority to a highly motivated expert agent, over time the principals can lend policy credibility to an initiative because it takes significant effort to reverse decisions of the agent. For example, the US government stacked the deck for Internet governance in favor of a technological community whose fundamental beliefs rejected forms of industrial policy that the government opposed.

The advantages of creating agents are partly offset by the costs of monitoring their performance. Agents possess specialized information and their own agendas that may exceed the comfort zones of their principals. This can lead to the familiar complaint about "out-of-control" bureaucrats.[37] Nonetheless, principals employ a variety of methods to monitor, provide incentives to, and even overrule their agents. Structuring the process of decision making, and participation in decisions, is an important feature of this subtle control. By cleverly setting these terms, principals can rely on stakeholders to call their attention to problematic decisions that might otherwise go unnoticed.[38] Or, as with the Internet, the principals can threaten to intervene to curtail the authority of ICANN in various ways.

In sum, the preferences of principals powerfully, if imperfectly, determine the general pattern of outcomes of agents. The principals may not know much about agents' detailed initiatives, but they have the ability to enforce their underlying agendas. If necessary, as happened in global communications, the market leaders will decide that an agent such as the ITU is locked into a rigid decision structure that cripples any efforts for it to change and evolve. They then alter the mix of agents to steer events. Indeed, the case studies show a critical element of changing ICT governance is the shift in the agents delegated to coordinate global markets. In view of the large stakes involved at the inflection point, we expect more such changes.

Choices about delegation are also closely tied to the emergence of problem-solving communities that permit the day-to-day coordination of a marketplace.[39] Indeed, a central feature of delegation can be awarding disproportionate influence to a selected problem-solving community.[40] Political maneuvering matters in networked marketplaces, but routine problem solving requires expectations among stakeholders about the logic of how market governance should work. This allows for decentralized problem solving.[41] The worldwide shift from monopoly to competition made trade experts more important for resolving issues related to communications policy. The expectations of expert communities provide an anchor for the many participants in complicated international marketplaces that go beyond the formal code.[42] Principals do not just hand over authority to experts, so transparent decision making for governance helps political leaders by allowing the contending parties to monitor the behavior of technocrats.[43] More important, certain principles and norms emerge (either by legislation or by informal guidance) in the governance of marketplaces. These principles and norms help guide decision making.

Understanding the Implications of Changes in Global Governance

We care about governance because it can change the path of a market.[44] The overall pattern of organizing markets and their consequences for economic performance are the ultimate outcome, the dependent variable, that drives our inquiry.

Large economic stakes are buried in global governance arrangements. They powerfully influence property rights, technical efficiency, the path of global innovation, and who wins and loses in the global arena. Critically, political leaders do not just choose between monopoly and competition; they chose specific forms of competition that favor certain types of new entrants and stakeholders. They do not just choose between letting technologists control Internet governance and handing it over to government decision makers. They select particular tradeoffs involving authority. Innovations in global governance can improve global welfare, but they usually do less than is theoretically possible because forces of political economy and imperfect knowledge are formidable. Imperfect reform provides the foundation of "pretty good" governance. As analysts we want to understand the imperfections and the realm of possible change in order to develop a realistic picture of the alternatives.

Students of international cooperation often are enamored of whatever functional gains emerge from cooperation. We began this book by noting that global coordination on standards can improve economies of scales, and that this was a standard explanation of cooperation for decades. But mandating uniform standards also reinforced a particular business structure and a particular set of competitive advantages by making it more difficult for newcomers to build innovative alternative designs. Standardization on functional requirements, rather than detailed design, was challenging to achieve because of its market implications, even if it was better for competitive efficiency and innovation.

The lesson from standards, or countless other choices, is that a clear idea is needed of what governance is attempting to accomplish. It is crucial to embrace a guiding theory and detailed policies to implement it. Our discussion of the three eras of ICT policy defined the theory as the "principles" guiding policy and the guidelines for policies as "norms." These are categories invented to capture the central thinking that ordered problem solving and political bargaining. Focusing on principles and norms allowed us go to the core of the political economic and intellectual underpinnings of governance. By stating these premises explicitly, it illuminates the underlying logic of governance and its implications for economic performance and equity.

Until the 1960s, global governance of telecommunications rested on the principle that "monopolies of services and equipment were the most efficient and equitable way of providing public service both domestically and internationally. This principle assumed state control over international communications."[45] From this followed a series of norms for organizing global communications capabilities. As we explained earlier, a result of the rise of "value-added governance" in the United States was that the old system was challenged by alternative principles and norms backed by the force of the American marketplace, by technological innovation, and by diplomacy. Both monopoly and state control began to be displaced. Later, the switch of the US to "managed market entry" governance introduced yet another dramatic change to global governance. Similar debates were stirring in other advanced economies, but the US breakthroughs both anchored the global agenda and added urgency to debates in other countries. The case studies that follow analyze these changes in three aspects of ICT governance.

The market-governance arrangements captured by principles and norms shape economic performance by influencing the allocation and assignment of property rights, the entitlement that allows an actor to own and manage an economic asset.[46] Governments can alter property rights to strengthen or weaken the powers and responsibilities of owners. Some rules, such as restrictions on foreign ownership of infrastructures using radio spectrum, limit who can own an asset. Other rules dictate whether owners can freely sell their assets to buyers that have not first been approved for license by government authorities. Other rules, such as those about pricing, influence the ability of owners to manage their assets. Students of political economy have shown that property rights help structure the dynamics of marketplaces.[47]

More generally, global governance influences the degree and the forms of competition in the world marketplace. If government rules tightly constrict competition in broadcasting, for example, but allow relatively free entry in Web content, that will channel competition and innovation in certain ways. It also will set up predictable struggles, such as the one now unfolding between digital universality of content on the Web and regulatory nationalism for broadcast.

Global governance also influences the transactional efficiencies of markets. For years, the regulation of global communications services imposed a specific way of paying for the termination of traffic from one country to another, and this system had incentives to inflate costs and profits. An elaborate "gray market" skirting the official system emerged in the 1980s and the 1990s that arbitraged inefficiencies of the existing system. But it took a reorganization of the global market through WTO rules to begin allowing new business models operating in transparent markets to emerge on a widespread basis.

The rules and institutions of global governance matter a great deal because of their distributional implications. Political infighting shapes governance rules and institutions and the form of governance has important consequences for understanding equity issues. Some changes in governance directly alter who wins and loses from the global marketplace.

Older electronic equipment firms faced major displacement as global services became more competitive. The failure of some national and regional economies to adjust to their decline hurt them in world markets. Some shifts in governance may not change who wins but do alter the terms on which leading firms or countries participate in the world economy. For example, IBM remains formidable but is less preeminent than it once was. The basis for IBM's business success is different today than it was in the 1970s. Other alternations in governance may have surprising consequences for stakeholders. Many developing countries thought that more widespread competition and privatization in communications markets would harm universal service. Although some countries so botched the transition away from monopoly that it did no good, most countries ended up with more investment and connectivity as a result of the efficiencies of even somewhat competitive markets.

In ways not imagined in the late 1980s, some wealthier developing economies, including Mexico and South Africa, now are home to large multinational communications companies that invest heavily in developing economies. As changes in governance occur in other aspects of the global ICT infrastructure, the challenge will be for new arrangements of property rights and transaction institutions to enable a broader range of information applications in poorer countries.

Summing Up

Technology disrupts by shifting levels of interdependence and stakeholder interests with regard to market strategies and governance. These catalysts are filtered through domestic markets and political institutions. The time is ripe to confront significant internal changes, reorganize their domestic governance, and restructure of global governance in various powerful markets. The United States already has triggered two such shifts: the rise of value-added competition and managed market entry. These domestic changes sent a credible diplomatic message and created a transnational channel of change that led many other countries to simultaneously reconsider their market interests. These governance changes reflected the impact of the global negotiation process and the "supply-side" constraints on the alternatives for institutional arrangements. Yet the ensuing shifts in the delegation of power to institutions and expert communities and the reorganization of property rights altered the structure, the conduct, and the consequences of world markets. Today, a third shift in global governance is under way.

III   Three Dimensions of Global Market Governance

7 Trade and the Global Network Revolution

Markets undergoing significant technological transformation face questions about global market governance. Technological changes were catalysts that led to the transformation of domestic market policies in the first two ICT eras. Eventually these changes in domestic markets created challenges that existing international market governance could not resolve. One response by governments was to grant more of a role to trade agreements in the global governance of ICT markets.

Initially, trade rules had no jurisdiction over communications and information services. Over time, trade rules emerged and evolved in response to the rise of value-added competition. Governance reflecting managed market-entry arrangements finally were put into place in the Agreement on Basic Telecommunications Services negotiated at the World Trade Organization in 1997. This was a fundamental change in governance.

The introduction of WTO disciplines for ICT service markets altered three features of the global market's governance.[1] First, the major market centers delegated significant power over competition arrangements for global communications to the WTO instead of the ITU. This changed the agenda and the expertise governing the international communications market. Second, the WTO rules, especially in the 1997 agreement, dramatically altered competition rules and property rights in the market, thereby changing its efficiency and the winners and losers in global markets. Later, developing countries made a failed attempt to redirect part of this authority back to the ITU. Third, the first two shifts altered the composition of the expert community influencing global governance. Figuring out how to rationalize and administer a natural monopoly was no longer the central goal. Instead, demonstrated expertise in managing competition policy and trade rules became critically important. The new organizing question was "What is the best way to harness competition to improve consumer welfare while maintaining a framework of strong regulatory guidance?"

international negotiations on VANs were difficult because many countries claimed that it was a purely domestic matter or governed by ITU rules. Moreover, there was no clear sense of what framework of trade arrangements could sustain global governance of VANs. Agreement proved difficult to attain. Eventually, the US government worked to incorporate these initiatives into more comprehensive bilateral and regional trade agreements. The North American Free Trade Agreement (NAFTA) followed early experiments with bilateral trade agreements. At the same time, from 1986 to 1994, the Uruguay Round WTO negotiators worked to craft a global agreement on VANs and corporate networks.

In retrospect, the often-contentious negotiations on global governance reform for value-added services may seem oddly disproportionate to the commercial stakes. In 1994, the Web was in its infancy and the international role of value-added services still was tiny. Global communication services revenues slightly exceeded $500 billion. The international (cross-border) services market amounted to about $50 billion, more than 30 percent of which involved the United States. The cross-border market consisted mostly of basic "switched services" (phone and fax) that relied on the use of phone switches to deliver services. The global cross-border market for value-added services, including data networking, was small. Precise numbers were never reliable, but it amounted to about 5 percent of the total, approximately $2.5 billion. But this sufficed to let the US move the equilibrium because it remained the technological leader and the largest market.

In short, the value-added market was less than 0.5 percent of the total world market, but its significance was greater for two reasons. In some countries this was a battle over the computer industry, because until the early 1990s superior computer networking provided a major advantage in the world of mainframe computers. Thus, Japan resisted entry into its domestic market by US VANs to limit the influence of US computer firms, especially IBM. This produced bitter US-Japan bilateral trade confrontations that culminated in agreement on international Value-Added Networks.[10] For developing countries, corporate traffic was an extremely profitable source of high-value traffic because it was delivered under traditional market regulations that inflated pricing. Private corporate networks reduced the potential margins of national post, telegraph, and telephone authorities ("PTTs"). In addition, incumbent carriers such as Mexico's Telmex worried that value-added services might allow sophisticated customers to "leak" traffic off the public phone network by sending it through their private networks.

National PTTs also resisted value-added regimes because they feared that the rise of private networking threatened their plans for profitable growth, including expanding computer networking on a monopoly model at a stately pace.[11] The introduction of VANs predictably created advocates that argued that the old PTTs were incapable of delivering a network with the cost efficiencies and the technical flexibility needed for value-added services to thrive. This happened in Europe when the EU tried this approach.

The trade negotiations over VANs confirmed the PTTs' fears. In the 1980s US trade negotiators, for example, conceded that they could not force foreign monopolies to relinquish their hold on basic services markets or the public network infrastructure. Instead, they pursued the same regulatory measure that prevailed in the United States in the 1970s—guarantees that corporate users could establish or use private networks on terms that would negate the monopoly power of the incumbent phone company. This meant that US trade authorities were classifying certain domestic regulatory practices as unacceptable, a touchy issue for all sovereign nations.

The tension over telecom became embedded in a larger story involving the management of the world economy. To traditional telecom experts, it seemed that "the gods must be crazy" when top economic leaders gambled that changing the global telecom governance would help to achieve a new world trade agreement. The politics of trade policy always is a defining issue for political parties and for national political economies. This is politics at a grander scale than ICT interest-group battles, and ICT got caught up in it.

In 1986 the Uruguay Round of trade negotiations was launched at the Punte del Este, Uruguay Ministerial meeting of the General Agreement on Tariffs and Trade (GATT), the WTO's predecessor. This came after a failed attempt to launch negotiations in late 1982 at a time of global recession and increasing gloom about the prospects for the world economy and the fate of free trade. Many suspected that declining US power would weaken the political glue holding the free trade system together. The Japan-US trade confrontations seemed to augur an era of trade wars. The earlier Tokyo Round negotiations had removed most significant tariffs on goods that industrial countries most wanted to liberalize. With no enthusiasm for liberalization of agriculture and textiles, proponents of free trade needed to find a different agenda to revive the momentum for global trade talks.[12]

One priority was to make the benefits of previous agreements more reliable. This led to the objective of a binding system for resolving trade disputes at the WTO.[13] Another goal was to create a potent new constituency for trade negotiations by putting selected items about intellectual property and foreign investment on the negotiating agenda. Above all, the Uruguay Round proposed to make the service industries subject to trade disciplines. Services accounted for the bulk of every industrialized country's domestic economy, and trade in services was growing rapidly. Further, all service markets were inefficient. They were ripe for showing how trade agreements could bolster global growth. In addition, a huge political clientele of service and equipment firms favored the opening of these world markets, thereby boosting political support for the Uruguay Round. Trade policy experts saw telecom as a leading edge issue because, unlike banking, a global deal seemed possible that would convert the general principles of service liberalization into a practical set of market access commitments.[14] Moreover, competition in ICT services was high on the request list of global service companies because ICT was a major cost and performance factor for them.

When the world's trade and finance ministers proposed to transfer authority over ICT services to the GATT, this did not reflect harmonious agreement. The Round's trade in services agenda was an idealistic and politically pragmatic gamble.

Several lessons emerged that illuminated how change unfolds in world markets. Crucially, "original" international jurisdiction over critical aspects of international telecom markets was transferred to the GATT (and later the WTO). Once relocated in that venue, the trading system's rules and negotiating logic-usurped agendas previously administered by the ITU, an organization rooted in monopoly, whose expert community believed that telecom markets were unique and therefore required special treatment. In contrast, trade experts viewed ICT services as just another market; the arcane details might require innovative features for trade deals, but the logic of market liberalization through the GATT still applied.[15]

In response to the skeptics, the United States tried something akin to a "proof of concept" for the Uruguay Round by incorporating services into various bilateral and regional free trade area negotiations. This happened in the 1985 US-Israel agreement and in the 1988 US-Canada Free Trade Agreement. Logically, it then became the basis for incorporating services into the NAFTA agenda.

As the Uruguay Round negotiations dragged on, the regional free-trade agreements took on a new significance in the American strategy. NAFTA and APEC (the Asia Pacific Economic Community), in particular, were advertised as alternatives to the conclusion of the Uruguay Round. Washington indicated to Europe that it could live with a failure at the

WTO because it would pursue liberalization through Free Trade Agreements in the fast-growing Pacific Rim. American policy makers predicted that America's deep economic ties around the Pacific would put Europe at a disadvantage. This was a crucial implied threat because the main obstacle to the conclusion of the Uruguay Round was the dispute over agriculture with Europe.

The backdrop to NAFTA was the United States' success in introducing long-distance competition that seemed to augur well for potential competitors to the Mexican incumbent, Telmex.[16] This disparity generated interest in both Mexican and US companies. US firms also were attracted by Canada's data and long-distance telecom markets.[17] The linkage of NAFTA to the Uruguay Round's closing negotiations meant that the US needed comparable concessions in both venues. NAFTA ultimately created bargaining leverage that hastened the Uruguay Round's conclusion. For example, NAFTA gave American and Canadian providers of voice mail or packet-switched services nondiscriminatory access to the Mexican public-telephone network and eliminated all investment restrictions for value-added, enhanced, and packet-switched services. It also required Telmex to provide cost-based access to its network for the competitive (or self) provision of enhanced or value-added services.[18] The NAFTA terms showed that trade liberalization of value-added services was possible between a developed and a developing country. The US thought it important to demonstrate this possibility to the developing world.

For equipment markets, the NAFTA negotiations took place during major industry adjustments and a soaring US trade deficit in equipment and concomitant major adjustments in US labor staffing of telecom manufacturers. The US industry was eager to expand internationally, but faced closed foreign markets. Canada wanted to lock in unrestricted access to the US market. Its main telecom equipment producer, Northern Telecom (Nortel), was a huge, early beneficiary of the breakup of AT&T. The seven original regional Bell operating companies bought heavily from Nortel to lessen their dependence on AT&T's equipment subsidiary, Lucent.[19] NAFTA also eliminated the tariffs on most equipment[20] and also assured users of the right to choose equipment attachments without undue interference from phone compnies.[21] This freedom was essential to business users configuring corporate telecommunications and computing systems.

North American liberalization further fueled the demand for a broad agreement on ICT equipment. The largest non-US markets were in the European Union and Japan. The fastest-growing markets were in rapidly industrializing countries. Nortel, Lucent, and other equipment companies favored global service liberalization because it supported new entrants into foreign markets that were potential customers. As the Internet boom expanded, the impetus for global networking innovation grew and equipment sales expanded. Global networking also facilitated high technology supply chains for manufacturing that persuaded several countries to embrace complementary suppliers of components and ICT equipment. Thus, in the Information Technology Agreement of 1996, the major trading partners in the WTO agreed on simultaneous unilateral liberalization of tariffs on many new forms of network and computing equipment. The agreement, signed by 52 nations, was consistent with a new pattern of intra-industry ICT trade. These equipment supply centers constituted 95 percent of the global demand for the products. Thus, simultaneous unilateral liberalization served the interests of both producer and consumer countries.[22]

In short, getting NAFTA to match the Uruguay Round terms reinforced the United States' bargaining strategy. It also served as a proof of concept for liberalization in general and accords with an industrializing country in particular. However, the successful conclusion of the Uruguay Round superseded the NAFTA accords.[23]

Achieving Managed-Entry Governance

NAFTA and the Uruguay Round concluded at about the same time. They had similar achievements on telecom equipment and services, but the Uruguay Round was slightly more inclusive than NAFTA. The Uruguay Round further demonstrated that a successful outcome in a networked service industry for multilateral trade policy was possible.

As the Uruguay Round dragged on, a more far-reaching change became conceivable. In the 1980s only a few countries accepted general competition in basic telecommunications services, and even those nations significantly limited competition. By the early 1990s, however, most industrial countries were moving to domestic market-entry rules that reopened questions about the global agenda. Thus, when the Uruguay Round ended in 1994, governments extended the deadline for negotiations on basic telecommunications services. The national differences over adjustment costs to global liberalization nearly sank the talks.

Cross-Border Services

In 1995, international traffic accounted for about 10 percent of the $500 billion world revenues for telephone services. This amount did not reflect the real economic importance of international services. The market for international calls and other cross-border telecom services shrouded a lucrative system of monopoly profits. The system's complexities shielded it from critical review. Let us draw back the curtain.

The ITU system for telecommunications services created a set of property rights in international telephone services that produced fundamentally anti-competitive consequences. These rules favored the "joint supply" of international phone services using settlement rates.[24] Settlement rates were paid to a country for terminating a call originating in another country. The settlement rate represented the cost of an input to production of an international phone call, just as iron is an input to producing steel. It influenced the pricing of international calling, but did not set the end price for consumers. The lack of competition in the retail market further inflated these prices.

When every country had its own monopoly, the accounting and settlement rate system reflected the property right of the local monopolist to charge for the use of its network and worked against the provision of end-to-end international services with pricing disciplined by a competitive global market. Monopolists often inflated settlement rates to cross-subsidize domestic customers and suppliers of labor or equipment, or simply to pad profits.

The introduction of competition in the United States further inflated the profits from international telephony for many countries. Increased competition in the US drove down international calling prices for its consumers and increased service options, thus stimulating US demand and driving up the volume of calls originating from the US to the rest of the world. With rare exceptions (Finland was one), more calls flowed from the US to other countries than vice versa. This led to a worsening of the imbalance in global traffic, and "net settlement payments" to PTTs became a lucrative source of dollars.

As an illustration of the net settlement payment, suppose the United States sent 10 minutes of calls to Mexico at a settlement rate of 50 cents per minute and Mexico sent the US 5 minutes of calls at the same rate. Then the net settlement payment from the US to Mexico for the period would be $2.50. To break even, the US carrier needed to recover this $2.50 payment from its customers ($0.25 per minute), a significant cost element. Because settlement rates bore little relationship to efficient economic costs, this also represented a large subsidy from competitive markets to monopoly markets. Furthermore, the Federal Communications Commission had to institute special controls to stop foreign monopolists from playing competitive US carriers off against each other on negotiating settlement rates for terminating their traffic. Although the US devised a clever patch, these FCC rules also weakened competition among US carriers.[25]

In mid 1997, after more than 10 years of competition, the FCC estimated that the average price of an international phone call from the United States was 88 cents per minute. This compared to 13 cents per minute for domestic long-distance calls. These price differences existed despite negligible differences in the costs of transmission between the two types of calls.

Exorbitant settlement rates inflated prices. In 1996 the average settlement rate paid by US carriers was 39 cents per minute; outside the OECD area and Mexico the average cost for US carriers was more than 60 cents per minute.[26] The FCC believed that the efficient cost of termination (the function paid for by a settlement rate) for most countries should not exceed 5 to 10 cents per minute.

In 1995, US carriers sent $5.4 billion in net settlement payments to other countries. This total reached about $6 billion in 1997. US consumers paid for this in their phone bills. The FCC calculated that roughly 70 percent of the total net settlement payments represented a subsidy paid by US consumers to foreign carriers. Moreover, changing patterns of international traffic induced by early competition suggested that US net settlement payments would continue to rise.[27]

The settlement rate issue also delayed the FCC from allowing increased foreign carrier entry into the US market for international phone services, a logical goal for boosting competition. The FCC took even longer to waive US restrictions on foreign investment in basic telecom carriers. In 1995, when the FCC adopted rules to systematize its case-by-case liberalization of US restrictions on foreign investment, the FCC still recognized that bilateral market openings would move slower than was ideal.[28] Efforts to prevent foreign carriers from abusing their market power also limited the potential benefits that they could bring to the US market by fostering more competition. Even if the FCC allowed British firms (for example) easier entry into the US market, this would not achieve effective international services competition. The settlement rate system still would need reform. Thus, in 1996 the FCC laid down conditions for "flexibility" under which the FCC would waive the use of settlement rates and other restrictions on international services.[29] Although an advance to liberalization, the 1996 rules did not alter the FCC's case-by-case approach to bilateral liberalization; the FCC still had to declare the home market of a foreign carrier to be effectively competitive for international services. This greatly narrowed the potential for flexibility.[30] In short, "flexibility" was supposed to undermine inflated settlement rates, but high rates limited the use of "flexibility." This contradiction in policy reflected a strategic market dilemma.

If the FCC made it easier for foreign carriers to provide international telephone services originating from the United States, it could reinforce their incentives to continue monopolies and high settlement rates.[31] A monopoly or near-monopoly carrier from a developing country, such as Telmex in 1996, could enter the US market and use various devices to increase the flow of international traffic back to their home from the US. This would increase the net settlement payment from the US to its home market.[32] If, say, 70 percent of this payment represented a subsidy from US consumers to the foreign carrier, Congress would punish the FCC for permitting a foreign carrier to generate larger net settlement payments.

Meanwhile, large US phone companies were not truly global operations. Their revenues from operations outside the United States provided only a minor share of their total revenue. Thus, they were not prepared to gamble that unleashing all regulatory restrictions would work out well. The consequence of this parochialism was that all major US carriers preferred the FCC to micro-manage the international market to lower settlement rates (and thus lower net settlement payments), rather than approve reforms designed to introduce more sweeping global competition.[33]

Changes in technology were eroding the old monopoly telecom system. But in many markets (e.g., textiles, where incumbents rake in huge profits and exercise huge political clout), delays of decades can precede "inevitable" market changes. The price structure of international services could have remained wildly inflated for many years if international service markets did not arrive at a political bargain to back reform.

These political and regulatory challenges led to a branching point for global negotiations. The status quo would liberalize VANs through the WTO and some basic services through bilateral agreements. Or, as a second option, VAN coverage might be expanded upon through a WTO agreement on basic communications services to open foreign entry only into domestic service markets. For example, foreign carriers might provide domestic cell phone carriers, but not international phone services. Alternatively, as a third option, all basic services for domestic and cross-national traffic could be brought into the WTO.

Even the second option was a formidable challenge. At minimum, well-defined property rights were needed to encourage private firms to make the required investment to provide services in foreign domestic markets. Establishing such rights would allow all domestic markets to benefit from inflows of new foreign entrants with money, technology, and management innovations. Reflecting the domestic policies of industrial countries, trade leaders concluded that such property rights required effective enforcement of competition rights. An independent regulatory authority was needed that was obliged to favor competition. This was a dramatic innovation in trade policy.

The United States concluded that efficient global networks were essential for the ICT revolution. Thus, it was essential to include international services in any agreement.[34] Moreover, the US political economy required addressing the link between domestic services and cross-border international services in a WTO agreement. This made inter-governmental action into an all or nothing game: agree on comprehensive new rules for all aspects of the market or rely on ad hoc bilateral agreements that would slow liberalized global competition.[35] The differences in the strategic positions and domestic institutions of the US and the EU made the WTO deal difficult.

Domestic Politics and International Markets: The US and the EU

Through the 1990s there was a general political logic to WTO negotiations. Most countries decided on their "best efforts" at commitments in the negotiations only after they observed what US-EU talks yielded. No sensible country would table major concessions before knowing what the two most active trading powers could agree on. This was the case for the basic telecom negotiations. EU and US negotiators reminded each other that if they did not agree on their "best offers" on a timely basis, there would be insufficient time to solicit better offers from other countries.[36] Progress depended on the two protagonists.

US and EU preferences reflected their domestic political economic institutions and their international strategic positioning. Domestic political economy led both to prefer some form of managed market entry. But their distinctive international positions led them to different calculations about the cost of switching from the status quo. Moreover, the US and EU political institutions faced different challenges for making credible promises on trade liberalization.

The US accounted for nearly one-third of international traffic flows. Its large, diverse exposure to the international telecommunications market meant that it confronted international telecom competition issues that had barely surfaced or registered elsewhere. The US therefore insisted that international services be part of any WTO agreement, and sought liberalization from large developing markets where international phone services were growing rapidly.[37]

In contrast, the EU preferred to handle international telephony issues matters with EU directives, not WTO talks. The EU members' international traffic was mainly intra-European, and fell under the jurisdiction of EU directives. Unlike US carriers that paid billions of dollars to foreign carriers in settlement payments, the EU made only modest net payments outside Europe. Therefore, the EU viewed the global negotiations as a way to secure unconditional access to the US market. Its secondary objective was to obtain something close to that in Japan. As a result, the EU did not consider developing countries as crucial to the success of the talks.

The variations between US and EU domestic institutions buttressed these international differences. In the US, the division of powers and the logic of congressional politics raised three critical issues. In each instance the EU embraced a different position.

First, the division of powers in the US meant that the EU questioned the credibility of the US commitments, particularly on foreign investment.[38] The US strategy relied on the FCC using its legal discretion to lift restrictions on foreign investment, and did not seek congressional legislation to implement a WTO agreement. The EU team cared more about how to judge the reliability of this commitment than anything else.[39] The division of powers between the EU and its member states also created a credibility problem that worried the US. Washington feared that EU commitments on telecom liberalization would not be implemented reliably by national governments. The US pushed successfully to remove any exceptions to full liberalization by large EU members on January 1, 2008.

Second, congressional incentives for foreign policy and international trade decisions shaped the US negotiating agenda. Congressional politics mean that US negotiating teams need a large package of concession to win congressional backing.[40] A small deal could not generate enough political interest to protect it against entrenched congressional skeptics of trade. Although the US crafted a strategy that avoided the need for legislative approval, if Congress were opposed, the FCC would not undertake sweeping regulatory changes. The Office of the US Trade Representative also would lose congressional backing for the rest of its trade agenda if the FCC forged ahead regardless of political criticism. This political strategy required three accomplishments: (1) The US negotiating team needed significant concessions from the industrializing countries of Asia, South America, and Eastern Europe. Otherwise, Congress would reject a deal that opened the US market without adequate coverage from all major markets. It did not have to show breakthroughs with most poor countries. (2) The agreement had to lower the price of international phone services. This was a significant benefit to trumpet to the press. (3) The agreement had to credibly protect long-distance carriers from anti-competitive behavior by foreign carriers entering the US market for international services. Congress required long-distance carriers to at least register cautious approval. A strong vote of "no confidence" would signal that the WTO deal was suspect. Thus, domestic politics made the US negotiating team push for a "big deal" providing comprehensive global reforms and winning commitments from virtually every significant market. In comparison, the EU trade negotiation process was less obsessed about external commitments. It focused at least as much on negotiations among European states over the organization of the internal market and on the powers delegated to the EU. The larger and more complicated the WTO deal, the tougher was the internal market negotiation process. So the EU would accept a more limited deal than the US.

Third, the special problems posed by international telephone services exposed how domestic institutions shaped regulatory options. At the WTO the US often advocated preemptive controls to curb these problems. EU negotiators always responded that such measures might diminish the rights of European carriers entering the US market. The EU argued that the US should act against problems only after they surfaced. Whatever the intellectual merits of the EU's view, it ignored the realities of the regulatory process in a country with highly divided powers, such as the US.[41] The FCC must go through a lengthy investigation, rulemaking, and enforcement procedure before intervening in the marketplace.[42] US carriers believed that problems were inevitable, but any FCC response was likely to be too late if it waited until a problem arose.[43] Divided powers led to a US preference for a WTO deal that authorized specific measures to prevent problems in the international services market over ad hoc enforcement to correct market distortions.

Although the division of powers shaped the US negotiating options, EU bargaining positions reflected the delegation of negotiating authority from member states to the EU, an overriding imperative to stifle unilateral US trade initiatives, and the need for internal bargaining over external commitments. These three factors led the EU to prefer limited multilateral arrangements that would stifle US unilateral forays.

The EU occupies a unique space in international trade diplomacy: it bargains as a single unit in WTO negotiations but lacks authority for unilateral initiatives outside trade negotiations. The EU thus prefers multilateral trade negotiations to unilateral initiatives, in which it lacks authority. The potential of multilateral agreements to hamper US unilateralism in trade added further impetus to EU support for a multilateral agreement housed in the WTO. Finally, a trade agreement opening the US market also made it easier to get member states to agree to internal market reforms in Europe.

The nature of internal EU politics and international strategic positioning reinforce this jurisdictional point. EU positions in trade negotiations are as much about external negotiations as about achieving internal agreement on a negotiating stance. Altering negotiating positions quickly and on ad hoc basis raises internal problems of re-negotiation.[44] The need for internal agreement on external positions means that the larger and more complicated any WTO deal, the tougher the process of internal market negotiation.

A final issue for the negotiation was credibility of commitments to enact pro-competitive regulations that would, for example, force incumbent phone companies to share or rent their network facilities to newcomers. Every country had rigidities remaining in their domestic markets that limited competition. The US was just unwinding local monopolies on telecom facilities. The EU had incumbents where governments still controlled large equity holdings and politically powerful workforces. In the US, federalism limited central government power. In the EU, the complicated inter-governmental division of authorities raised major issues about the credibility of promises to regulate in ways that curbed incumbents' market power.

Ultimately, both sides thought, perhaps wrongly, that the analogy to long-distance service competition in the US was accurate. If held strictly accountable, governments had the legal authority and know-how to compel incumbents to cooperate enough with new entrants to spur competition.[45]

The WTO Agreement

The WTO pact on basic telecommunications services nearly fell apart because of the way the political economy of the major negotiators interacted with the rules governing the WTO.[46]

Negotiations before 1997

Until early 1996 the negotiations showed promise but were incomplete. There was a good beginning, a remarkable achievement, and one huge stumbling block. The promising beginning was on national commitments to liberalize markets, although only OECD states made strong offers of market access. The achievement was on the reference paper of Pro-Competitive Regulatory Principles. What was problematic was the treatment of international services.

Countries that were committed to managed-entry governance at home led the negotiation. They did not accept the notion that a government should remove legal barriers to entry and see what happened (keeping antitrust action in reserve if something went wrong). Many governments placed specific limits on competition. Japan, for example, designated how many entrants could participate in particular market segments. Others retained ownership shares of the old monopolies and cobbled together elaborate bargains to protect the current labor forces of these companies. All the negotiators believed that government sometimes needed to micromanage the early stages of competition to make entry practical.

Between 1994 and 1996 the WTO negotiations produced a revolution in trade policy. A group of nations produced a "reference paper" that stated critical competition principles and specified how an independent regulatory authority operating transparently should uphold competition. They distilled the essence of the major regulatory regimes of countries that had or were about to introduce competition. Then, countries were asked to "schedule" the reference paper as an additional WTO commitment on market access for basic telecommunications services. Nothing quite like it existed in trade policy; it represented a "manual" for how to judge competition policy in a country. Agreeing on the document proved politically difficult, but once it was widely endorsed it became a credible signal to the ITU and to the poorer countries. They finally had a measuring stick of what the top industrialized and industrializing countries judged to be efficient market management. Even countries that made few or no WTO commitments during the negotiations began to use the reference paper as a starting point for discussions in changing their markets unilaterally.[47]

The issue of international services deadlocked the negotiations in 1996 and required an extension of the talks until February 1997.[48] The negotiations were hung up by questions about to what degree foreign carriers faced competition in their home markets and to what degree settlement rates were significantly higher than efficient economic costs. The former determined whether the foreign carrier could use control of its bottleneck network facilities at home to employ anti-competitive tactics; the latter determined the financial significance (and thus the financial incentives) of anti-competitive tactics.

Everyone in the informal WTO negotiating group on international services saw no problem if countries just opened their markets to carriers from countries that permitted general competition in all communications services subject to regulatory safeguards. But here the logic of delegation worked with a vengeance. The WTO would lose its credibility if it ignored its "most favored nation" rule.[49] Any commitment to open the US market to international traffic and carriers from Europe and Japan also automatically opened it to WTO countries with monopolies.

The United States floated several ideas about how it could distinguish between regulation of carriers from competitive and uncompetitive markets. But no country accepted this kind of national discretion for fear that it would weaken the central WTO principles of most favored nation and national treatment.[50] The US withheld its support from the WTO agreement because of this impasse, and the negotiating deadline had to be extended beyond April 1996. Multilateral negotiations could not achieve a US-EU consensus on how to restructure rules for the world market.

The 1997 Solution

In mid 1996, when negotiations resumed, some European governments quietly suggested that if a WTO pact could be agreed upon, the EU could create counterpart rules to the FCC's "flexibility order." Parallel regulatory action by the two trading powers would amount to a tacit back-door initiative to complement the multilateral trade deal.

The United States remained skeptical for two reasons. First, the industrializing countries, where international traffic growth was greatest, typically delayed the introduction of competition for 3–7 years in their WTO commitments. Second, many poorer countries made weak WTO commitments or none at all. The "most favored nation" obligations of industrial countries on international telecom services made getting post-WTO competition in international services more difficult because developing country carriers could plausibly generate higher net settlement payments once they had unilateral access to the US market. Why would they abandon their monopoly and high settlement rates under these circumstances?[51]

In 1996 the United States reluctantly decided that it might have to revert to bilateral liberalization, but the next year it hit upon a third path. It decided it could accept a WTO pact if two conditions were satisfied.[52] First, Europe had to join the US in making a final major push to improve the market opening commitments of industrializing countries. Second, the EU and other industrial countries had to accept that the US would undertake a unilateral regulatory action outside the WTO. This initiative—dubbed "benchmarks"—would apply to all countries. It was designed to knock the underpinning out of inflated settlement rates. The US government declared that it would not negotiate this regulatory measure at the WTO, but it pledged that the new policy would meet the WTO obligations requiring competition regulations to honor the principles of "most favored nation treatment" and nondiscrimination. If not, other countries could challenge the policy under the new WTO telecom rules. After the EU agreed to this tacit compromise, Brussels and Washington together quickly won significant improvement in the WTO commitments by several important industrializing countries.[53]

The US unilateral regulatory initiative caused a sensation because it directly targeted settlement rates. The benchmarks were price caps (legal limits on the maximum price) on the level of settlement rates that US carriers could pay to terminate their international traffic in other countries. Levels varied because calculations showed that poorer countries had higher costs for terminating US traffic.[54] Benchmarks were designed to remove the bulk of the economic rents that could fuel anti-competitive behavior in the market. They also were intended to lower the net settlement payments for US carriers, thereby easing the financial sting of imperfections that existed in the WTO arrangements.

Benchmarks required an extraordinary level of coordination between the FCC and the Office of the US Trade Representative (USTR). But the agency leaders (Reed Hundt at the FCC and Charlene Barshefsky at USTR) saw the larger economic and political story clearly and agreed to make the effort. As a result, benchmarks solved a policy and political problem for the US related to international phone services and allowed the US to accept a WTO deal. The combination of lower settlement rates and more competition in world markets also helped lower the price of international phone services, a major policy and political goal.

Ultimately, 69 countries, including all the OECD member states, signed the WTO pact. Commitments on opening markets covered about 85 percent of the world market for basic domestic and international telecom services. For all OECD countries except Korea and Mexico, the commitments covered almost all forms of domestic and international telecommunications services. The commitments included guarantees of foreign investment rights for new entrants. All signatories also agreed to a set of "pro-competitive regulatory principles" that created obligations for how national regulators would protect new entrants from anti-competitive behavior by incumbents with market power.[55]

These advances allowed the FCC to rule that easier entry into the US market was now in the public interest because US carriers would gain rights in all major industrial markets. Simultaneous opening of the major industrial markets helped liberalize FCC rules on foreign entry to permit 100 percent indirect foreign ownership of US common carriers employing radio spectrum.[56] It was no longer necessary to rely solely on piecemeal bilateral liberalization. In short, the WTO pact was a remarkable achievement, but did not by itself solve all the problems of cross-border networks and services.

Assessing the New Rules

Did the WTO agreement induce a real global market change? Change already was underway in the largest industrial markets. In these countries the WTO helped produce a better way to efficiently open markets to foreign investment and cross-border networking. It steered the world away from lengthy, bureaucratically complex bilateral reciprocity negotiations. This was a major net benefit that accompanied the shift to competition in the OECD nations. Note, however, that this system continued to support some aspects of a managed market-entry regime.

The pact also accelerated the speed of market reform in industrializing countries in the short term and in poorer nations in the medium term. The forays of poorer countries into competition had often been more limited than in OECD countries. The WTO negotiations, and complementary diplomatic activities, let industrial countries focus the attention of multinational users of advanced communications services, the international financial community, and telecommunications investors on the decisions of these industrializing countries.[57] Industrializing countries came to recognize that their reputations as a host to communications investments were tied to their WTO positions. WTO negotiators had created a set of market opening and regulatory commitments that approximated a standard for judging whether national policy dealt adequately with the emerging global realities. Telecommunications policy officials in these countries were charged with attracting billions of dollars or euros in investment capital to upgrade their communications infrastructure. In time they accepted that a WTO commitment would provide property rights for foreign investors and new market entrants that would bolster the credibility of their pledges to achieve a modern communications infrastructure.

Political games continued. For instance, Mexico often adjusted its policies to accommodate the concerns of Telmex, Mexico's most influential company. This prompted a high-profile dispute with the United States over

Mexico's effort to forbid "flexibility" on international traffic and retain the use of settlement rates that continued until a WTO ruling favored the US.[58] Still, a new dynamic emerged where newly privatized carriers from industrializing countries that suddenly were facing competition at home became multinational firms expanding across their regions.

After 1997 an accelerating tide of market reform swept across poorer countries. Early market reforms often privatized monopolists without introducing competition. Awareness increased that it was preferable to tightly couple privatization and competition. China and India have embraced competition, following the lead of Hong Kong, Singapore, Korea, and Taiwan and then Thailand, Malaysia, and even Indonesia. A few Latin American countries, including Chile, embraced significant competition. Many settled for markets characterized by de facto duopoly or regulatory schemes that so segmented markets that it sapped much of the potential for competition.

Africa moved more slowly. Even some sub-Saharan Africa countries, once bastions of resistance to competition, now regularly cooperate with the development banks on introducing competition regimes that conform to WTO principles even if they have not scheduled WTO commitments.[59] Still, in South Africa, in March 2008 the government still owned almost 39 percent of Telkom, the wireline monopoly, and its newly licensed national competitor, Neotel, did not launch test service until the summer of 2007. The cost of broadband Internet access in South Africa is among the highest in the world, exceeding prices in Morocco, Egypt, Botswana, and Mozambique. In frustration, Capetown and Johannesburg plan to construct municipal broadband networks to provide less expensive services than available from Telekom.[60] Despite all these imperfections, African-owned mobile wireless operators now compete with each other across Africa. Similarly, in Bolivia, one of the poorest countries in South America, ownership of a cell phone is no longer considered a sign of having escaped poverty. Cell phone ownership and use costs only $4 per month, a price within the reach of the poor. Even limited competition has made connectivity more available.[61]

Numerous restrictions on the number of competitors and the terms of competition remain. Governments retain large equity stakes in old monopolists and limit the number of licensees to ensure the financial viability of new competitors. They maintain pricing rules that hinder competitive innovation. Moreover, communications ministers in India and in other countries with parliamentary governments continue to override telecom regulators in ways that blunt their effectiveness. Other countries, including

China, still lack any semblance of an independent regulator. Still, most countries are moving toward an independent regulator with reasonable power. These emerging regulators increasingly rely on transparent decision-making procedures, gather evidence on proposed decisions through public comment, and then issue a written record and justification tied to the final decision.

When the largest supplier and user markets for ICT embraced global markets, the consequences for global governance was huge. Their support empowered the WTO to promote global competition and market integration. Nominally, developing countries have an equal say at the WTO, but in practice it takes a large block of cooperating developing countries or the leadership of those with growth markets to make a difference. In the 1990s, most developing countries were indifferent to the WTO telecom negotiations, because they did not see any benefits to their economies (as support for monopolies was still strong) and because industrial countries were so focused on commitments from a few of its economic leaders. However, the rise of the WTO provided a powerful signal to the ITU that its main financial contributors no longer would tolerate the ITU's antagonism to competition and trade reforms. The ITU's mindset shifted significantly by 2000. In effect, wealthy countries sanctioned the ITU by stripping away some of its authority.

After the close of negotiations on the WTO pact and the US benchmark initiative on settlement rates, some developing countries continued to press to return the authority over international services to the ITU. This came in two forms. When the FCC imposed benchmarks in August 1997, the backlash showed that many developing countries preferred to maintain the old system.[62] They lobbied to allow the ITU to produce its own benchmarks as an alternative to the FCC formulation. The draft ITU proposals that emerged would have yielded only minimal changes in the level of settlement rates. For that reason, the US rejected this plan out of hand, and most of the OECD countries quietly concurred.[63] A more serious attempt, supported by some smaller industrial countries (e.g., Australia) that believed that they were at the edge of the Internet, pursued an effort to recast the ITU as a central actor on the prices charged for the international exchange of data traffic serving Internet Service Providers (ISPs) while accessing the World Wide Web. As of 2008, this effort has produced no result except much discussion and a few international resolutions of dubious value. The major markets so far have treated the exchange of Internet traffic as a matter of competition policy within the confines of the WTO reference paper.[64]

Appellate Body, in its decision on the "Internet Gambling" case (a dispute over US regulations restricting gambling on the Internet), suggested an important precedent. When a country opens a sector for cross-border market access under the General Agreement on Trade in Services (the specific legal framework in the WTO that serves as the umbrella for service agreements like the one on basic telecommunications), foreign Internet-based services can enter the market and demand that any services barriers including filters, bans, or other rules be justified or eliminated.[68] The Appellate Body's recognition that GATT obligations evolve to fit changes in technology is likely to make the WTO a receptive forum for addressing Internet services issues.

Change also brings big challenges. The first challenge is the changing composition of domestic telecom governance because of the inflection point. A large regulatory divide has emerged between the US market and many major countries. Over time this could create stress.

One source of tension flows from specific policies that reflect the differences in national network infrastructure. The United States now has two wired broadband infrastructures, and wireless technologies might evolve into additional national networks. Most European and Asian advanced economies have one infrastructure and use detailed rules on network sharing (unbundling rules) to spur competition, as the US once did. They are achieving lower prices and higher speeds than US networks in many cases, but they are subject to detailed government oversight.

Another source of tension is the philosophical difference over the likelihood that companies controlling a technology platform will have the incentive and ability to use it for anti-competitive purposes. Washington has grown more skeptical that there is a threat to competition while other industrial countries have concluded otherwise, believing that the ability of US firms to manipulate these technology platforms is critical to their continuing dominance over ICT markets. Thus, some other industrial countries have extended their anti-competition oversight from telecom networks and software operating systems to careful scrutiny of the kinds of Web-based platforms emerging at the inflection point. This split in the premises of competition policy could hamper efforts to find global rules for many of the largest market developments before 2025.

There also are huge gaps in global governance as a result of the limits of governance in the era of managed entry. Managed-entry governance made limited progress on competition in audio-visual services in most countries. Predictably, a conspicuous shortcoming of the WTO process was the governments' decision to withhold practical jurisdiction of over most audio-visual services (media content and broadcast) from the WTO. France and other countries demanded that "cultural" industries be excluded.[69] As convergence proceeds, the lack of trade commitments allows the potential for the creation of barriers to the free flow of audio-visual products and services. In short, without an obligation to offer market access to broadcast, or broadcast-like services on the Internet, governments are free to erect new barriers to uses of ICT. The EU is attempting to tackle this by distinguishing between "linear" and "non-linear" services. Using this logic, a television broadcast program webcast over the Internet would be considered a linear service and, thus, subject to broadcast service rules. Conversely, a television program accessible to consumers through a search engine would be considered a non-linear service and, thus, not subject to broadcast rules.[70] Such distinctions are difficult to maintain in the modular "mix-and-match" design of modern Web services.

Equally troublesome is the ambiguity of trade coverage for Internet services. The emergence of the Internet was just taking place as the WTO pact was forged. In the mid 1990s the negotiators were advised by technologists that voice service over the Internet would never approximate the clarity of voice sent over the circuit-switched network. Today, efforts to block Internet telephony ("VoIP") or to make it conform to the precise rules and pricing schemes of traditional phone services show the ambiguity of trade treatments of packet-based services. More broadly, the gaps between the jurisdiction of the WTO and the ITU are sufficiently vague to fuel a heated global debate over what forum is best suited for a discussion of Internet governance. This new space is also contested.

Finally, the WTO regulatory principles tiptoed around some difficult technical issues. The WTO agreement adopted weak provisions on property rights and governance systems for radio spectrum. These decisions could be important for future ICT infrastructures. Can these trade arrangements evolve to advance a system emphasizing trading rights? Everyone recognized that governments could manipulate how they allocate and assign spectrum or set standards for wireless licensees in ways that distort competition. There also was acknowledgment that existing WTO rules (in the Agreement on Technical Barriers to Trade or the Standards Code) already provided trade rules on standards-related matters. However, there was concern that trade lawyers should not complicate the tasks of spectrum engineers in national government who had the unenviable task of balancing complex national interests from defense, civil aviation, law enforcement, and commercial uses of spectrum. For this reason, trade provisions on spectrum policy provisions tend to use relatively guarded terms—e.g., requiring policy measures that might restrict foreign market access to be "least burdensome" and "competitively neutral." These strictures are useful, but are far short of trying to raise the minimum bar on how to allocate and assign spectrum in a more market efficient manner. Yet spectrum is essential to ICT infrastructure innovation. Thus, enormous tension exists between the most innovative national regimes for spectrum policy and the traditional ITU process. These tensions are heightened by the fact that spectrum and standards policies are among the last bastions for industrial policy. The resulting mismatch between the direction of technological trends and policy practices are producing huge challenges for the evolution of wireless ICT infrastructures.

The substantive weaknesses in trade agreements for ICT could be compounded if US support for trade and investment integration through bilateral and multilateral pacts slackens. If disillusionment with trade deals pre-empts the American agenda through 2025, then policy entrepreneurs would have to delegate problem-solving to other venues. This might include voluntary harmonization of domestic regulatory arrangements among important markets. If the agenda for trade changed, it is equally possible that the political prospects for trade agreements might improve. Thus, a compelling new trade agenda might include balanced responses to worries over the social and environmental impacts of economic change. Complementing these changes, a bolder approach to tackling the issues facing the global ICT infrastructure through trade agreements might strongly engage the political commitment of producers and large users of ICT to new trade deals. The current WTO round is, in many respects, a timid exercise in terms of tackling the larger problems confronting the world economy. The time may be ripe for a different approach, especially in light of the failure in July 2008 to reach an agreement on concluding the WTO Doha Round of trade negotiations.

8 Wireless Infrastructure

The ascendance of the wireless infrastructure was a major ICT innovation. This chapter examines the political economy of the changing governance of the wireless infrastructure by analyzing the introduction of wireless broadband (third-generation, abbreviated 3G) services.

Governments strongly influenced the wireless innovation processes because they controlled the radio spectrum, the essential wireless real estate, set general competition policy for wireless services, and often set the technical standards for the market. The traditional justification for government's central role was that radio spectrum constituted a scarce public resource that could be degraded by radio interference among competing uses. Government policies almost always over-reacted when addressing the risk of interference. "Under traditional spectrum regulation . . . it is the mere possibility of interference, not the reality of it, that governs when, where and what devices can be used. Therein lies the problem."[1] This principle of preemptive control of possible interference underpinned an unduly restrictive policy, even for traditional technology, because it relied on government command and control to resolve unlikely interference scenarios rather than on techniques routinely used to sort out other market clashes (e.g., tort law and commercial negotiations). An accompanying principle was the affirmation that spectrum was a scarce public resource under government control whose use by the private sector had to be carefully controlled. This weakened property rights, thereby limiting market flexibility.

In the traditional system, experienced radio engineers, armed with a mandate to preempt all interference, dominated the spectrum-governance community. Slow, conservative grants of spectrum allocation and assignment made their lives easier. As a result, governments usually doled out spectrum in small dollops to a few carefully specified competitors that provided a pre-approved list of services on the licensed spectrum. Three norms for spectrum policy permeated domestic and global governance. First, spectrum was allocated to specific uses (and countries coordinated on a specific band of spectrum for a designated use). Second, the number of suppliers was restricted to protect against interference. In addition, as a third norm, governments routinely dictated which technical standards would prevail. The rationale was that the standard would be the best technology to preempt interference and a single standard would also build economies of scale, thereby lowering equipment costs.

This approach to spectrum management cozily co-existed with a general market-governance system that emphasized monopoly or limited competition. The first generation (1G) and the second generation (2G) of wireless phone and data services emerged from this governance tradition. First-generation, analog wireless service was a niche market with minimal influence on the general telecom market. Governance of 2G reflected the dynamics of the managed-entry era. Governments knew 2G would be a bigger commercial market (although early adopters still vastly underestimated its ultimate import) and introduced competition in a measured way that balanced costs and benefits for former telecom monopolists and their equipment suppliers. Unlike other ICT segments, the European Union extensively shaped global market governance because the United States, with its low-price, robust wired infrastructure, lagged on the switch to 2G.

Even the prospects of a fundamentally different 3G technological architecture and service mix (high-speed data) did not initially alter the old approaches to governance. Governments and companies had charted a manageable balance between regional preferences and global coordination for 2G, and a dominant global technology, the Global System for Mobile Communications (GSM), emerged out of the mix. Europe and Japan, in particular, hoped to build on this platform. They envisioned a single technology design for 3G services deployed on one global band of radio spectrum, which would be upgraded at a predictable pace. To the shock of market leaders, their plan for 3G deployment fizzled.

Three challenges eroded traditional spectrum governance. First, the Cheap Revolution transformed the equipment and networking industry and transformed competition in telecommunications services. This created a new set of stakeholders in every major market. Second, increasing modularity gave carriers much more flexibility in the mix of spectrum and equipment to provide wireless services as services became digital and broadband.[2] Third, the United States became fully engaged in market-governance issues for third-generation broadband services. Its different approach to domestic market governance led the US to dissent from plans for a comprehensive global blueprint for 3G.

Together, these factors forced a reorganization of the delegation of authority over global market governance and a new policy approach. Instead of a single global standard for 3G, governments agreed to sanction a platform of related but disparate 3G standards. Instead of a single global band for 3G, governments came to accept a variety of frequency bands. These developments weakened the norms of government dictated standards and designation of a preferred spectrum band for services. At the same time, governments recognized that more competitors and bigger releases of spectrum for flexible uses were compatible with sound spectrum practice and contributed to larger goals for ICT markets. As a result, the rollout of 3G services (and their successors) and the business models for the market diverged sharply from early expectations. By 2008, more countries were strengthening the property rights of spectrum holders in order to encourage market transactions to swap spectrum. Cumulatively, the principles of a strong presumption of likely interference and treatment of spectrum as a scarce public resource were eroding.

As a result of an erosion of norms and principles, the authority of the ITU over standards, spectrum, and services declined. Initially there were changes in regional decision making for standards, such as the rise of the European Telecommunications Standards Institute (ETSI).[3] Later, cutting-edge standards processes were dispersed to industry associations built around each technology camp. A further change in delegation involved the World Trade Organization. The changes in global trade rules described in chapter 7 boosted competition in wireless, including competitive entry through foreign-owned carriers. The WTO also limited, but did not eliminate, how governments could manipulate technical standards associated with wireless licenses to promote industrial policy. It also made the decisions of standards bodies, even those associated with the ITU process, subject to trade policy reviews.

Property Rights, Balancing Stakeholder Interests, and the Politics of Market Transitions

Our theory emphasizes the role of the leading powers in the world market in changing global governance. Their preferences reflect the intersection of their strategic position globally and the interests generated by their domestic political economies. In the 3G case there was intense political bargaining between the United States and an entente of Europe and Japan.[4]

This case reflects a situation where market leadership was more broadly dispersed than in other ICT markets because in the 1990s mobile deployment in the EU and in Japan outpaced US deployment. Moreover, the triumph of mobile over fixed networks in many developing countries further altered global bargaining dynamics by making outcomes in those markets central to global strategies.

The next four figures provide a snapshot overview of the wireless, mobile, and broadband trends since the early 1990s. Figure 8.1 tracks the surging growth of mobile lines compared to fixed lines worldwide. The number of fixed lines increased from about 600 million in 1993 to almost 1.2 billion in 2004. Mobile lines surged from extremely low numbers in 1993 to 1.75 billion in 2004. Mobile lines surpassed fixed lines in 2002 and the gap continues to widen. Figures 8.2 and 8.3 trace the rapid growth in mobile subscribers and the penetration of mobile services across important countries and regions. By mid-2008 there were 3.3 billion mobile subscribers worldwide. About 1.2 million new subscribers were being added each day.[5]

More narrowly, figure 8.4 compares the recent growth of mobile data subscribers in different regions. By early 2007, there were about 600 million

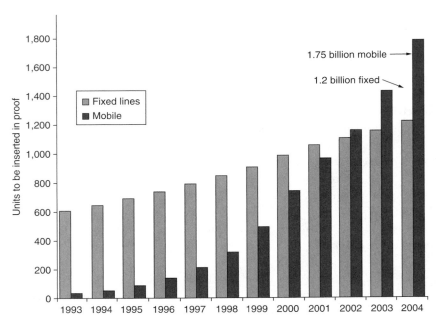

Figure 8.1
2002 was the turning point. Source: International Telecommunication Union.

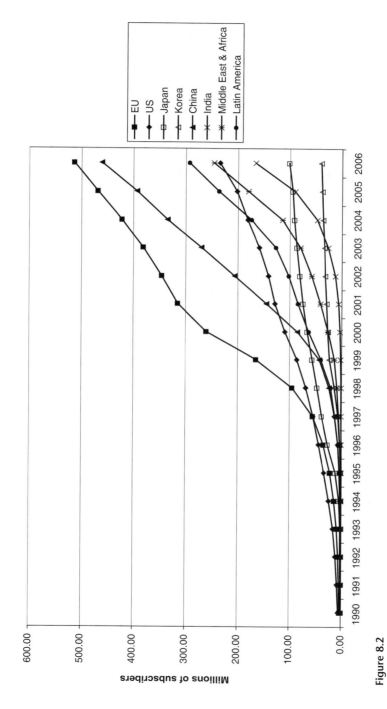

Figure 8.2

Comparative growth of mobile networks: mobile subscribers, 1990–2006. Source: International Telecommunication Union.

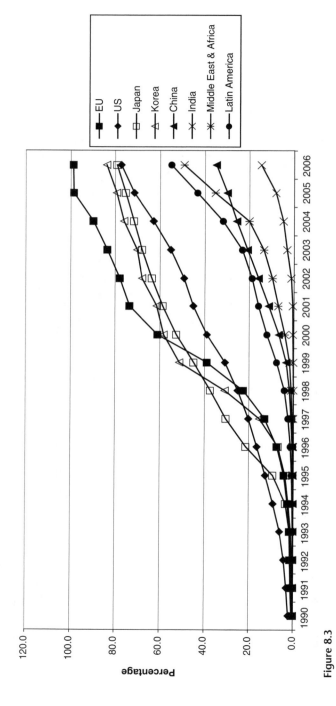

Figure 8.3

Comparative growth of mobile penetration, 1990–2006. Source: International Telecommunication Union.

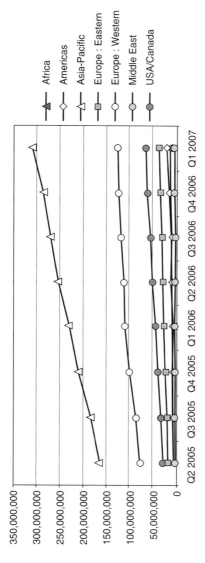

Figure 8.4

Mobile data subscribers by region. Source: Informa Telecoms and Media.

politically difficult transitions formal and informal restrictions on foreign investment often transfer rents to domestic competitors or to business partners of foreign investors. Licensing policies tilting toward domestic technology firms are another favorite.

On top of raw politics, government institutions dealing with these technically complex markets faced information challenges. The stakeholders often possess information not known to the regulators, so there are incentives for trying to induce consensus through bargaining among stakeholders. Government institutions sometimes can facilitate agreement by requiring all participants to accept pre-conditions before participating in rule making. However, in the case of 3G the ITU could not restrict participation on standard setting to those agreeing beforehand to limit their IPR claims.

When consensus building stumbles, government institutions may have to choose among players, but they vary in their ability to make binding decisions. As the number of decision points or veto points in a policy process increases it becomes more likely that the status quo will persist or that the decision will be skewed to serve the needs of players with the strongest veto power.[11] Most national regulators use majority decision making to resolve deadlocks more credibly, even if they try to induce consensus-oriented outcomes. The ITU and other international institutions have more stringent decision-making rules that require unanimity. This increases veto power, although political and economic pressure may induce reluctant parties to acquiesce.[12]

Because consensus building was critical, a grand plan for 3G was supposed to please everyone by providing incumbents with the rewards of a big new market in return for accepting more competitors. In 1985, when the undertaking began, the ambitious level of global coordination envisioned by 3G planners assumed that policy decisions would be largely an insiders' game. But the consensus-driven process in the ITU broke down. The pace and complexity of standards setting increased as the Cheap Revolution got underway. Traditional standard-setting bodies seemed cumbersome and expensive, so firms and governments turned elsewhere for faster decisions.[13]

Consensus also was undermined as the number of stakeholders increased and their interests diverged. The ITU, an inter-governmental organization in which governments decide and others observe, was designed to deadlock when normal bargaining could not produce consensus. As differences in the preferences of regional groups of nations caused the interests of stakeholders to diverge, standards and spectrum plans diverged from the initial global blueprint. A single blueprint became a menu of approved choices from which players could pick and choose.

Defining Property Rights for 3G

The prominent role of government in wireless markets is the cumulative product of weak property rights because it was presumed that spectrum was a public resource leased to private operators.[14] Governments only licensed spectrum for a fixed time period, subject to many constraints. Private bargaining among property rights holders about interference broke down because government restricted many market functions (such as the ability to easily buy and sell licenses) and the regulatory process created large uncertainties about the value of spectrum licenses. For this reason, property rights were not secure, and private bargaining among companies often was ineffective. In response, the private sector encouraged government to micromanage spectrum problems in regard to three sets of decisions influencing property rights.

The first set of property rights defined intellectual property rights (IPR) in the standards for global wireless networks. A new generation of wireless services emerged from the global collaborative planning of carriers and equipment suppliers coordinated through the ITU and through regional and national standard-setting processes. Participation in these processes and the conditions imposed on the use of IPR in the standards process influenced the selection of global technology.

The second set of property rights stipulated rules governing the allocation of spectrum, including the use of licensed spectrum, for specific purposes. "Allocation" refers to the decision about how much spectrum to allot to particular services or groups of services, and on which frequency ranges.[15] Revisiting spectrum allocations opened the way for politicians to earn credit by micromanaging a valuable resource. In addition, government control made it easier to satisfy the demands for large amounts of spectrum by military and police services, which few political leaders wanted to oppose.[16]

Governments granted licenses in predictable but restrictive ways. For example, US spectrum licenses traditionally limited the ability of spectrum owners to change the type of service in three ways. First, they could not shift licenses between services from fixed to mobile wireless. Second, they restricted ownership transfer. Licenses usually were granted for a set period of time, often 15 years, although since the late 1990s this mix has been changing. Third, Asian and European governments often went further, dictating the type of technology platform that spectrum users could employ to offer services. These types of process typically favored incumbents with operational or informational advantages.[17] As a result, private property rights for spectrum were weak.[18]

The third set of property rights involved the assignment of licenses. The number of licenses, the method for selecting licensees, and the sequence of assignment of licenses shape market efficiency. After the mid 1980s, the number of licenses slowly increased, thereby creating more competition in services. But since the early 1970s the sequence of licensing decisions provided hefty market rents for the original incumbents and their initial challengers.

In short, more competition in telecommunications markets improved market performance in many countries. Yet political leaders usually eased the risks for large competitors during the transition to greater competition. The politics of transition, explored next, raised the costs of the transition to 3G and often helped some competitors at the expense of others. These challenges ultimately delayed 3G rollouts.

The Political Economy of Three Generations of Wireless Service

Property rights define the rules of the game under which economic actors pursue their interests. They influence the economics of markets and the strategies of governments and firms. Institutional structures then shape bargaining and outcomes. This section shows why this mattered for wireless.

The political economy of 3G begins in technology and policies chosen for the first two generations of wireless services. As 1G and 2G market growth soared, mobile wireless became the darling of the financial community and a strategic focus for former monopolists. Political considerations shackled the former monopolists with high costs and inefficient work forces in their traditional businesses. Fortuitously, mobile services allowed them to create new subsidiaries that earned dramatically higher revenue per employee.[19]

The reinvigorated profits for former monopolists eased some political tensions about transitions to competition. However, by the late 1990s wireless competition increased while the industry foresaw slowing market growth for voice services. This combination threatened to reduce the profitability of major carriers, so companies and regulators faced a fundamental political dilemma: how could they increase competition while also restoring growth?[20] The quick answer for many industrial countries was to license more competitors while betting that 3G networks could boost market growth in two ways. The idea was to first reenergize growth as the number of cell phones with data connections increased rapidly.[21] Second, by the late 1990s they believed that a unified global technology and spectrum plan for 3G would stimulate cross-national networks that would boost margins by charging lucrative fees for providing services to business customers when they roamed across national borders. This expectation prevailed until 2001's crash of telecom markets and began to re-emerge around 2007.[22]

Standard Setting and Intellectual Property

Governments were heavily involved in the standard-setting process until the 1980s because they owned and operated the telephone carriers. These carriers worked with a small set of preferred national or regional suppliers in a closed standard-setting process. Global standards processes at the ITU reflected this legacy of limited competition.[23] Significant variations in national standards for 1G were common; efforts to coordinate new global services and standards, such as 2G, had to accommodate these variations because ITU decision making was consensual.

Second-generation digital wireless services involved technologies that promised better quality, lower costs, and more user capacity. They promised to expand the global market significantly, thereby stirring interest in new export markets. At the same time, even as equipment market competition stepped up in the 1980s, the incumbent carriers and their preferred equipment suppliers still treated technology development as a long-term, collective planning process involving international coordination of standards and industrial policy planning. Reconciling regional policies with global coordination was the challenge.

Regional Features of 2G

The earliest major plan for coordinated 2G emerged in Europe, where political leaders saw it as a chance to dramatize the benefits of integrating European markets and policy. In 1982, European elites endorsed a single common standard: the Global System for Mobile Communications (GSM), a variant of time division multiplexing access (TDMA).[24] The process, designed to create standards for GSM, took place within the European Telecommunications Standards Institute, which used a weighted voting process to ensure a prominent role for incumbents.[25]

Motorola, the only prominent non-European firm in the market, held a wide array of GSM patents. It became locked in a dispute over the terms for licensing its intellectual property. Despite its major global position,

Motorola lacked switching systems and was smaller than its EU rivals. Thus, it compromised by cross-licensing its patents to the major European incumbent suppliers, a deal that allowed it to thrive in Europe as a supplier of selective radio equipment. Predictably, second-tier and Japanese equipment suppliers complained that GSM patent pooling terms favored the largest European companies.[26] Indeed, the main purpose of the bargain was to deflect Asian challengers.

ETSI standards are voluntary, but the EU had the power to adopt an ETSI standard as a European norm. It did so by creating policies that de facto required all carriers to use GSM.[27] This built economies of scale for GSM service, allowing it to evolve into the dominant global technology for 2G, especially because of its dominance in the emerging Asian market. The EU still considers GSM to be one of its two great successes in industrial policy.

Japan's second-generation decisions took place in an era of industrial policy, so it chose standards that differed enough from those of other nations to impede foreign suppliers and favor a few Japanese suppliers.[28] The Japanese standard—Personal Digital Cellular (PDC)—made some headway in the Asian market but never flourished outside Japan. Still, the big, closed Japanese market provided large-scale economies and high profit margins that financed Japanese suppliers as they adapted their equipment for sale in foreign markets.

In the 1980s, when Japan's exports of telecommunications equipment to the United States surged and US importers had little success in Japan, raucous trade disputes proliferated. Initially the US government worked to force Japan to reform its standard-setting and procurement systems. Then the US insisted that Japan license a Japanese wireless carrier that proposed to use Motorola technology. Next, Japan was pushed to reallocate spectrum to make the new competitor viable in the Tokyo market.[29] Still, despite this foothold for Motorola, the rest of the Japanese equipment market was not compatible with US and European standards.

The strategy of the United States focused on market competition rather than global coordination. Its continent-size national market allowed the US to create large economies of scale for whatever standard it chose. By the 1970s, a few industry associations, not an individual carrier, dominated the standards process. The Telecommunications Industry Association (TIA) and the Cellular and Telecommunications Industry Association (CTIA) featured open membership and voluntary standards. The US satellite and cellular industries regularly clashed over spectrum policy. As a result, US deployment of 2G lagged Europe and Japan. Even when 2G was licensed, the FCC's norm of technology neutrality resulted in two dominant technology camps: CDMA (code division multiple access) and TDMA (time division multiple access) and some variants of the latter.[30] This division slowed the initial rollout of a cohesive national network while creating intense pressure for competition between technologies. This weakened American influence on 2G markets, while setting the stage for the disruption of global planning for 3G.

The Challenge of 3G

In the 1990s, the technology of a new player added another wrinkle to the process. By charging large sums for spectrum, the American 2G spectrum auctions made carriers keenly appreciative of any technology that could allow more traffic on less spectrum. Qualcomm emerged as a rising technology star when its CDMA technology was selected by Verizon, Sprint, and other US carriers because of its efficient use of spectrum.

Except for 3G, CDMA might have remained just another regional technology, similar to Japan's PDC. European and Japanese companies decided to base the 3G successor to GSM on CDMA (or a variant, W-CDMA) rather than on TDMA because CDMA's spectrum efficiency extended to transmitting large amounts of data.[31] This decision created a huge problem, which was underestimated at the time, because a single US company, Qualcomm, controlled the essential intellectual property rights of CDMA. A series of patent suits did not weaken Qualcomm's IPR supremacy.[32]

Qualcomm's control over critical IPR ultimately undercut the typical arrangements for telecom networks in global standards bodies. Traditionally, major suppliers cross-licensed their intellectual property rights on a cost-free basis while developing major new standards. Rather than deadlock about the precise distribution of payments, the top-tier suppliers benefited by using low-cost or zero-cost licensing to grow the market on their preferred terms. (Second-tier suppliers paid significantly more for licenses.) These arrangements proliferated so rapidly that by the late 1990s large regional bodies would not embrace a standard unless everyone agreed to license the relevant IPR to every IPR holder under the standard.

With 3G, the International Telecommunication Union faced a new problem. The formal ITU licensing rules are artfully ambiguous about expected licensing terms, but no standard can emerge unless all of the significant IPR holders consent.[33] In this case Qualcomm controlled the essential IPR. As with many newer ICT firms, this IPR was its main competitive asset. If Qualcomm gave it away, it could not survive because in the 1990s the company was too new and too small to win a competition that hinged on advantages in global economies of scale in manufacturing, distribution, and marketing. So Qualcomm insisted on collecting royalties and playing a central role in designing the emerging 3G architecture, even though it was quite new to the inner corridors of global standard setting. Nonetheless, Qualcomm had virtually no profile in Europe, where ETSI dominated. This meant that the strategic information available to all major players was spottier than normal. It was easy to miscalculate during the bargaining process. Nobody expected that Qualcomm could strike a tough bargain.

Major players slowly recognized the implications of Qualcomm's claims. European and Japanese incumbent suppliers wanted business as usual and therefore wanted to erode Qualcomm's licensing position. They introduced W-CDMA, a variant of CDMA that incorporated design features from GSM that they claimed would improve 3G's performance. They intended that these features also generate new intellectual property to weaken Qualcomm's control and provide the Japanese and Europeans with IPR bargaining chips to obtain improved licensing terms.[34] Qualcomm considered these design features arbitrary and predicted (correctly, as it turned out) that the design changes would make the transition to 3G more complex and time consuming. Qualcomm also worried that the numerous changes incorporating features of GSM architectures would undermine a principal advantage of its 2G CDMA systems, the promise that it could be upgraded cheaply and quickly to 3G. Qualcomm was concerned because 2G systems would continue to be a large part of the world market for wireless equipment for years.[35] In view of the high stakes, the major carriers soon chose their version of 3G depending on their 2G architectures. Second-generation carriers with a base in TDMA or GSM, mainly from Europe and Japan, supported W-CDMA. Those with a CDMA base, mainly in North America and Korea, supported extending CDMA to 3G.[36]

The European Union recognized that any attempt to dictate a mandatory standard for 3G had potential liabilities under new WTO telecom rules. For this reason, it crafted a position that required each member country to ensure that at least one carrier in its market would employ W-CDMA (called UMTS in Europe). In this way the EU allowed for multiple 3G-technology standards, but the rule was intended to "tip" the market toward W-CDMA because of network externalities. The guarantee of comprehensive European coverage for one standard gave an incentive to all carriers to deploy it so that their customers had European coverage while traveling.[37]

Carriers in markets with multiple technology standards for 2G had to resolve conflicting interests. In Canada, the dominant incumbent chose CDMA. Other countries championed Qualcomm in the ITU process. Usually one of the newer entrants favored CDMA. Competitive business reasons persuaded most dominant incumbents to favor W-CDMA. NTT's DoCoMo urged the ITU to designate W-CDMA as the only 3G option. Had the ITU done so, this would, for technology reasons, have rendered the 2G network of its rival DDI (now KDDI) less valuable for 3G.[38] As Korea and China introduced greater competition, similar stories with their own national nuances appeared. In short, the potential for gain in 3G influenced the positions of the players.[39]

At the ITU, the European Union and Japan favored a single 3G standard, arguing that this would yield the largest economies of scale and simplest interoperability of systems worldwide. They favored W-CDMA, the version of 3G backed by their largest carriers and equipment vendors. The European Commission understood how standards bodies could be strategic for the market.[40] Qualcomm responded by refusing to license its IPR to this proposed ITU standard.[41] It was then that the logic of the ITU mattered. Under ITU rules, without Qualcomm's agreement it became nearly impossible to set a global standard.

The ITU uses a "one country, one vote" system for decision making. It avoids deadlock because government and commercial interests seek common ground on standards and spectrum allocation. Although informal polls sometimes gauge relative standings of positions on some spectrum allocation debates, in practice consensus is needed to make progress. Member governments also have committed to work within the ITU on spectrum allocation, but major market powers can paralyze ITU decision processes.

Support from the United States and a few other governments strengthened Qualcomm's position. Qualcomm worked intensively with Lucent (which had virtually no sales in Europe and had not yet merged with Alcatel) and US carriers using CDMA to rally political support in Washington.[42] It won strong support from the US government despite objections from GSM carriers, in part because CDMA and Qualcomm had become a political poster child for the FCC spectrum auctions. The Clinton administration viewed the emergence of US-brewed CDMA in the technology-neutral auctions as proof that its policies could induce new technological successes and US exports.

The CDMA dispute illustrates how high-level politics goes beyond interest-group dynamics. Any free-trade-oriented Democratic administration

On one level, the European experiment was successful; the GSM technology thrived. Consumers responded enthusiastically to truly continental service. During the 1980s, the market-oriented features of wireless were appealing when compared to the moribund marketing for traditional phone service. The European success fueled the growth of global mobile services and thus emphasized international harmonization of band plans. African administrations, long tied to European suppliers, again agreed to follow Europe. Asia adopted a mixture of band plans, but the European consumer success led national governments to tilt toward the European plan.[50]

The United States took a different path toward spectrum management. Unlike the EU, the US already enjoyed unified spectrum band allocations. A single analog network covered the US, and its continental market generated large economies of scale in equipment supply even without global harmonization. Its political economy tilted against a consensus on a single technology option. Not only did powerful players already occupy the European 2G bands, the US satellite industry had ambitious plans for mobile satellite services using low-earth-orbit systems that needed spectrum overlapping with possible 2G and 3G systems.[51] The administrations of George H. W. Bush and Bill Clinton selected more flexible bands for 2G. Canada followed the US plan because Nortel, its flagship equipment firm, depended on US sales. Other countries in the western hemisphere followed the US allocation decision, at least in modified fashion.

Regional dynamics determined the bargaining positions of actors during 3G spectrum planning. European suppliers and carriers began the 3G process hoping to create a uniform global band and a homogenous network environment (W-CDMA).[52] The dominance of GSM in Asia meant that Asian 3G spectrum bands approximated those in the EU. Therefore, from the start, many European and Asian carriers systematically considered building a global footprint. In contrast, beginning at the 1992 World Radiocommunication Conference, the US backed a plan to facilitate mobile services that gave no special priority to 3G over 2G or mobile satellite services. Other countries were irritated that until late 2002 the US did not clear the spectrum designated elsewhere for 3G.[53] Even then, the US declared that 2G spectrum could be used for 3G, thereby creating diversity in the global spectrum band. Critics of the US approach argued that it would reduce global economies of scale in equipment while raising the costs for consumers who desired global roaming with their mobile phones. (If band plans differed, even phones on the same standard would require chips designed to work on two sets of frequencies.[54])

Assignment of Licenses

Licenses are the third form of property rights. As in standard setting and spectrum allocation, regional patterns of market behavior held steady in the assignment of licenses. Predictably, the United States led the charge for more competition in license assignment. Each of the original seven regional Bell operating companies received one of two wireless licenses in its home territory. As had previous creators of duopoly, the US embraced non-market-based criteria for awarding the second wireless license. Methods for selecting licensees varied, but lotteries and administrative selection of a sound company promising good performance ("beauty contests") were popular. This practice helped equipment suppliers that were clamoring for new customers. Some of these new entrants became prominent players in the regulatory process, helping to determine future spectrum allocation and assignment policies.

In a major policy innovation, the 2G US spectrum licenses were auctioned off. Winners could choose which services to offer and which technology to use. By the mid 1990s the US had at least five competitors and rival technology camps in every region. However, foreign investors were barred from controlling interests in wireless carriers until the 1997 WTO telecom services agreement liberalized foreign investment rights.[55]

One consequence of US licensing policies was that, if the operator wished, 3G could be deployed on 2G spectrum. Thus, 3G could be deployed on a band not recommended by the ITU. When the additional spectrum conforming to ITU band plans for 3G was made available, it also was assigned by auction with technology-neutral licenses. Incumbents that already were heavily invested dominated the bidding. (This pattern held true in the auction completed in March 2008 for valuable spectrum previously held by analog television broadcasters.)

Around 1983, when wireless mobile phones became possible, most European governments licensed the traditional operator. Competitors gradually were introduced through the assignment of a second license using "beauty contests," especially in the 2G era.

The EU hoped to recreate the success of GSM through quick deployment of 3G using uniform spectrum and standards. The goal set in 1998 was extensive deployment by 2002. As with 2G, the EU required separate licenses for 3G services on a single designated band.[56] Thus, a 2G carrier could not upgrade to 3G on its old 2G spectrum. The net effect on the equipment side was to reinforce the dominance of European suppliers for the GSM family of mobile network equipment. For example, in 2004 Lehman Brothers calculated that Ericsson, Nokia, Siemens, and Alcatel held

81 percent of the market for 2G and 2.5G in the GSM family. Their combined share for W-CDMA was 84 percent, although Siemens and Alcatel teamed with Japanese partners (NEC and Fujitsu respectively).[57]

Because 3G was designed to operate on "virgin" spectrum, incumbents had to win new licenses in major markets in order to participate. By now the EU had embraced general telecom competition and several major countries, including the United Kingdom, France, Germany, and the Netherlands, chose to auction licenses by a more competitively neutral approach. More than $100 billion was spent in EU 3G auctions. In Europe, four traditional incumbents (British Telecom, Deutsche Telecom, France Telecom, and Telefónica) and two newer supercarriers (Vodafone and Hutchinson) commanded the largest share of the critical licenses.[58] This was preordained by the high cost of auction licenses and the advantages the large carriers might reap by spanning multiple national markets.

In 2001, 3G temporarily imploded, especially in Europe, under the weight of the collapse of the Internet and telecommunications bubble. The collapse of European carriers' stock market valuations and their heavy debt burdens foreshadowed possible deep job cuts. Bankruptcies became possible. The downturn dramatically increased pressure on many European countries to revisit their licensing strategies. Some began to seek ways to ease the financial burdens on carriers deploying 3G.[59]

In general, Asia relied less on auctions, allowed fewer competitors, and often dictated the choice of technology in its service licenses.[60] Fewer competitors generally translated into less financial pressure on carriers during the telecom slump of 2001. For example, when Japan allowed expanded entry in the mid 1980s, the government explicitly reviewed technology plans of applicants when selecting 2G licensees in a "beauty contest."[61] This helped Japan to indirectly steer the equipment and services markets. For 3G, Japan again opted for a "beauty contest" to advantage its three largest wireless carriers.[62] The government fashioned a dual market by selecting companies on both sides of the 3G-technology debate. The KDDI group, a descendant of the carrier involved in the Motorola trade war, adopted the cdmaOne and cdma2000 standards. DoCoMo, NTT's mobile wireless group, embraced W-CDMA, as did the group affiliated with Vodafone. In 2005, when Softbank acquired the Vodafone license and Japan licensed a fourth 3G competitor, eMobile, both companies selected an evolved version of W-CDMA technology.

Major emerging economies usually made explicit policy choices over the choice of permitted technology. But variety slowly won the day. Korea allowed only three competitors (KTF, SK Telecom, and LG Telecom). It required CDMA for 2G to build its export position in the CDMA equipment market. More variety emerged in 3G licensing. Hong Kong and then China carefully split their operators' licenses for 2G so that the largest went to the GSM camp while CDMA was assigned to a newer entrant. China then took until 2008 to reorganize its telecom carriers in an effort to create three major competitors, each equipped with a wired and mobile network. Each competitor had a different version of 3G, including one using TD-SCDMA (the Chinese-promoted standard).

India gave the earliest 2G licenses to GSM carriers but a myriad of regulatory disputes slowed the market's growth. The correction of these problems plus licenses for CDMA to two major companies stimulated market growth to the point that India emerged as the largest growth market for wireless by 2008. GSM and CDMA carriers furiously battled over transition plans to 3G with rival claims over how spectrum should be allocated among different 3G technologies. The decision to license 3G finally emerged in 2008, but by then the largest carriers were also contemplating complementary networks utilizing WiMAX.[63]

In sum, the licensing for 3G in most countries permitted or mandated more than one 3G standard.[64] Nonetheless, by March 2008 W-CDMA, like GSM, had emerged as the major approach to 3G. GSM reached 1 billion users by 2004, 2 billion by June 2006, and 2.5 billion by June 2007.[65] The Global Mobile Suppliers Association identified 211 W-CDMA operators in 91 countries. It calculated that during 2007 80 million new W-CDMA subscribers were added worldwide, a year-to-year growth rate of 81 percent.[66] More important, the worldwide crossover point on wireless infrastructure spending tipped in 2005 as spending on 3G exceeded 2G for the first time. The number of 3G customers reached parity with 2G customers in Western Europe in 2005. Moreover, the total number of 3G customers surpassed 2G by 2006 in Japan and Japan introduced a new carrier, eMobile, which only supported a 3G network.

Implications for the Next Transition

Delays in 3G build-out plans had important consequences for the economics of the market and its political economy. The delays altered technological options, policies of spectrum allocation, and assignment. This may change how the global ICT regime handles wireless policies that are central to the inflection point.

The delay in 3G opened more technological options. As was argued in chapter 3, modularity and the Cheap Revolution has created more versatile

Japan used a "beauty contest" to award WiMAX licenses on the 2.5-GHz band to KDDI and Willcom (a small second-generation operator). Korea's WiBro deployment was on 2.3 GHz, a spectrum band that is heavily crowded in the US.

At the same time, 3G innovation sped up markedly because of continuing rivalry among the different 3G camps. Various revisions are evolving 3G to provide high-quality video and multi-media for large numbers of users.[73] A reliable, minimum symmetric speed of around 2 megabits per second is scheduled, and one upgrade announced in 2007 has peak download speeds of 9.3 megabits per second, more than ample for simultaneous mobile television and VoIP uses on a terminal.[74] The 3G vendors claim that even higher speeds will be possible as a set of hybrid technologies—some overlapping with features from alternatives to 3G—are melded into 3G. The magic number of 70 megabits per second for WiMAX is touted by some 3G plans. (Proponents of "4G" are arguing that 100-MB/s systems are a proper goal.[75])

For technologies to provide very high speed for large numbers of users requires huge swaths of high-quality spectrum and sophisticated engineering. Not surprisingly, the further variations in evolved 3G open the door to more efforts to manipulate markets. The Japanese communications ministry worried, for example, that DoCoMo would attempt once again to build a slightly idiosyncratic standard for Japan. This would ultimately make Japanese equipment suppliers less competitive on world markets while forcing DoCoMo's smaller rivals to adapt at added expense to the DoCoMo standards if they wished to roam on DoCoMo's network.[76]

The race for high-speed, wireless broadband—fixed and mobile—will feature a newer but less tested set of technological alternatives, backed by Samsung, Intel, Nortel, and other technological giants, as well as by the Korean government, against a rapidly evolving 3G architecture that itself may be somewhat fragmented. If newcomers' performance and cost margins are compelling, they may make substantial inroads if they do not bicker over standards. If the performance of new technologies is only as good or slightly better, it will be harder to challenge 3G leaders, which have a head start in the market.

The political economy tale of this market remains as much about business models as it is about engineering. Despite the bewildering array of acronyms for the various 3G upgrades, all 3G systems (except WiMAX) are based on CDMA. Critics complain that Qualcomm charges a royalty, but this is economically irrelevant for understanding the total cost of the system. The cost of R&D, including profits on the investment, is included in every technology development whether by a royalty or by bundling it into the price of the end product. The royalty is significant only for how profits are distributed, not for the total level of costs for consumers (unless Qualcomm has the ability to charge much higher rents than other producers).

More significantly, the economics of modularity and multi-sided platforms are complex. So long as 3G, or its descendants, is organized on its current business model, everyone pays Qualcomm about the same fee (about 5 percent of the price of a handset) for licensing its IPR.[77] For Qualcomm this builds a complementary, highly competitive ecology of end system providers. It also removes a traditional economic advantage enjoyed by top system vendors (which cross-licensed their IPR for little or nothing). (Removing this advantage allowed Korean vendors to crack the top ranks of world suppliers of CDMA terminals.) Qualcomm claims that its present royalty level will optimize total returns on the platform. Its critics counter that the royalty is far too high to achieve this goal.[78] But even the "correct" royalty rate automatically creates tensions with the largest equipment suppliers that seek every cost advantage. They face increasing competition from modular innovation systems with more specialized ODMAs and design shops plus the formidable Chinese entrant, Huawei.[79] Besides forcing further consolidation to build scale and cut costs (such as the Alcatel-Lucent merger), this gives industry giants an interest in experimenting with technologies where royalty arrangements might be more advantageous.[80]

The continual evolution of competition also changed the close alignment of carriers and equipment vendors. Since prices remain under pressure, carriers are examining options that reduce costs and multiply revenue alternatives. They are discovering that much of the promise in data markets requires multi-media capabilities. Loyalty to their traditional equipment vendors matters less as they seek to expand capabilities quickly and reduce costs. This has expanded opportunities for Huawei and other Chinese vendors. Critically, they are discovering that the expanded broadband capabilities require more spectrum, used more flexibly, than in the past. Since companies cannot flexibly buy and sell spectrum or rededicate the services on a spectrum band freely, they must assemble capabilities by combining available spectrum through "smart terminals" operating on more than frequency and technology format. The decreasing cost of engineering these terminals is prompting a rapid evolution in networking. For example, television on wireless devices is being delivered on a different band than the one for data and voice. Terminals combine the services and bands seamlessly. Samsung has designed a terminal that will use an advanced version of 3G for voice while employing mobile WiMAX for data.

Significantly, the latest chip sets for wireless devices only need about 20 percent of their space for radio functions. The rest can provide advanced functions, and in view of the modularity of terminal design there is ample room for co-invention of functions on the terminals as it approaches the capabilities of a personal computer. Arguably, the most important advances for ICT will now be on the terminal, as it becomes an anchor for the many new applications. Leaders in information technology, such as Intel, already view mobile terminals as a key growth market. Conversely, telecommunications firms may use their expertise on terminals to take aim at information technology markets.

In short, modularity and the Cheap Revolution grew in importance during the delay in rolling out 3G. The traditional principle of a presumption that interference was likely and had to be dealt with preemptively weakened. Digital smart terminals could reduce (not eliminate) spectrum risks and allow more spectrum flexibility. This flexibility also meant that spectrum was not quite so scarce because more bands of spectrum could support a particular use. Digital radios used spectrum more efficiently and Internet protocols could allow for more service mixing on the same terminal. Thus, the norms of government restricting users and uses heavily to protect against interference began to fade. And, above all, modular terminals meant that operators wanted flexibility in technological formats to seize opportunities to utilize different bands spectrum. For example, European carriers quietly backed more flexible use of spectrum and technology licensing polices as they transitioned to broadband after 2001. The Northern European group of Norwegian, Swedish, and Danish carriers deployed cdma2000 in 2006 on the 450-MHz band. Moreover, the enthusiasm for more spectrum flexibility and property rights that began in the US quickly migrated to the United Kingdom.[81] Beginning in July 2003, the EU even permitted 3G licensees to trade spectrum and licenses as a way of providing financial relief to carriers.[82] Eventually, the EU decided to generalize some of the spectrum policy models created by Britain while expanding its power over spectrum policy.

As old principles and norms weakened, the mix of expertise changed in the United States, in Europe, and in other market centers. Economists' influence on spectrum allocation increased. They preferred to release larger blocks more quickly to promote market entry and innovation. To assign spectrum, a growing number of economists favored auctions, which conferred stronger property rights and allowed for flexible choices of technology and services. They also preferred substantial leeway to trade and resell spectrum. (Alternatively, when technological ingenuity substantially erased scarcity and interference problems for certain applications, many economists preferred no license at all.) Their analysis of spectrum markets reflected the forces of modular innovation at the inflection point. This shift in North American and Europe domestic markets may force further changes in global governance toward a more market-driven, bottom-up model of change.

Still, major government intervention in markets continues in India, China, and Japan even as they introduce more competition and technological variety in their wireless markets. Outside of the US and the EU, most countries agreed to introduce more wireless technologies but governments selected preferred technologies for licensees in an effort to create an optimal mix of technologies. They also tried to balance advantages among competitors, not to maximize competition or technological flexibility.[83] Thus although countries were clearly embracing the view that they should allow more technologies and license them more quickly, no clear alternative principle and norms emerged by 2008. The ITU's control over standards and competition has diminished while the WTO and other standards organizations play a larger role in the decision landscape.

Through 2008 concerns over non-interference and the possible gains from a single spectrum band for a wireless application to build economies of scale kept the elaborate process of regional and world ITU spectrum coordination meetings in place. The ambiguity of the WTO obligations related to spectrum policies also restricts its role. However, the inflection point creates incentives in more markets (starting with the US and the EU) to inch toward domestic trading-rights systems to enable multi-technology, multi-band networks that do not fit easily fit within traditional spectrum planning. If this projection is correct, the current international discussions about planning 4G are unlikely to yield a single technology or market model. Although 3G offered the opportunity to integrate multiple standards, 4G may create the possibility of integrating multiple technologies. As chipsets become more powerful and more complex devices with integrative capacity through technology becomes more realistic. For many of the 4G advocates, 3G was the right idea but failed because of bad timing (prematurely pushing for high-speed wireless before better technologies were available) or poor execution (including the corporate battles over rollouts). This misses the big picture.

9 Internet Governance[1]

The Internet is credited with incubating new forms of networked governance.[2] As the first ICT network infrastructure designed for the digital age, the Internet is an indicator of how governance of ICT could evolve.

There are three interrelated layers of Internet governance.[3] First, development, specification, and adoption of the technical standards are voluntary, and the benefits of compatibility are widely distributed, so there are incentives to cooperate. Still, agreement can be elusive. Second, the allocation and assignment of exclusive resources, such as addresses and domain names, resembles the allocation of resources in other domains, except that it requires technical knowledge and is technically constrained. Decisions on policies and procedures must address scarcity, efficiency, equity, and the role of markets versus administrative planning. Decisions made in this layer can facilitate the enforcement of policies not related to the technical resources themselves—e.g., policies for the assigning of domain names may enforce copyright claims. The third layer concerns the policies and procedures related to the interconnection and interoperability (e.g., identity systems or DRM) of internet service providers (ISPs) and their use of physical telecommunication facilities to transport data.[4]

The Internet and ICT Governance

The Internet took advantage of broad underlying changes in technology by creating a digital packet network that could efficiently inter-network telecommunications networks and computing infrastructures. The expert community that pioneered the Internet was primarily American because of the dominant US position in computer sciences and markets. Nonetheless, this community was inclusive and global in its scope. The Internet's ultimate commercial triumph was also a product of the specific political economy context of the United States.

Remarkably, the technological leadership of the Internet community succeeded in creating specialized governance arrangements that co-opted global support and largely preempted roles for other international organizations.

Internet governance seemed radically new and different in many respects. It was not a pure creation either of industry or of government. Instead, it was explicitly rooted in a technological community that saw itself as global and as not shackled by conventional political and market boundaries. This perspective was reflected in four of the Internet's features. (1) Its architecture ignored national boundaries. (2) Its coordination depended on global technological communities that were not internally organized around national boundaries and representation. These communities' decisions often relied on consensus led by a recognized technical authority. Unanimous consent and formal voting rules were not required, although a process of transparent posting and consultation existed. (3) Many important coordination points in the Internet resided in non-profit, nongovernmental organizations.[5] (4) Governance activities relied heavily on email, online documentation, and other forms of networked collaboration enabled by the Internet itself.

This organizing vision of decision making reflected the Internet's underlying principles and norms. The principles and most of the norms descended philosophically from the expert community that designed the Internet.

Three of the guiding principles of the Internet underpinned the specific norms for its governance. First, the "end-to-end principle" required that intelligence be predominantly placed at the edge of the network, in contrast with the traditional phone network and many early data networks. The idea was to create decentralized, flexible networking that would use the full capabilities of digital packet networking. Second, it was decided that the architecture should support genuine interoperability among networks and devices. This is a significant test that the standards-setting authority uses to assess any proposed standard. Third, an open decision process was designed to create technological progress by enlisting users and producers in a global community that would operate outside the traditional channels of governments and companies.[6]

The four norms that emerged to implement these principles were consistent with both the formal rules and the working expectations of the expert community. First, the introduction of competition in the provision of network infrastructure and services made digital networking more efficient and innovative. The Internet emerged from the US computer community, which championed competition in data networking. As it evolved, its governance institutions opted for architectures and processes favoring competition. The second norm, which is more controversial among governments outside the US than the first, is to limit intrusion by governments and certain corporate interests in managing the creation and administration of virtual infrastructure resources, such as Internet numbers and names or Internet standards. The third norm is to embrace open standards that do not create proprietary technological advantages out of the virtual infrastructure resources. The fourth norm, as a later addition emerging from debates on social policy, is to take positive measures to extend universal access to the Internet and information services without necessarily replicating the traditional universal service models for telecommunications.[7]

Internet governance is more than an experiment with technology; it also is a clue to the emerging dynamics of the governance of "trading rights." From the start, those concerned with Internet governance assumed the possibility of convergence among applications and consciously aided this development. It also was assumed that competition and modularity were parts of the ICT infrastructure. Internet governance recognized property rights and the development of markets in virtual resources (e.g., domain names) while complementing them with processes to facilitate the sharing of specialized innovations to advance technical progress.[8] The creation of specialized governance institutions also was tailored to the needs of the Internet.

But governance is never seamless or friction free. The strengths and weaknesses of Internet governance also sprang from the reality that the global Internet infrastructure was a product of a US government technology program. Washington implicitly and explicitly ceded much of the authority to govern the Internet to a global technological community drawn primarily from elite American IT research and engineering institutions. These people were principled and ambitious. They wanted to break from the prevailing standards-setting approaches, in which time-consuming processes and restrictive participation rules for major infrastructure projects were the norm. Their governance approach managed to co-opt the international scientific world so that the Internet's "made in USA" stamp did not doom it internationally. More recently, ICANN (the Internet Corporation for Assigned Names and Numbers) and Internet governance have struggled to retain this authority because many global stakeholders, especially the governments of developing countries, grew restless with its structure and some of its priorities.

Four tensions emerged. First, Internet governance could not easily handle issues related to the creation and distribution of economic rents that emerged from the management of important virtual resources, such as domain names. Internet management was not purely technical; it had implications for market efficiency and conduct. Second, the role of traditional state authority (the Sovereignty principle) was tested by the need to devise new Internet policy in a more dynamic and efficient manner (the second norm of Internet governance). Inevitably, other governments chafed at ceding jurisdiction over all of the world's domain-name disputes to US courts. Third, as the scale and scope of the Internet's virtual infrastructure grows, and as security issues become more pressing, it was challenging to keep decision making speedy and resilient. Fourth, it was necessary to balance the traditional political economy of universal service goals with achieving efficiency of the Internet infrastructure. This raised equity and efficiency issues as companies bargained over reciprocal compensation when interconnecting national networks. It also injected an extended dose of global conference diplomacy, the World Summit on the Information Society (WSIS), which featured networked non-governmental organizations focused on complaints about digital divide issues and on proposed remedies. For example, one proposal, that was not adopted, was to cross-subsidize digital access by taxing domain names.

The US Political Economy

The governance of the Internet is a function of the political economy of the United States. The US political and market institutions gave a particular spin to the evolution of competition, and sent it down a particular path.

Recall that the political economy of US competition in the value-added era and in the managed-entry era favored technology neutrality in regulating ICT markets. This did not preclude support for technology development, as was demonstrated by government support for the DARPA project that led to the Internet protocols.[9] The US Department of Defense sped up progress in other ways. It needed lighter weight and higher speeds in electronic circuits, so it paid huge premiums for early ICT industry products. For example, in 1960 Fairchild sold 80 percent of its transistors and all of its early production of integrated circuits to the Department of Defense.[10] When Congress gave DARPA wide discretion to spend money to keep the United States ahead of the Soviet Union, the Department of Defense responded with brilliant management that included politically shrewd spending. Its spending, including on research, built a strong sustainable base of congressional support because the Department of Defense distributed its funding and thus the benefits across all of the states.[11]

The Internet's full commercial significance emerged during the years 1993–2000. The Clinton administration tried diligently to brand their ICT policies as technology-friendly and pro-market.[12] The full implications of the Internet and its complementary innovation, the Web, came into focus in 1993, when the first successful Web browser propelled the mass popularity of the Internet. Soon, a fundamental choice arose about how the Internet and e-commerce would align with traditional taxes, regulations, and government institutions. The Democrats were anxious to continue their courtship of the ICT community, which was commercially and technologically invigorated by the prospects of e-commerce and the infrastructure needed to enable it. The Republicans had gained majorities in the Senate and in the House of Representatives by pledging to oppose new taxes and regulations. Both parties pursued middle-class and upper-class voters, who voted in large numbers and who were caught up in Internet euphoria. Neither party wanted to seem to yield to France and its allies on matters of cultural protectionism. Thus, the Clinton administration's approach to Internet commercialization was to protect it from traditional regulations on commerce and to make its governance as free of direct government control as was possible. Both at home and in international negotiations, the United States also tried to forge a different policy mix in response to social concerns over "the digital divide." It tried to avoid the kinds of inefficient and often anti-competitive measures that had traditionally been used to subsidize telephone services.

Standard Setting and Institutional Innovation

The first aspect of Internet governance is standards setting for the software that enables inter-networking.[13] The Internet Engineering Task Force (IETF) is the primary vehicle used to coordinate this task. Cooperation on standards can produce welfare gains, but standards also can be manipulated for strategic advantage. Standards respond to the distribution of commercial or national interests and to the institutional framework used to address questions of collective action. This is a classic "coordination" problem in game theory: there are solutions that make everyone better off, but it is easy not to achieve them.[14] Why did the informal community of scientists that emerged from these projects and evolved into the IETF succeed in this case?[15]

The Internet evolved within a research community receiving government grants, not as a commercial research project intended for the market. Internet standard setting in this community emerged from a pioneering model of networked collaboration. The research community was an early champion of the use of email and email listservs to accomplish distributed collaboration. The community's status as both a user and designer of Internet standards created self-correcting feedback and positive incentives that accounted for much of its early success as a standard-setting nexus.

The research community self-consciously built on a set of design principles that constituted the de facto governance principles for the Internet. The end-to-end principle placed intelligence at the edge of the network. Interoperability among networks and devices was the bottom-line objective for the architecture. An open decision process of voluntary experimentation and collaboration promoted innovation by ICT users and producers working as a global networked community.

Three factors tipped the balance toward successful collaboration to create a single protocol for inter-networking and packet switching.[16] First, the US military needed a robust inter-networking solution that would make networks more reliable. Instead of trying to create its own standard-setting system, the government sought an end result: a robust system of data networking and the growth of computer science. It was content to let the computer science community provide the decision-making system for standards. This set the research agenda. In time, DARPA handed off its networking research to the National Science Foundation, which, in 1985, chose TCP/IP as the standard for NSFNET and which funded in 1986 the Internet Activities Board as the successor to DARPA funding.[17] Second, the military embedded its effort in the larger computer research community and then mostly left it alone; this allowed the convergent efforts of civilian computing network design in the United States and Europe (most critically in France) to be incorporated into the technical design debate. Third, there was no significant commercial interest in the Internet approach in the early 1980s. In this context, the research community that built the US military's trailblazing Arpanet became the model for standards setting that extended until the creation of the IETF in 1989.

The IETF now operates as a non-governmental expert system with membership open to all stakeholders, but with the rule that participants act as experts, not as representatives of governments or firms.[18] The products of the IETF Working Groups are reviewed by all members who wish to do so. It is an open process, with the work posted on the Web.[19] Two appointed bodies, the Internet Engineering Steering Group and the Internet Architecture Board, must approve the work products of the Working Groups. The Internet Society, an open global organization, appoints the members of these bodies.[20] This process contrasted with the traditional standards-setting process for the international telephone network, which was undertaken by expert ITU work groups in an inter-governmental process. (Representatives were chosen and organized by national governments.) Standards materials were only available through payment of fees that were high enough to bar all but the most serious companies from participation.[21]

In its early years, the IETF was an agent of its community of technologists, not of any government. Its leadership fiercely advocated for setting standards by using a strong dose of experimentation, especially by the leading users of computer networking.[22] Eventually, as commercial stakes grew, the US government had to decide whether to accept the IETF's activities as a reasonable reflection of American interests.

One reason for delegating power in complex technical areas is to benefit from expertise, especially when there are large policy externalities. This includes formally or informally ceding agenda-setting power to highly committed, expert partisans to deflect less welcome alternatives. Even if there is no formal decision on delegation, the interest and capacity of the government to intervene can shape the prospective agent's pattern of conduct. The IETF represented a raucous community of prestigious experts with strong views on networking, including resistance to domination of technical design by governments' industrial policies or by the plans of influential firms. The US government's deference to the IETF gave it the benefit of an agenda controlled by an expert community that did not routinely favor any individual company or tolerate the capture of the Internet on behalf of any country's industrial policy.[23]

How did the IETF establish itself as a "de facto agent" of the US government or other governments? As the significance of the Internet emerged, it became more salient to other companies in the computer and telecommunications industries. This question crystallized in the late 1970s, when the International Organization for Standardization (ISO) tried to craft standards for commercial networking. European researchers and companies led the ISO effort, but some US rivals to IBM and some leaders in the Internet community (seeing a possible ally against the ITU) also were enthusiastic.[24]

The ISO's work provided a more comprehensive map of the architecture of digital networking than the Internet community had designed.

As a mapping exercise, however, the ISO needed to include alternative standards, so its map was not a seamless way to guide development. Nonetheless, the ISO's early decision to incorporate the data networking standard setting efforts of the ITU's International Telegraph and Telephone Consultative Committee (CCITT) into the Open Systems Interconnection (OSI) Basic Reference Model eventually alarmed Internet advocates.[25] They saw the ITU's efforts as an effort to refocus computer networking around telephone monopolies seeking to preserve their power.

The IETF community soon enlisted the US Department of Defense and its supporters in a successful effort to sway OSI to accept Internet protocols as part of its "suite" of options for the OSI architecture.[26] They received assistance from many firms that saw the Internet Protocol as an alternative to IBM domination.[27] In addition, the IETF persuaded the US military to fund "translator" gateways that allowed interconnection of non-Internet and Internet networks. This effectively made the ITU's proposed protocol for data, backed by the phone companies, into a subset of TCP/IP for data networking.[28] Similarly, the preeminence of the TCP/IP protocol was cemented when NSFNET adopted it.

In summary, the Internet community established its cohesion and its unique working processes because of its incubation as a government-funded research project. This genesis meant that no company's strategic preferences dominated the handling of intellectual property rights for the Internet.[29] The subsequent success of the Internet standards community, as commercial stakes escalated, rested in part on persuading major government agencies to support its efforts to "tip" the marketplace toward Internet protocols. Then, the IETF had to continuously demonstrate that it could deliver the timeliest solutions.

When the senior political levels of the US and other major industrial governments finally focused on the Internet and its standards bodies, the Internet already was a mass-market service. The earliest, high profile event relating to governments and the emergence of the Internet was the 1995 Group of Eight (G8) Summit on the "Information Society," which set some underlying principles to guide specific government policies influencing the new digital Internet world, the Web, and e-commerce.

Internet networking already had achieved domination, and no major government wanted to argue with the large corporations that had embraced the Internet architecture. In addition, retaining the IETF as the locus of standards governance allayed the worst fears of the three major industrial regions. The US government worried that the EU or Japan might belatedly try to engage in industrial policy to overcome the lead that the US computer industry had gotten from the Internet computing revolution.[30] For the EU and Japan, the IETF was an instrument to keep the computer industry away from Microsoft's consolidated dominance.[31]

The issue became how to frame the IETF's influence in terms of broader principles that the industrial governments could support. Stakeholders agreed to a formula used in many trade agreements: international standards should be "voluntary and industry led." This principle would deflect any government from intervening strongly in the marketplace to seek competitive advantage for its firms.

As the Internet's prominence increased, the ITU tried to reassert itself in standards setting on behalf of the national phone companies' plans for data networking. But ITU efforts floundered because the United States and other major governments refused to undercut the control of the university research community and private information technology firms that bolstered the IETF's leadership.

The governments of the United States and other countries did not formally delegate dominance on Internet standards to the IETF, but they rejected a new formulation that would have moved pre-eminent control over standards away from it. The IETF discreetly defended its autonomy by acting as an acceptable "virtual agent" from the perspective of governments.

In view of the huge stakes, why did the IETF community sustain its position as the first choice of the major players? First, transparent decision making promoted its credibility. The community's history of detailed open comment, review of working groups by higher levels of authority, and spirited, open debate provided reassurance. Second, the IETF decision process was credible to governments because the community required extraordinary commitment by its leadership of noted international experts. In the language of bargaining theory, the costly and observable efforts of experts make them more believable. Third, their work is subject to verification by principals and there are large penalties for lying through peer opinion. These three conditions in combination create a situation in which a principal can rely on an agent (in this case, a virtual agent).[32]

Despites its past success as a focal point of networked governance, some worry that the IETF has reached the limits of its capacity. In a swiftly changing technological landscape where commercial applications evolve rapidly, time is a scarce resource for the commercial community that is a major part of the IETF constituency. Technical revisions of standards at the IETF are slow. The lack of time that leading participants can devote to its operations may force more hierarchy into the Internet governance system. This problem is likely linked to the IETF's organizational form and methods, which rely heavily on donated time, voluntary initiative, time-consuming consensus development, and review processes. In the future, more standardization activity likely will bypass it, or its organizational form will grow more formal. Parallel changes already are underway in the Internet Society.[33] If the IETF follows suit, greater hierarchy will cause the technical community and governments to revisit the terms of delegation. For example, more hierarchy may reduce the ability of group dynamics to provide for verification to principals.

Virtual Resources: Scarcity, Hierarchy, and ICANN

Like telephone numbers, domain names and IP addresses are virtual resources. Ways are needed to assign these resources to specific Internet users. Such allocation and assignment procedures introduce a need for hierarchy, which then creates issues of control and scarcity. These open up economic questions about how these points of control might be manipulated. As a result of some deep philosophical differences, there were disagreements within the technological community about how to assign domain names. Who should benefit from assignment of domain names, and how much deference should be given to commercial interests, which claim intellectual property relevant to domain names? Internet governance originated in the United States, and its political economy tilted toward support for strong trademarks and property rights to names. As a result, the initial outcome for this debate over economic policy was preordained. This section explains why there was a need for hierarchical authority with respect to the Internet's domain name system and how this translated into a policy for property rights.

Some see the Internet as a decentralized, flat network. This is a gross over-simplification. Centralization and hierarchy in networks vary over time because complexity increases faster than network growth. A linear increase in the number of network participants can produce an exponential increase in the number of possible interconnections or relationships. Managing this increasing complexity can require disproportionate increases in the need for administrative coordination. For example, as the number of telephone subscribers grew, the number of possible connections among them increased as the square of the number of subscribers.[34] Before the use of electronics for switching phone calls (matching calling and receiving numbers), mastering this growth in complexity was one reason for adopting a monopoly phone system that could impose a strict hierarchy of local, regional, and long-distance routing of calls that simplified the switching challenge.

This important challenge affects the growth of the Internet. As more networks and users join the Internet, the number of possible routes for packets grows exponentially. Information about each route must reside in every router, and must be referenced every time every packet moves through a router. Without route aggregation, which reduces the number of possible paths a router must know about, the Internet's growth would have ground to a halt years ago. But route aggregation is achieved at a steep price. It imposes a hierarchical structure on address allocation. This makes it extraordinarily difficult to trade IP address resources freely and for users to have IP address portability, which would make it easier to switch from one ISP to another. Even with an unlimited supply of Internet addresses,[35] the whole market structure of the Internet connectivity industry is severely constrained by the effects of the expanding possibilities of a growing network on routers. In short, if the Internet becomes more valuable as it increases in size, the increased complexity associated with continued growth may require structural changes in administration that fundamentally alter its character.

The Internet—literally, the internetworking of networks—depends heavily on hierarchical structures for its operation. The traditional telephone network was extremely hierarchical and was centralized at the top to conserve the then scarce resources of transmission capacity and intelligent switching capacity. Developed in an electrical-mechanical age, these resources were expensive to create and to expand.[36]

The Internet inverts the constraints of the telephone system. Bandwidth is relatively cheap and plentiful, and network intelligence grows in accord with Moore's Law. Over time the goal of achieving maximum reliability in an environment of scarce resources of intelligent guidance and capacity receded in importance. Relatively flat, decentralized architectures could improve transmission efficiency.[37] For example, a traditional phone call requires a dedicated circuit that is often idle during the call. In contrast, the Internet breaks all messages into separate, independently transmitted packets (a process that requires ample computer power), thereby allowing many users to share available transmission capacity.

A critical case of scarce resources helping to shape the organization of networks is the essential (or bottleneck) facility. As we argued in chapters 3 and 4, the local transmission network of phone companies is difficult to duplicate and remains critical for communications services. This scarce resource still is a central concern in the broadband era.[38]

The problem of scarce resources also pertains to the Internet. A prime example is a router's capacity to store and search routing tables. YouTube's popularity has heightened this concern. Similarly, the administrative capacity to coordinate unique domain name assignments is limited. The need for unique names produced a major coordination problem that only elements of hierarchy could resolve.[39]

In short, no matter how nominally flat and decentralized a network may be, a variety of elements may make it vulnerable and subject to hierarchical control. Scarce network resources, especially essential facilities, shape the design of networks, including the degree of hierarchy.

The issue of scarcity that shaped Internet governance centered on domain names, the user-friendly placeholders for numerical IP addresses.[40] Domain names have two technical requirements. First, each name must be globally unique, so that information going to or from a domain is not confused. Second, during its use on the Internet, each name must be bound to a numerical IP address, which is the "real" address as far as the Internet's packet-routing infrastructure is concerned.

The design of the domain name system (DNS) protocol provides for an inexhaustible number of domain names—there is no scarcity. But any individual name must be assigned exclusively to a responsible user so that the uniqueness of assignments is maintained. It was the need to coordinate the uniqueness of domain names that created the bottlenecks and scarcities that led to a hierarchical naming structure in DNS. To make this clearer, imagine a totally flat name space in which every computer connected to the Internet must receive a unique name. With tens of thousands of domains added and deleted every day, the process of compiling an exhaustive, authoritative, and accurate list of which names were already taken, and disseminating it to everyone who needed to reference it in a timely (every second or so) fashion, would be difficult. An additional problem is that names continually change their mapping to IP addresses as network configurations are modified.

How can a computer on the Internet know which names are available and which IP address goes with which domain? DNS solves these problems by making the name space and the mapping process hierarchical. A global central authority (ICANN) coordinates the registration of a small number of names at the top of the hierarchy (top-level domains, or TLDs). Top-level domain names include the familiar suffixes .edu, .com, .org, and .info and all the two-letter country codes, such as .uk and .mx. ICANN implements this system through the root zone file, the authoritative information source about which TLDs exist and which IP addresses to which they should be mapped. The root server system (a global system of 13 file servers that steers requests to the appropriate TLDs) draws on the root zone file to tell global Internet users which IP addresses are associated with those top-level names.

There are enormous practical benefits from this hierarchic system. Once the administrator of the root (the authority determining the TLDs) assigns names at the top of the hierarchy, the registries for each TLD (say, .com) can take over the task of assigning unique second-level names (say, aol. com), and operate their own name servers that match second-level names to their proper IP addresses. Likewise, the unique second-level name holders can distribute unique usernames or third-level names (e.g., John@aol.com). With this hierarchy in place, root-level administrators need not worry much about lower-level activities to maintain coordination. The hierarchical structure frees the lower levels from over-dependence on the top, and vice versa.[41] Essentially, this solution creates a highly distributed database, referenced billions of times daily, that depends on fast, inexpensive networking. When anyone uses a Web domain name, the software associated with that Web browser asks the nearest name server to find the appropriate information.[42]

In principle, any computer server on the Internet can distribute copies of the root zone file to users. There are no entry restrictions. In practice, hierarchy is a result of who controls or coordinates the content of the root zone file. Moreover, the 13 "official" root servers that distribute the root zone content have achieved strong inertia because BIND, the dominant DNS software,[43] points name servers to their IP addresses. This makes them the default servers for hundreds of millions of global Internet users. For any single DNS administrator to change the default values involves extra effort; for hundreds of thousands of administrators to coordinate a collective shift to new values would be extremely difficult.

In 1982, when its implementation started, the DNS name space hierarchy was an impressive solution to scaling issues facing the coordination of unique naming. It began to raise thorny political, economic, and institutional issues as the Internet in general and domain names in particular increased in value during the 1990s.[44] The DNS's hierarchical structure created an essential facility at the top of the hierarchy, raising issues about who would control it. The bottleneck character of the root was reinforced by the presence of strong network externalities. The more computers use the same naming hierarchy and name space, the easier it is for Internet users to interoperate efficiently using domain names. These network externalities, in turn, foster global convergence—and dependence—on a single, dominant root zone.[45] Getting users to migrate en masse to a competing root is virtually impossible. The DNS root becomes an essential facility, and its administrator achieves substantial leverage over the industry and users. The root zone file administrator controls the supply of top-level domain names and can manipulate value and control the distribution of benefits. Competition by existing TLD registries is affected by the root administrator's decisions. The creation of new top-level domains, or the reassignment of the right to operate a major top-level domain such as .org or .net, involves wealth transfers representing many hundreds of millions of dollars per year.

The institutional response to managing the problems of resource allocation and assignment is a classic example of delegation. ICANN represents a partial "de-nationalization" of a system of US control that relied on delegation to global decision-making arrangements. It has introduced a "chain of delegation." The US government delegates authority to certain institutions that, in turn, allow other actors to participate.[46] This delegation was designed to lock in a policy approach that America favored. The views of the private sector and technical experts were stressed, especially the views of the leaders of the Internet technical community. This permitted features to co-opt enough expert support in Europe and other technological centers to sustain control of ICANN over the root. Still, the root file zone and root server system represent essential facilities that are subject to struggles for control and disputes over distribution.

ICANN also demonstrated the advantages of controlling the negotiating agenda. The Internet already existed. It relied on the name and number system that had been created with funding from the US government. Other major countries might not have agreed to the ICANN structure if they had started to design this global capability from scratch. But the choice for these countries was to reinvent the digital wheel or to get the US government to allow more influence by global stakeholders over the conduct of the name and number system. If the US government tried to retain perfect control, it might have provoked other countries to attempt to create an alternative to the Internet or it could have fuelled heated diplomatic disputes over this function, perhaps leading to commercial retaliation against American ICT products.

ICANN's articles of incorporation and by-laws, and the "White Paper" process creating ICANN, invited international private sector entities to participate. The goal was to allow the strongest commercial interests outside the United States to play a role in ICANN's deliberations. The US strategy of "internationalization through privatization," also allowed it to bypass the lengthy, difficult process of creating a new intergovernmental organization or of harmonizing territorial jurisdiction. Instead, a private corporation empowered to issue global contracts to address the governance problems was created.[47] Policy decisions are vetted through a relatively open system of corporatist representation involving functional constituencies: DNS service suppliers, the Internet technical community, multinational Internet service providers, civil society, trademark holders, and country code Top Level Domain (ccTLD) managers. Participation in most ICANN meetings and processes is open to all, and seats on policy-making councils are distributed according to geographic representation rules. (We discuss complaints about this process shortly.) In a concession to European complaints, a "Governmental Advisory Committee" (GAC) provides an interface between governments and the ICANN board. GAC gradually grew in informal influence and is likely to continue to do so in response to the World Summit on the Information Society, two United Nations conferences held in 2003 and 2005.

Three instruments delegate powers to ICANN. First, a primary supervisory document regulates ICANN conduct, provides a list of ICANN's policy-making tasks, and sets specific priorities, milestones, or targets for ICANN. Second, ICANN formalized its authority to administer the root zone by contracting with the US government to perform the so-called IANA (Internet Assigned Numbers Authority) functions (the technical coordination of unique name and number assignments). A third instrument specifies the relationship between ICANN and VeriSign, Inc. and sets the parameters under which VeriSign implements root zone file modifications.[48]

ICANN's primary task is to set policy for the administration of the root zone.[49] The US government, however, retains "policy authority" over the root zone file, requiring ICANN to submit proposed changes to the Department of Commerce for approval. VeriSign, a US corporation, distributes the root zone file to the 13 publicly accessible root servers. It operates a hidden primary root zone server that updates all the others. The actual operation of the 13 root servers is performed by an informal, autonomous collection of engineering groups, a residue of the informal origins of the Internet. These operators have roots in the technical community that developed the Internet, and answer DNS queries, but do not set policies related to the root zone file.[50]

At the root server level, the technology and political economy suggest a new dimension for the Internet. Responding to political pressures to geographically distribute root servers more equitably to lessen US domination, some root server operators developed clever ways to create multiple distributed copies of the base root servers, a technique known as "anycast." This technique also improves the Internet's response time. Major websites ultimately realized that they could improve their response time by introducing a complementary innovation: "mirror" websites. Instead of "going" to Yahoo's US servers, a Web surfer could get the same content from Yahoo's Chinese server. Mirror websites and anycasts also allowed more national control over Web content because the Chinese government (for example) could more easily censor a server in China than one in the United States.

By providing a single, authoritative source for finding information needed to resolve top-level domain names, the root server system ensures the global uniqueness of names used for email, websites, and other purposes. This ensures global compatibility in Internet applications that rely on domain names. If any competing root server system attempted to do more than distribute copies of the ICANN/DoC-approved root zone, it would introduce incompatibilities into the DNS, and undermine the network externalities of the global Internet.[51]

Bottleneck facilities are also a source of vulnerability. The Internet's root server system reduces vulnerability through redundancy—if any individual root server is down, the DNS software redirects queries to another root server. Still, the absence of one authoritative source for setting the content of the root zone could introduce serious degradation and requires considerable time and effort to replace.

Internet vulnerabilities, such as the maintenance and definition of the DNS root zone file, ought to generate special protective institutional mechanisms. The centralization of power embodied in the DNS should attract political interest and substantial discretion for the agent.[52] When creating ICANN, the United States "stacked the deck" in favor of its priorities. It gave the Internet technical community substantial control over the agenda to help it solve coordination problems as well as limited dispute resolution powers. ICANN's board favored this community over government representatives and thus was at odds with governments seeking more authority. Predictably, its worldview made it a champion for the private sector's role in the Web's operation, a desirable propensity from the US viewpoint.[53] This community also opposed any use of the domain name system to extend government regulation over the Web. This preference largely fit the Clinton administration's priorities but later clashed with the Bush administration's concerns over social policy. The George W. Bush administration's priorities eventually led to a change in the terms of delegation.

One early concern of the US government was how the community might craft the balance of rights and duties in regard to trademark. Washington worried that a huge expansion of top-level domain names might drive up the costs for registering and protecting trademarks for major global companies. It also was sensitive to the question of how trademark disputes in regard to domain names would be resolved. The US responded, when the first ICANN board of directors was formed, by increasing the mix of telecommunications and information industry executives sensitive to trademark issues. The ultimate ICANN policy included dispute resolution conforming to US trademark law—an adequate solution to a complex challenge, but also a choice that was congenial to American preferences.[54]

The terms of the delegation also ensure that the composition of the ICANN board of directors will not veer far from the original median point. The regime's accountability to the public and to domain name consumers is weak, while industry is well represented. The original idea of holding public, global elections to select half the members of the ICANN board was tried in 2000 but was not repeated after the election results indicated that the distribution of power envisaged in the initial stacking of the deck might be undermined by global board elections.[55] Advocates for more influence at ICANN for a variety of non-governmental organizations and leaders were deflected. But government control may increase even if ICANN remains a non-profit corporation.

First, the US government, despite early promises to relinquish control over ICANN to complete its "privatization," retained residual control over ICANN. The administration of George W. Bush reasserted this control. Its June 30, 2005 statement of principles formally asserted a US right to retain policy authority over the root, and the US government continues to press for a reversal of ICANN's decision creating a new top-level domain for pornography (.xxx).[56] This was a classic example of the ultimate principal sanctioning an agent that was using unwelcome discretion.

Second, the unilateral authority of the United States over the root became a flash point during the WSIS debates on Internet governance when the EU and various countries decried the "pre-eminence" of the US and demanded parity.[57] The WSIS process escalated a long-term debate over ICANN governance. Many national governments seek greater authority. A wide divergence of preferences would occur if a consensus emerged to reduce the US sway over ICANN. The theory of delegation would predict that the discretion granted to ICANN would be reduced because even what was technical would be in question.[58] Late in the negotiations, the EU surprised the US by calling for a greater role for government in overseeing "public policy for the Internet" while maintaining ICANN's control over "technical management." The US responded to the EU at the senior political level. Secretary of State Rice rejected the EU idea. Washington reasserted its authority during the process, invoking Internet "security and stability."[59] Congress and business interests overwhelmingly backed the US government's claims because they opened the door to traditional intergovernmental processes that Internet governance attempted to sidestep. This provides a sharp reminder that power is delegated to serve a political and policy objective, and delegation is tied to stakeholders that define whether their general purposes are being met. The Internet governance delegation had a technological purpose (Internet design principles) and a political purpose (downgrade, not eliminate, the influence of routine government politics and processes). In the end, WSIS called on the United Nations to create an international Internet Governance Forum (IGF), but the IGF would have no real authority over ICANN. In return, the US agreed to a declaration committing countries to support actions (but not make binding financial commitments) to reduce the global digital divide.[60] Although demands to move ICANN functions into the ITU were rebuffed, many state actors still insist on a distinction between "public policy" and "technical management," reserving to states the former and consigning ICANN and private sector actors to the latter. As a result, the Governmental Advisory Committee has become more influential in ICANN's policy process.

Third, the importance of country codes seems to be increasing. Non-US participants in early Internet development insisted on creating national domains (ccTLDs). Since then, national governments have viewed the assignment of country codes to registries as undercutting their national sovereignty.[61] This creates an important national space within the global approach of the Internet design. ICANN's initial attempt to incorporate ccTLDs into its private contractual regime, making them mere contractors on the same level of generic TLD registries such as .com and .org, failed. The regime backed down, and ICANN now recognizes a national-sovereignty right of each government to regulate "its" country code domain.[62]

Governance and Interconnecting Internet Transport

A third function of Internet governance (along with setting standards and distributing domain names) is to address policy choices that facilitate interconnection among Internet service providers by influencing the price and availability of data transport over telecommunications networks, especially international telecommunications transport. This debate over international interconnection of Internet traffic focused on reciprocal compensation. How should a network that exchanges services with another network be compensated? If flows in each direction are of roughly the same magnitude, the best course may be to exchange on a reciprocal "courtesy" basis. If flows are regularly unbalanced, determining compensation is more difficult. Heated debates about what constitutes "equivalent" flows can arise, as happened in debates about Web traffic flow over the global Internet. If more Web traffic enters the US than exits, how should US and foreign Web traffic carriers compensate each other, if at all?

The governance rules and processes for setting technical standards and governing domain names were new arrangements tailored to the Internet. This was never the case for Internet transport, because transport was deeply entangled in the quirky economics of the traditional governance of global telecommunications interconnection. (See the discussion of settlement rates in chapter 7.) The perennial interconnection question of "reciprocal compensation" involves matters of efficiency and potential transfers of market rents.

The Internet facilitates the transport of data bits, which can be converted to voice, data, text, images, video, or music). Its economics depend on the cost and capacity for data transport that the Internet protocols organize. When it emerged, the Internet represented a challenge by the computer industry to the logic of communications engineering associated with the telephone industry. The Internet's designers embraced the efficiencies created by a competitive communications infrastructure. This became a norm of Internet governance.

A 1992 report to Congress by the National Science Foundation laid the groundwork, soon implemented, for introducing "network access points" into the Internet's architecture to allow competitive provision of high-speed, broadband backbone data transport.[63] The network access points also provided the infrastructure for interconnection among commercial rivals.[64] The US Internet backbone was switched to commercial provision in April 1995 when the National Science Foundation contracted out transport services to four commercial providers.[65] Thus, the basic policy decision on competitive infrastructure preceded any delegation of US authority to any international institution. The US policy reflected long-standing decisions, discussed earlier, mandating transmission resale designed to protect the computer networks from any commercial manipulation by the incumbent phone companies.

Companies (e.g., AOL and Earthlink) that ran national ISPs would purchase "backhaul" transmission capacity (network capacity needed to transport data over long distances) from one of several competitors.[66] From 1995 through 2000, particularly rapid growth of competitive supply of backbone transport in the US reduced the need for detailed regulation for the market to protect buyers or suppliers. Despite rapidly expanding supply, a controversy emerged concerning interconnection of Internet traffic. Initially, US backbone networks had responded to increasing volumes of domestic data traffic by exchanging traffic at no fee. As volume soared, the largest carriers started investing in private "exchange points" where traffic could be swapped more efficiently. The Big 5 carriers in particular began to recognize a hierarchy among carriers. With their "peers" on volume and geographic scope in the US, they negotiated private contracts to continue exchanging traffic at no cost. They charged smaller regional networks a transport fee. A new multi-tier pricing scheme for exchanging traffic arose that immediately evoked charges of unfair interconnection pricing in the US by smaller carriers. However, the Federal Communications Commission and the Department of Justice reasoned that there was enough first-tier competition to limit any potential harm to consumers.[67] The one exception to the "hands off" approach came in response to a wave of proposed mergers in the late 1990s. This led the US government to reject some mergers among the companies providing "backhaul" capacity to prevent excessive concentration of ownership of the broadband backbone.[68]

In contrast to its sanguine view about the market for US backbone transport, from 1993 through 1997 the US government worried about the cost and provisioning of international data transport. Until 1998, most international transport provisions were between competitive US carriers and foreign monopolies (or systems with limited competition). Prevailing international ITU rules for global communications strongly reinforced rigid, expensive networking arrangements. With the goal of introducing competitive networking across borders in order to promote greater efficiency, the US championed a shift in delegation of authority from the ITU to the WTO.[69] This effort succeeded in 1997. As a new framework for competition in global data trafficking emerged, other countries began to raise concerns about the practices of the US.

The Web drove up the volume of cross-border traffic as international users sought access to many popular US websites. Foreign carriers sought contracts with US carriers for international data transport (e.g., from the international network exchange point in Seattle to a Chicago website).

To large US backbone carriers, these international networks were the equivalent of small, low-volume, "second-tier" US carriers, so they charged them for exchanging traffic.[70] Foreign carriers complained that the US first-tier carriers' practices lacked transparency and took advantage of the less competitive supply of international transport to exercise market power for data transport. This concern was heightened because the US also provided many international transport links worldwide. For example, until 2000 the route from Cairo to Jakarta usually ran through the US. As noted earlier, the economics of networking mean that peering and interconnection always raise issues over how to apportion costs and revenues. In this case the low traffic flows of poorer countries seemed to doom them to higher prices.

The dispute over backbone peering occurred just when the US exercised its leverage on world markets. The Federal Communications Commission imposed a price cap to drive down the prices paid by US carriers to terminate US voice calls in other countries. The FCC believed that this measure, along with the WTO pact on telecom services, would boost investment in competitive cross-border networks and would also sharply lower the cost of data transport. (See chapter 7.) This FCC strategy provoked major economic controversy between 1997 and 2003. The controversy faded only after the FCC measure had changed the market decisively.

The combination of US efforts to force a reduction in what US carriers paid to foreign carriers for voice services and a claim that US carriers were jacking up prices to foreign carriers for Internet data transport was politically volatile. In 2000, in response, smaller industrial countries, led by Australia and Singapore and supported by non-governmental organizations, made Internet transport pricing a major issue.[71] Later, in another effort to shift the delegation of global power over communications markets, developing countries raised Internet pricing as an issue at WSIS.

The ITU had long served as the delegated agent of governments for conducting international communications policy. The ITU rules supported a formula for reciprocal compensation method on international calls that heavily subsidized domestic networks and restricted competition. A large coalition of developing countries strongly supported the rules. As described in chapter 7, the industrial countries went around the ITU by shifting the delegation of authority partly to the WTO co-jurisdiction. Predictably, this pushed the ITU to revamp its approach to competition to defend against further trespassing by the WTO.

After the WTO pact, Internet transport became subject to greater scrutiny from national competition authorities and world trade rules also applied.

Payments for Internet connectivity became normal commercial transactions subject to regulatory oversight that are negotiated individually among local, national, and global Internet service providers. Many governments protested that the new contractual Internet arrangements did not sufficiently protect the interests of poorer countries. But there was no plausible case that the US market for peering was uncompetitive or discriminatory, the only grounds for successful WTO trade actions.

In response, critics used the WSIS to push for new government oversight to make international pricing more favorable to developing countries. Governments that were critical of the US peering arrangements enlisted NGOs to assist them at the WSIS. Any commercial practice that seemed to increase costs for developing countries, even if produced by a competitively efficient market, was decried because it would worsen the "digital divide." These NGOs often focused more on assistance than on data transport market efficiency. Many of them were critics of competitive markets for socially sensitive services. Most of their proposals envisioned a larger renewed role for the ITU and government formulas for mutual compensation.[72]

This Internet traffic case shows how classic distributional disputes tend to draw more direct intervention and control by governments. In this case the battle over distribution translated into a debate over how to delegate authority. Countries emphasizing market competition preferred a larger role for the WTO. Countries emphasizing regulation to lower prices for poor countries wanted the ITU to have more authority.

The WSIS process concluded in the Tunis Declaration, which acknowledged many countries' concerns over Internet transport services, urged careful consideration of trends toward developing more backbone infrastructure (including network access points) in regions of developing economies, emphasized the need for transparent and non-discriminatory pricing practices, and urged the ITU to continue looking at international Internet connectivity as a "digital divide" issue at the Secretary General's Internet Governance Forum.[73]

In a highly dynamic market an impasse on global negotiations can permit commercial developments to change the interests of stakeholders. During the peering dispute the price of fiber-optic backbone traffic plummeted after the "telecom crash" in the late 1990s, when over-building of new fiber networks precipitated the collapse of many of them. In addition, new technological developments, including "anycasting" and Web mirror sites, reduced the need to send data to the US in order to access the content of Yahoo, Google, and other US-based Web services. Thus, the controversy over pricing for international traffic exchanges somewhat abated. More-over, some analysts shifted their focus from complaints over pricing to proposals for stimulating traffic to and from poor countries. More traffic would improve the position of poorer countries when negotiating "peering" agreements.[74] Finally, opposition by the OECD countries and by some emerging markets (including India and Singapore) that are investing in international fiber-optic networks makes any concrete results unlikely. Unless there is a finding of anti-competitive behavior that contradicts WTO obligations on basic telecommunications services, the pricing system will be left to market negotiations.

Altogether, the WSIS debate on peering did not alter an important Inter-net governance norm: competitive networking is the logical building block of the Internet. The success of this approach is demonstrated by the rapid growth of global networking. Figure 9.1 tracks the growth of submarine fiber capacity linking five important routes.

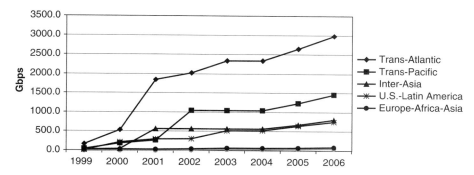

Figure 9.1

Lit submarine cable capacity, 1999–2006, in gigabytes per second. Source: Telegeography Research, Primetrica Inc. Capacity figures denote lit, protected capacity at the end of the respective year. Capacity for 2004 was projected from capacity upgrade announcements and new cable construction information as of March 2004. Capacity for 2005 and 2006 was projected on the assumption that cables with upgradeable capacity will increase total capacity 20 percent each year until fully upgradeable capacity is achieved. Intra-Asia capacity includes cables with landings in both Hong Kong and Japan. Trans-Pacific capacity excludes Southern Cross and PacRim East. Trans-Atlantic capacity excludes Atlantis-2. Cables retired before end of 2004 are excluded from Fully Upgraded capacity. Fully Upgraded capacity is based on system design capacity. Does not include dark cable laid but not in use.

Summary and Conclusions

(with Donald Abelson)

Here we offer a preliminary blueprint for future ICT governance policies. Specific suggestions show how to begin the process of reformulating domestic and international governance to meet the challenges presented at the inflection point. Most of our proposals begin with a test of political economic feasibility in the United States, because for the foreseeable future America will continue to have the most influence on global arrangements. We also employ our theory of how global governance changes to connect shifts in US policy to global policy decisions.

We address several important questions, including these:

- Which policy choices should shape ICT's governance at the inflection point?
- How will changes to the environment and future political economic struggles over ICT influence governance rules?
- How can governance rules benefit from the technological opportunities that they seek to advance?
- What kinds of principles might enhance market transactions in a modular supply environment with blurred jurisdictional geography?

The technological potential for innovation through 2025 is enormous. Broadband networks can deliver services (including such advanced services as ad networks) built with modular architectures that allow networked data applications to break out of their traditional geographic areas and standard business models. These modular, ubiquitous networks and services facilitate innovation at the low end (cheap mash-up experiments) and at the high end (giant research networks working at unprecedented scales). How can politics and markets unlock this potential? Overall, we argue that using the metaphor of "trading rights" (as defined on p. 16) is the right direction for governance because it emphasizes the principle of modularity; this principle will best enable governments to enhance consumer welfare and foster innovation.[1] A system based on trading rights will perform more efficiently as it supplants poorly specified property rights and inefficient market exchange mechanisms.[2]

Although major governance shifts typically begin in the largest domestic markets, the governance challenge is global because the reach of modular networks is ubiquitous. Thus, national borders and market segments blur, and it becomes impractical to regulate solely on a national basis. For example, websites that offer multi-media audio-visual content cannot be regulated as if they were traditional broadcast or cable television networks. Although physical assets (such as cell phone towers and fiber-optic cables) remain geographically fixed, the services they deliver are combined and recombined in ways that defy geography.[3] National policy choices thus have an inevitable international component.

These policy choices will be grounded in the political economy analysis that we explored in chapter 5. This analysis can be summarized in five political guidelines for designing new policies. First, the fragmented goals of the hardware and software industries for networked ICT policies makes broad policy initiatives difficult. The narrower agenda of large corporate users for network issues further reinforces the shrinking of options for future policy initiatives. At the inflection point pressure increases on all pricing structures, further undermining old political economy bargains concerning cross-subsidies in prices for services. Second, changing politics and technological opportunities mean that winning policies will rely on interventions that attempt pinpoint accuracy. Narrower interventions can identify common denominators that do not broadly shift advantages among different classes of stakeholders. Third, the "sweet spot" for bipartisan policy in the United States favors approaches that facilitate open entry for networks, suppliers, and applications. The preference is to ease the way towards interoperability (modularity). An additional preference is to enhance property rights and make it easier to exchange those rights (by building on such precedents as spectrum auctions). The domestic political economy in other countries' markets may work against this approach, but international bargaining will focus on finding a common denominator about elements of the open entry agenda. Fourth, there is potential political support for entrepreneurs who facilitate new avenues of innovation (e.g., co-ownership of Grids) or new classes of networked services (such as research tools that advance wireless sensor networks). Fifth, the growing sophistication of networked ICT services creates a new set of issues involving privacy, content rights, and control of data that are ripe for policy entrepreneurship. Modularity in services means that entrepreneurial political leaders can benefit from making broadcast and content policies more flexible and attuned to the full possibilities of digital markets.

In light of these political economic guidelines, we propose four basic principles (and compare them to three alternative ones). These principles are high-level theories about cause and effect that organize problem solving through governance. Next, we highlight ten norms that implement the principles and advance "trading rights" as an approach to problem solving through specific policies and delegations of authority. Although the norms cover a variety of specific challenges concerning the inflection point, they share some underlying concerns that are specified here.[4]

- How can new approaches to delegating governance authority make decision making more flexible, specialized, and timely while also meeting political demands for accountability?
- How can past policy approaches be modified to advance modularity in the supply chain? For example, how can lessons learned from earlier efforts to foster the Internet be applied today?
- At the inflection point, is there an optimal way to encourage the emergence of competitive, ubiquitous broadband networks that respond to market demand? Furthermore, how should network build-out challenges and net-neutrality issues be resolved?
- How should regulations be adapted to new services that break the traditional categories and geographic boundaries for markets, especially on digital content and broadcast?
- How should property rights and market mechanisms be reorganized to account for inputs from networked applications, especially those involved in the Personal Network Platform (PNP)? (PNPs will thrive only if issues underlying data-management issues such as digital rights management, personal information, and data ownership are addressed.)

Principles for Governance at the Inflection Point

Four Guiding Principles

As with all good platforms, ours has a central guiding principle. Principle 1 is "*Enable profitable transactions among modular ICT building blocks using a flexible mix of public, private, and non-profit agents.*" This should be done without regard to geographic boundaries or technologies (e.g., broadcast, data, and voice). This broad principle suggests three complementary principles.

Principle 2 is "*Governance should facilitate the interconnection of modular capabilities at every stage in the supply and distribution chain.*" (Recall that we follow Farrell and Weiser in defining modularity as a means of organizing complements—products that work with one another—to interoperate through public, nondiscriminatory, well-understood interfaces.) Governance should accelerate ubiquitous broadband deployment, which should itself feature modularity.

Featuring modularity as the central component of the future ICT infrastructure is both a narrower and a more generally applicable approach than that used since the 1980s. It is a narrower approach because it does not lock policy into supporting any particular network architecture. This will matter in the future as the Internet continues to evolve.[5] But modularity also is a more generally applicable approach because it allows any number of architectures while reducing risks to innovation and consumer welfare. The point is not to explicitly or presumptively oppose vertical or horizontal integration or tiering, but rather to look especially closely at developments that promote or inhibit the growth of modular alternatives. For example, online advertising networks are increasingly part of the networked applications and should be examined in light of modularity. Do individual ad networks permit customers to mix and match their ad services with a variety of services from other providers? If they do not, this would hinder modularity and deserve careful scrutiny. Promoting modularity also highlights the importance of public investments in building research tools and network protocols for advanced networked ICT applications.

Principle 3 is *"Governance should facilitate 'mix-and-match' efficiencies at every stage in the supply chain by reducing transaction costs."* New applications will mix and match ICT capabilities. Their variety should elicit a range of specialized governance structures. The current regulatory environment resembles periods of great financial innovation when a variety of stock and commodity exchanges, each with somewhat different disclosure and trading rules, emerged. All of these exchanges were ultimately accountable to government, but the variety in exchanges was crucial to maximizing transactional efficiencies. In addition, these exchanges only were possible because governance had evolved useful frameworks for specifying property rights. Similarly, spectrum management and digital rights management both could benefit from changes in the way that government regulators treat property rights and transactional markets. The application of this principle should also apply to new areas not traditionally treated as part of the network, including ad networks and personal data.

Principle 4 is *"Major market leaders should reform their domestic governance to set the stage for reorganizing global governance."* A clear message is that international diplomacy should follow domestic market reform. In the first two eras, new domestic market-governance structures in the United States were mirrored by energetic US diplomatic initiatives. Conversely, Washington demonstrated its seriousness in these new initiatives by making powerful changes in US governance regimes. The diplomacy was reinforced by the impact of changes in the US market on the self-interests of stakeholders in other major markets. Today the US is still the most important market for setting the direction of global governance, but domestic inertia could squander this pivotal position. In contrast, the European Union crafts reforms inside Europe in light of goals for regional and global governance. By advancing the goal of a single integrated European market, it also gains experience in crafting governance rules while it enhances its global bargaining position. India, Japan, Korea, China, and Brazil will influence decisions considerably, but they do not yet combine the market muscle and policy leadership globally to lead major transformations.

Politics make any transition in global governance quirky. No country will easily abandon its domestic constituents or blithely cede special market advantages. Which country leads, and how, always matters for global outcomes, because international negotiations are based on the strength of the participants' starting positions and the forcefulness of their commitment to succeed. For example, there will be tremendous political ramifications stemming from the significant changes in the intellectual property rights of content industries that are inevitable as modularity makes possible the personalization of content. As with trademark policy at ICANN, US leadership of future discussions probably will lead to more protection of the intellectual property rights of content holders than other countries might prefer. Conversely, if Washington allows governance at the inflection point to drift, the changes will be less supportive of content property owners. Similarly, Washington's leadership also will weaken industrial policies globally because the US has a long bipartisan history of rejecting government interference in its private-sector industrial base.

Three Paths Not Taken

Expert opinion is divided about the best principles for guiding networked ICT. Although we believe that our principles and norms are politically feasible and offer the best potential for continued innovation and economic growth, it is easier to understand the tradeoffs embodied in these principles by comparing them to some major alternatives. (We understand that a brief characterization of these alternatives invites caricature, and we acknowledge that our critiques of three possible alternatives do not give them their full due.)

rather than impose them. One prominent success in governance in the 1990s was the decision to largely abstain from detailed governance rules for the new turbulent space of the Web and its commercial frontiers while promoting a series of targeted national and global responses to specific problems (e.g., assignment of domain names, treatment of trademarks, and cybercrime).

Ten Norms Needed to Implement the Principles

We now can suggest ten norms needed to implement the principles that were just explained. Norms are not detailed blueprints, but they test the appropriateness of policies. We propose ten norms that should be embraced at the inflection point, and we illustrate these norms with examples of policies and delegated authority at the national, regional, and international levels. This is not a comprehensive package, because not all of the policy ideas will emerge as the best choices. It is a starting point.

Norm 1: Institutional Design

Norm 1 is "*When delegating authority globally, emphasize flexible, sometimes experimental, choices of agents, including mixed authority structures.*" This norm addresses the challenges of institutional design that accompany all policy guidelines. At the same time, we recognize that any arrangements at the global level to delegate authority must be accompanied by mechanisms for global accountability.

Chapters 7–9 showed that global delegations of authority for ICT shifted substantially since the 1950s. Sometimes authority was split between the International Telecommunication Union and the World Trade Organization. At other times new decision-making prototypes were developed (e.g., ICANN and the rise of alternative forums for setting standards). These shifts adjusted a system rooted in support of monopoly and national control to a more global and dynamic market. What is next?

No decisive trend toward any single mix of authority is evident. Most decisions with binding consequences for international trade and global security will require a larger direct government role. Often the choice will be between informal trans-governmental arrangements operating among national bureaucracies and formal international organizations. The choice of appropriate venue is critical because each organization has its own logic of decision making that shapes outcomes.

If the Internet did not curtail the authority of national governments, it did chart new ways to exercise shared authority. There are significant opportunities for innovations in delegated authority because networked ICT (e.g., websites and email lists) allows for more flexible, and yet readily monitored, decision-making networks that mix private and public authority in new ways. Processes can be quicker and more expert.

There is considerable potential in two venues. The WTO bargaining process has produced greater harmonization of regulatory codes for markets than anyone imagined was possible in 1980. In addition, parallel synchronization of national rules through specialized global forums or exclusionary regional groups also has proven useful.

Four guidelines for implementing norm 1 follow: (1) Rely on private and non-profit leadership whenever possible, because inter-governmental forums typically are less flexible and slower.[10] In addition, embrace non-discriminatory membership rules for non-governmental organizations that set influential rules for markets. There may be qualifications for membership in private/non-governmental authority structures such as standards setting, but these restrictions should be tied to expertise and funding of reasonable expenses. For example, expensive fees for documents (such as the old ITU standards system required) would be suspect under this guideline. Similarly, transparent decision making and public comment are essential, even to the extent of mandating Web posting to ensure transparency. (2) Emphasize mixed government and non-governmental fact finding to build credible information for policy coordination in both the public and non-profit sectors. As we explained in chapter 6, a principal task of global governance is to improve the credibility of information in order to make coordination easier in a world of decentralized public authority. (3) Promote limited harmonization of national rules. Specifically, introduce flexibility in governance mechanisms while encouraging global coordination by agreeing on minimum international practices (so-called core essential requirements) that will be honored by all national or regional schemes. These techniques were honed through much experience in global financial markets (e.g., the Basel accords for banking) and EU market integration. They allow experimentation while benefiting from global coordination on the elements that ensure a maximum amount of unrestricted competition and market openness. The WTO telecommunications agreement, particularly the "pro-competitive regulatory principles," shows considerable promise as a precedent for other ICT exercises. (4) Use accountability mechanisms to blend national initiatives with global infrastructure needs. The US created a global collective resource, the Internet name and numbering system, and tried to cement certain national preferences (greater openness, competition, and accountability) through its contract with ICANN.[11]

will block "plug and play" add-ons and their substitutes than on the dangers of bundling. Moreover, favoring open-source in procurement may be reminiscent of other preferential purchasing policies, such as those favoring small business. These policies have mixed records.

Indeed, the worries about bundling on proprietary platforms may blind officials to the risks created by gigantic system solutions or new forms of "platforms." One implication of norm 3 pertains to public funding for many ICT projects, such as smart transportation infrastructures, which in effect can become "new platforms" tied to new forms of data and related information services. By defining the risks associated with these new platforms in the context of "offline" markets (for example, "transportation services" in the case of smart roads) or by ignoring central elements of business activities that limit modularity, governments may miss the ability to enhance modularity in a way that creates consumer welfare. Put differently, these projects boast high payoffs but also raise significant competition risks. To begin, there is the familiar and substantial challenge of inducing competitive behavior by suppliers of large government projects. In addition, there is a risk of a high degree of infrastructure lock-in. The original suppliers of major hardware and component systems in the project are hard to replace because of their deep knowledge of the application. They also have the opportunity for vendors to price at marginal cost (zero) for new services that evolve from the original "platform investment." The prospect for anti-competitive lock-in of solution applications increases when the speed of turnover in expensive hardware and software systems lags behind that for typical consumer and enterprise equipment. It becomes even more acute when many stakeholders have to approve new applications (as is common for public-sector applications). It will be a challenge to keep these complex, large-scale, public system applications in the flow of innovative processes and competitive opportunities. The task is harder because significant stakeholders may profit from slower innovation and stronger lock-in.

Competition authorities now consult internationally, but formal harmonization of major rules on platforms seems unlikely. Differences in philosophy and the huge commercial stakes work against agreement. Disagreements exist within countries (many aggrieved parties filing in EU cases are American) and between countries. Leadership by positive example and by veto will be important. If the US disagrees with the policy strategy on competition elsewhere, it should articulate and enforce a clearer alternative at home. If US competition policy choices generally are viewed internationally as right and appropriate, the US choices should tee up reassessments elsewhere. In the meantime, it will be essential to use "negative agenda control," politely saying No to any efforts to codify international principles on these competition questions for the time being.

Norms 4 and 5: Norms to Strengthen the Network Infrastructure

The build-out and deployment of the ICT infrastructure, especially ubiquitous competitive broadband, is critical. Norms 4 and 5 lay out, in considerable detail, a policy approach to achieving these capabilities as efficiently and rapidly as possible.

Norm 4 is "*Spur the build-out of ubiquitous, competitive broadband networks by using a light regulatory touch regarding pricing, investment, and assets crucial to providing ICT networks and services.*" This norm supports new business models, financial engineering, and technological opportunities. The inflection point permits new ways to create value and to finance it. Government policies should be conducive to these types of innovative arrangements. Indeed, once created, competitive infrastructures will reduce even further the need for heavy-handed government regulation. Infrastructures organized around new business plans also would encourage innovative deal making between companies, thereby further supporting and encouraging the growth of novel ICT applications. What can be done?

First, some existing pricing and investment measures should become more prevalent. Greater freedom for telecommunications pricing, to take advantage of the economics of multi-sided platforms, is desirable. Although politically tricky, allowing flexibility improves price signals for efficient investment and consumption. Greater pricing freedom would also remove perverse incentives that cause major suppliers to restrict competition because they cannot price flexibly to earn profits efficiently. But pricing is inextricably tied to legacies of domestic political bargains and cannot be unwound quickly or by international compact. Although more freedom for pricing does not negate the responsibility of governments concerning competition policy, including their WTO obligations, the primary international needs are for better information sharing and for global consensus on the best regulatory practices. This consensus could be reached at the International Telecommunication Union (if it were to restore its credibility with major government, industry, and civil society interests) or at the Organization for Economic Cooperation and Development, Asia-Pacific Economic Community, or other international consultative organizations focusing on economic policy.

Second, restrictions on ownership and trading of investment assets (except for legitimate competition and security concerns) and on providing services across borders make little sense in the highly mobile world of communications. The World Trade Organization already is a venue of action for removing foreign ownership and cross-border restrictions. An expansion of WTO commitments permitting all types of cross-border services and foreign ownership of all aspects of communications networks would introduce stronger property rights and more liquid global markets.[19] There are two big questions here: Can rights of foreign investors be enforced when countries seem willing to invoke vague security rationales to protect domestic investors?[20] Can investment rights be generalized from telecom assets to broadcast assets, for which most countries have taken limited commitments under the WTO?

Release of more radio spectrum for flexible uses on a technology-neutral basis also would promote modularity.[21] The deployment of RFIDs and other sensors may lead to novel network infrastructures requiring considerable spectrum flexibility.

In general, it is desirable to use auctions to assign spectrum when there is scarcity. Conversely, when spectrum is abundant it also is desirable to provide unlicensed uses of spectrum.[22] The holder of the spectrum should have more complete property rights, such as the right to lease or resell licensed spectrum, as long as there is continued adherence to terms and conditions of the original license.[23] This right would provide more liquidity for network assets and more flexible responses to demand.

The spectrum-management regime of today is ill suited for the realities of tomorrow's modular environment: National governments manage spectrum within the confines of their geographical borders, and most spectrum-management regimes are only fitfully evolving away from old-style command-and-control policies. The World Radio Conference, a global exercise in spectrum coordination, is organized on the basis of national representation. It is a spectacle that mixes naked politics and engineering objectives while teetering between absurdity and inspired kludges. As the European Union experiments with regionalization of spectrum management suggest, entirely new mechanisms for cross-national spectrum deployment could emerge. Cross-national, regional band managers might evolve, as was discussed in chapter 5. If so, this could foster a more market-oriented form of management that would enhance consumer welfare. This might substitute private contract negotiation and dispute resolution among the participants in the band-management plan for many traditional regulatory processes. It is worth speculating: How would the world spectrum talks evolve if largely left in the hands of these international band managers?

In the case of band managers, credible domestic or regional experiments in the European Union and elsewhere would have to precede action on a broader international stage. In view of its unique "confederal" structure for economic policy, the EU might be the pioneer in forging such precedents. The United States could adopt a formal approach with Canada and Mexico to allocate and assign selected spectrum on a regional basis. This would be particularly valuable within 100 miles of the borders, as these North American economies and populations are increasingly integrated and could benefit from more flexible spectrum rules to enable the greatest possible use of new modular networks and services. These regional experiments could provide detailed information sharing and fact finding that could be used to establish principles and procedures that might be embraced at the international level. For example, these regional groups might develop general principles for good spectrum management that could later be used to augment WTO market access commitments for spectrum-related networks and services. Although current WTO commitments are ambiguous, future WTO commitments on good spectrum-management practices could lend credibility to market reforms. Global and regional economic groupings also might foster domestic institutional innovations.[24]

More creative options exist. One idea is the experiment with business models featuring "shared user systems" that build on modularity. The advocates of spectrum commons have envisioned these possibilities. The earliest (circa 2001) model of shared investment in the consumer market was the growth of WiFi, which allowed users to invest in equipment to share a broadband connection over an extended space (the home residence) or user base (Starbucks).[25]

The success of WiFi suggested the possibility of expanded user co-investments in networking. Examples were efforts to "daisy chain" WiFi connectivity for a neighborhood and efforts to develop a business model for urban WiFi coverage. So far these have met with limited success. Charging for WiFi access has attracted few customers (perhaps because of rival 3G services). Entities that provide free service have yet to find alternate revenue sources.[26]

Other models loom for shared user financing. For example, Google or Microsoft might finance municipal WiFi networks to win "eyeballs" for their ad services. The idea would be to substitute an intermediary user, the Web service, for household consumers in the co-financing model. In a similar spirit, there are proposals for "underlay" networks that allow smart radio terminals to use idle spectrum within spectrum bands designated for other purposes. The Frontline proposal described in chapter 5 adapted this model by advocating shared use networks between public service and private users.

Another possibility is emerging for fiber networks; high bandwidth may be a sufficiently distinctive benefit to entice co-investment by upper end small and medium-size users and by still-underserved larger users. Advocates envision metropolitan governments providing limited incentives such as favorable zoning rules for fiber co-location facilities and aggressive policies to make municipal ducts and rights of way conveniently and inexpensively open for fiber deployment. "Power households" and institutional users such as schools and medium-size businesses then purchase one or more dark fiber pairs on a cable that terminates into a local co-location center. The users are responsible for the electronics on their own strand. (The cost of coarse wavelength division multiplexing electronics for less "dense" utilization of fiber capacity has plummeted.) The users can negotiate aggressively as a "club" or individually with regional and national carriers for backbone connectivity from the co-location center. The users obtain a 100 megabits per second to 1 gigabit per second pipe that enables essentially free video, Internet, phone, and data services. Early experiments in Canada suggest that the investment should pay for itself in 2–3 years.

Other commercial providers, such as electric utilities (which could add energy-management services to buildings on the pipe) or information services or content providers might co-finance such schemes to bundle their services. In addition, if necessary, local or national governments could offer tax incentives for builders and operators of co-location facilities meeting certain functional requirements tied to enhancing ubiquitous broadband and co-ownership of the "last mile" with end users.[27] Although these experiments may be less salient to the United States, where the fiber network boom of the 1990s and the efforts by cable companies to rival the Bells have created substantial local fiber, many countries lack a local fiber infrastructure, especially one that is competitive supplied. Modularity tied to new business models is one possible remedy.

New business models also pertain to high-end ultra-broadband development. For example, a research consortium, an industry association, or some other global community could jointly finance Grids. Carlos Casasus, head of Internet 2 in Mexico, notes that an association could set caps on the total use by any individual user of a shared Grid, perhaps on a dynamic time-of-day or traffic-flow basis.[28] The individual user co-financing the Grid would be no worse off (if it draws on its financed share of the total capacity), and almost always better off (by freely tapping idle capacity).[29] This kind of Grid can operate as a form of peer-to-peer network within the larger Internet complex.

Two items relevant to global governance might arise from the ferment around new business models. First, detailed information sharing in the major international forums that address ICT policy will be needed. This began around 2000, but it was lost in the debate over the merits of the "commons," a subset of a larger range of innovative possibilities. Information sharing is extremely valuable at these windows of opportunity. Second, and more surprisingly, new business models upset existing stakeholders. Policy can make innovation easier by clarifying the rights to invest and take risks with novel business plans. In this case, the major innovation is "shared use" of a network. Instead of renting the network, users co-invest in it.

Although the details are arcane, most major markets have WTO commitments that cover both shared use networks (for communications within the group of users, such as in the Grid) and the right to deploy competitive infrastructure networks. These commitments open the way to ensuring the right of foreign investors and cross-border service suppliers to create these networks and to removing local regulations that would prevent them from doing so. The WTO commitments for this innovation can be clarified to provide even greater assurance.

The other implication of modularity and financial innovation pertains to the perennial struggles tied to funding "universal service." It is difficult to make such schemes economically efficient; many of them cross-subsidize rural or other groups of middle-class users. These measures are not targeted to serve the poor. In general, politicians prefer price manipulation of services to make them "affordable" rather than providing outright subsidies for purchasing services. Cross-subsidies among rate payers to lower prices do not appear in the public budget.

At the inflection point, the cost of networking is lower because there are more options for developing networks. The expanded ICT applications now emerging outside urban business and service centers also increase the returns from expanding broadband in rural areas. Therefore, building out networks to serve the incremental, low-income or low-volume rural market grows more attractive.

The International Telecommunication Union is the proper institution for setting a positive goal for making consumer broadband at a specified target speed available, even in poor regions. The terminal revolution should make this goal feasible. For example, Vocera Communications, a provider of hands-free wireless platform in a networked building or campus, promotes

third-party traffic.[36] Global best practices can inform the discussions about the proper parameters of the access service.

Users should have freedom of choice of terminal and software applications. The right of users to choose terminals as long as they do not harm the network has been an anchor of wired network policy. This right should be extended to wireless, mobile, nomadic, and hybrid networks, as has already occurred in many countries, and could be added to WTO commitments. The right of the user to freely choose software and Web applications is more difficult to formulate, because some premium services might choose to "manage" acceptable services. However, if there is an adequate "basic access service" (as described above) or a commitment to resell network capacity on wholesale terms to others, carriers will not be able to restrict access to end Web services.

Provide transparency. Customers should receive clear, understandable terms and conditions of service that explain how any network operator, Internet service provider, or Internet content provider will use their personal information and how it will prioritize or otherwise control content that reaches them.

This approach treads lightly because modularity makes many forms of regulatory controls counter-productive. Still, it recognizes the risks of duopoly while also acknowledging the fragmented politics of net neutrality. The split of the old corporate competition coalition makes it difficult to sustain traditional unbundling or detailed price-control rules. The basic access service for consumer and small business broadband addresses the biggest worry of the software and technology research community while also addressing some of the worries of consumer group. Major carriers oppose compulsory service offerings, but they care more about their freedom to offer other services without micromanagement through burdensome regulation. Freedom of terminal and software choices for mobile devices and services should win support from corporate customers and consumer groups. Transparency requirements also appeal to advocates of consumer rights. With appropriate tweaking, either American political party could adapt this package.

Globalizing this platform for net neutrality requires reversing the policies on unbundling that dominate the telecom regulatory environment outside the United States. The US must craft a coherent policy at home that other governments can observe in practice before the US policy can become a credible basis for reforms of global governance.[37]

Eventually, the success of measures to increase the number of infrastructure providers and the variety of business models will result in a decline of the significance of network neutrality rules. However, the evolution of broadband networks also creates new challenges tied to next-generation interconnection that require some oversight by governments. Although often conflated with network neutrality, these issues are conceptually distinct and politically more tractable than network neutrality. This problem arises from the desirability of allowing carriers and users flexibility to explore the best ways to provide value-added features that enhance network security, robustness, quality of service (e.g., prioritization of traffic to reduce latency), and network management (e.g., segmentation by type of traffic).[38] These capabilities raise two important questions: (1) Who should qualify as a peer for exchanging traffic between networks? (As was explained in chapter 9, peers are eligible for traffic exchanges without a fee.) If one network provider decides that another network does not match up on quality of service and security features, should it be treated as a peer? (2) Who gets to provide value added in network functionality? Value-added functions are prone to manipulation for anti-competitive purposes because they are central to competing visions of how to design architectures at the inflection point and to profit from them. This might occur as result of strategic bargaining by entrenched carriers or as an offshoot of national industrial policy (for example, China's experiments with mandatory security standards for Web traffic).

Fortunately, there is an incipient consensus on how to address these challenges that is reflected in the wide endorsement by diverse business groups of the "Four Freedoms" put forward by former FCC Chairman Michael Powell. This leads directly to Corollary 5.3: *"Separate decisions about peering from decisions about interconnection when dealing with the provision of value-added network functions."*

A starting framework for policy might begin with three thoughts:

• All value-added functions, including quality of service, security, and filtering, should be treated as separate issues from network interconnection. Users should always be able to choose who supplies these functions. Networks should not insist on providing these functions as a condition for interconnection with another network.

• Governments should not impose mandatory technical regulations for these functions. Instead, governments ought to define functional requirements at the application and network layer interfaces.

• To qualify technically for peering "least burdensome" distinctions should be used. For example, imagine one network denies a peering relationship (reciprocal free access) to another network that does not perform "deep packet inspection" because of legitimate security concerns. In this situation regulators might set out a series of broad functional requirements (not technical specifications) necessary to qualify as a peer network with respect to interconnection.[39] Those meeting the requirements would enjoy rights not extended to others.

The security elements of next-generation interconnection mean that governments will play a large role. Global consultation, at the International Telecommunication Union or another international technical institution, will be necessary before forging approaches at the national or regional levels. International discussions might produce recommended technical functional requirements. There could be a separate international discussion, perhaps at the World Trade Organization, about the impact of these technical requirements on competition. For instance, at the WTO governments could consider expanding the pro-competitive regulatory principles already contained in the Fourth protocol to include next-generation interconnection.[40]

Countries must resolve whether WTO commitments to provide market access and full national treatment cover the situations where peering is denied for security or other quality of service reasons. The WTO Services Agreement contains provisions that permit governments to maintain legitimate domestic measures, as long as they are "least burdensome." In other words, a government has to show that it is in reasonable conformity with an approach that has the least burdensome impact on international trade. Alternatively, the authority to monitor whether peering rules are fair and impartial could be delegated to a forum involving carriers, other suppliers, and users. This forum might issue certificates attesting to the fact that peering rules comply with agreed norms. Privately managed quality certifications now are a major feature in international commerce. Research shows that environmental standards, for example, adopted by firms in major markets, such as the United States, diffuse to their suppliers in other countries.[41] An internationally accountable process for network certification could be developed in a non-governmental venue and could set off a diffusion process that could supplant or reinforce inter-governmental discussions.

Norms 6–10: Norms for Consumer Services

The inflection point more likely will lead to advances if the regulatory conventions for end services allow the potential for innovation, convergence (including mash-ups), and competition. Convergence should not lead to more restrictions on innovations. For example, a few national regulatory schemes, after ignoring VoIP, are becoming hostile to the convergence of broadband and voice.

Norm 6 is *"Government policies generally should promote experiments with new applications."* In general governments should not restrict experimentation by using regulatory limits on the mixing and matching of services (including on cross-border supply) or through rules on pricing that limit experiments with multi-sided platform packages. There will be exceptions to this norm on security and other grounds, but exceptions should be narrowly defined and should aim to be competitively neutral. The increase in multi-sided platforms for ICT services (see chapter 3) will challenge the instincts of regulators concerning pricing policy. Regulators may have to redefine the relevant definition of the market to encompass these multi-dimensional service products.

The next norm relates to content markets. Norm 7 is *"Create rules for the globalization of multimedia audio-visual content that balance the goals of encouraging trade in services and fostering legitimate domestic media policies."* For example, governments should promote localism, pluralism, and diversity of content.

Until now, national media rules were based on over-the-air, terrestrial broadcast technologies, which were limited geographically and restrained politically. Governments manipulated the broadcasting rules to achieve laudable objectives, but also less liberal goals. In some countries, broadcast services are explicitly used to subsidize the production of audio-visual content. Many governments have rules intended to influence or control the editorial content of news programs, and elected officials everywhere have a vested interest in attracting media coverage to their campaigns. The United States built its broadcast regulatory regime on the basic principles of localism, pluralism, and diversity. It also incorporated into its regulatory system certain advertising restrictions, such as bans on alcohol and tobacco ads for children's programming. The US regime includes often-challenged rules on obscenity and pornography (such as the Janet Jackson–Justin Timberlake Super Bowl "wardrobe malfunction"). Finally, the US regime contains limits on the ownership of broadcast station licenses, both for domestic entities and foreigners (i.e., no more than 20 percent of direct foreign ownership, and 25 percent indirect ownership). Predictably, other countries' regimes contain similar provisions. Indeed, the goals of promoting localism, pluralism, and diversity are nearly universally shared by governments.

The inflection point requires a wholesale revision in the way that regulatory authorities and officials responsible for cultural and trade matters treat

The PNP will make it much easier to accomplish transactions in the networked world. Three issues that already are contentious are digital rights management (DRM), privacy, and data lock-in.

The prevailing framework for DRM is too rigid for new realities. DRM tries to write contracts and controls in advance of market conditions. The erosion of market segmentation and the implosion of traditional content pricing make traditional means of achieving DRM (selling exclusive rights to a piece of content for a set time or use) less efficient because they no longer provide a predictable business model for a large share of copyrighted content. Meanwhile, there is evidence that eBay and other online markets are becoming more efficient at clearing markets of goods that were not traditionally traded. Intellectual property rights will remain important, but the economics and politics at the inflection point severely hamper the technological fixes that might uphold current business models through a strict DRM system.[47]

Outside the United States the situation is even more in flux. For example, in Europe the legal challenges to iTunes argue that the DRM system for the iPod is so rigid that it violates competition laws by locking iPod tunes out from other devices thus inhibiting consumer switching to other devices. In Belgium a ruling on Google caching found that Google was impinging on the intellectual property rights of Belgian newspapers. Similarly, as YouTube becomes more global, the struggles between content owners and YouTube over unauthorized use of copyrighted materials will escalate.

It would require another volume to fully discuss international IPR and DRM issues. Here we merely suggest how the inflection point could change the governance options. To focus on this challenge, norm 8 suggests "*Use networked ICT techniques and changes in policies to tip practices toward new markets for trading and transacting digital rights.*" Digital modularity is rapidly undermining traditional business models for DRM. The same technological forces, if encouraged by policy, might allow for a smoother transition to a more flexible system of intellectual property rights.

We believe that the forces undermining the status quo for DRM produce changes even if there is no official revision of intellectual property rights for content. But selectively pruning and modifying these rights for content might further spur growth and innovation. Bruce Abramson argues provocatively that companies should be able to use either copyright or trademark, but not both.[48] Many critics deplore the prolonged copyright extensions approved in the Sonny Bono Copyright Term Extension Act of 1998 as a monopoly that produces no added incentive for innovation.[49] As we argued in chapter 5, there is no political basis for thinking that intellectual property rights will be legislatively drastically curtailed, but some selective reforms would advance a more realistic system.

The goal should be to "tip" the market toward new practices. This approach is in the spirit of Sunstein and Thaler's "liberal paternalism." They suggest that "In many domains people lack clear, stable, or well-ordered preferences. What they choose is a product of framing effects, starting points, and default rules. . . . We argue for self-conscious efforts, by private and public institutions, to steer people's choices in directions that will improve their own welfare."[50] At the same time, the policy interventions should present choices that are not compulsory, so that anyone may opt out. Applied to DRM, this approach might argue for two policy innovations.

First, government could, as a condition for copyright protection on new applications or on extensions, require the registration of owner/agent contact information to make it easier to find someone to negotiate with in regard to DRM. As a condition for maintaining the copyright, the information would have to be updated, perhaps within 180 days after the copyright office received notice that the contact information was no longer operative.[51] This compulsory information would place only a minor burden on the rights holder, but would make market transactions easier.

Second, applicants could be required to respond to a set of standard contract options and terms that define the content and the use of the protected material. This contract would have options for standard terms (e.g., length of right granted and price) and a standard structure (entire content, sub-sections, audio or video components, geographic breakdowns, etc.) to define differentiated rights that could be split off. We believe this standard contract approach could yield vastly more profitable exchanges of content for "lower-value-added" content than are currently taking place. For example, regional sporting events—the Five Nations Rugby Tournament, local football games, or the final round of a pay-per-view fight—are "untraded goods" that might be opened up by standard contract terms to ease the costs of legal management of these assets. These separable rights might include replay and versioning rights as well as the ability to choose "open-source" styles of contract options (such as the "Creative Commons" license).[52] The applicant could opt out and decline to accept the terms of the contract, or could substitute one of the other license packages now sprouting on the Web.

The standard contracts would bring forth a wave of websites with advice on how to select among the contract terms; these sites alone might suffice for most applicants. Copyright holders could revise their offer terms periodically, but they could not void existing contracts. All revisions to the standard contract would be posted on the government website. This kind of standard contract does not compel particular terms of use. Rather it creates a market exchange or tipping mechanism in favor of standard reference terms, to ease transactions. This is important because there will be a cascade of material created by individual creators and users. Inevitably they will remix materials from the large digital content companies in their offerings. For that reason, standard contracts for buying and selling rights that go beyond fair use are desirable.

As new market mechanisms arise, more sophisticated contracting options, such as futures contracts and trading for digital rights, will appear. These will allow rights holders to more imaginatively unlock the value of the content they own. It also will give new options to users while allowing better market mechanisms to discipline pricing and terms of contracts for suppliers.

Imagine the growth of more sophisticated trading exchanges involving buying and selling the rights to use DRMs and even the development of futures options on those rights. How would one value the future rights to music of the Beatles or Eminem? Politically, private mechanisms to enhance the trading of rights also require accountability rules and methods for enforcing them. Wall Street has the Securities and Exchange Commission, for example. If futures markets in digital rights emerge, how can they be overseen?[53]

The first market center to create viable exchange mechanisms that operate under a framework of public principles will wield enormous international influence. The United States, as the dominant content center, could play this role. Its political leadership could transform a problem into a political opportunity. But if the US does not innovate institutionally, alternative formats will arise that may be less favorable for US holders of intellectual property rights.

It makes sense to hold international discussions on guidelines for minimum government obligations in regard to the conduct and accountability of such exchanges. A major strategic choice will involve the negotiating venue, because venues embed policies in broader frameworks. In this instance, an ad hoc group of national competition and securities exchange authorities might be the optimal starting point. Governments will first have to carefully consider their own domestic organization of authority. They will be less concerned about writing general international rules for these new exchanges than with "testing" their consistency with existing national and global rules for intellectual property rights.

The content issue is critical on its own, but it is also part of the larger issues related to the control of data in the Personal Network Platform. Who owns data, and how should data privacy be insured? The precise answers are not clear, but those debating the options might consider how better-defined property rights to data could address both challenges. This leads to norms 9 and 10.

Norm 9 is "*Enhance property rights for personal data and create mechanisms to allow commercial exchanges involving those rights on standard terms.*" The modularity at the inflection point allows mash-ups and functionalities that will reach across a person's life in the large enterprise or institutional world and in the person's private realm. As more applications and more interactions are conducted online a consumer adds to his or her "click-stream profile" every day. The applications and the flexibility afforded by the Web are extremely appealing, but they raise significant privacy issues. For example, recent efforts by Google and Microsoft to become providers of physicians' services promise to make sharing data among scattered physicians' offices easier for consumers, but they raise serious privacy challenges to the extent that the physicians are not covered by HIPAA rules.[54]

One way to move forward is to set different default rules about privacy. Crudely put, Europe represents the notion of "opt in," requiring an explicit permission from the individual to access personal data. The United States tilts toward "opt out": the individual must request that his or her data not be released. Both regions treat this issue primarily as a legal, not a market, transaction. This misses an opportunity.

Over time, the Personal Network Platform will induce individuals to develop personal data profiles of greater complexity. Individuals will sign contracts with their employers that specify how to share these profiles. The same contractual situation will arise with providers of health care. Facebook entries show that some individuals already have adopted this practice. Since commercial enterprises prize personal data, why not introduce incentives for creative data sharing that elicit the real value of the data (and by implication of privacy) and the real value of the acquisition of private data to the parties involved? Well-functioning markets could help to price individual data better and more accurately, could yield more optimal exchanges between consumers and products, and could lead to a new set of innovative exchanges and business models based on them.

A plausible technological challenge is to develop the equivalent of eBay markets for personal data. Companies already sell or share large amounts of private data, and individuals' social network connections and e-commerce ratings are readily searchable through Web services such as

extensive set of user data. Traditionally, it was reluctant to curb its efforts to track all user behavior on Google servers. In addition to search data, many privacy experts believe that Google scans user emails for keywords to more effectively target ads on its Gmail service. Microsoft, Yahoo, and Ask.com have been keener to focus on user privacy in order to differentiate them on this point.[57] More recently, Google called for international standards on the use and retention of end-user data in the industry. This followed a Privacy International report that ranked Google last in end-user privacy.[58]

As in the case of content, we believe the focus on privacy misses the opportunity for policy innovation and also misses the important challenge that "closed data archives" raise (i.e., the possibility of consumer lock-in in specific services can deter modularity and stifle innovation). If you cannot "take your Zillow profile with you," are you likely to switch services? In short, elements of information services intended to make them "sticky" also open the possibility of lock-in. One reason for encouraging the Personal Network Platform with ownership rights to personal data is that it will tend to promote co-ownership of the data in cases like that of Zillow. (Zillow and the individual would have a right to the data.) For policy, governments should carefully examine the possibility of data lock-ins. Hence, norm 10 is *"Users may take their information with them when they depart from specific applications and experiences and own their 'click streams.'"* This is like the principle in telecommunications competition policy that a regulator should enforce the right to "number portability"—that is, a user's ability to switch networks and still keep his or her present phone number. Thus, number portability undermines customer lock-in.

Table S.1 reprises our four principles and the ten norms that could help with their implementation.

The Way Forward

We have emphasized the variety of venues for action and subjects for initiatives in order to adapt governance to the concept of "trading rights." The advantage of this diversity is that meaningful initiatives can develop on the most opportune front for substance and policy deliberation. We also have emphasized some advantages of trade agreements as an anchor for harmonizing significant elements of national policies. We will close by examining initiatives on trade to illustrate how these principles and norms could be pulled together. Of course, if trade venues stall, other avenues will emerge.

Table S.1

Four guiding principles and ten norms to help implement them.

Principles

1. Enable transactions among modular ICT building blocks.
2. Facilitate interconnection of modular capabilities.
3. Facilitate supply chain efficiency, reduce transaction costs.
4. Reform domestically to help reorganize global governance.

Norms

1. Delegate authority flexibly.
2. Invest in virtual common capabilities; be competitively neutral.
3. Use competition policy to reinforce competitive supply chains.
4. Intervene lightly to promote broadband networks.
5. Narrow and reset network competition policy. All networks must accept all traffic from other networks. Narrow scope of rules to assure network neutrality. Separate peering and interconnection for provision of VANs.
6. Government should allow experiments with new applications.
7. Create rules for globalization of multimedia audiovisual content services that encourage international trade and foster localism, pluralism, and diversity.
8. Tip practices toward new markets for digital rights.
9. Promote commercial exchanges that enhance property rights for personal data and mechanisms to do so.
10. Users own their information and may freely transfer it.

Using the WTO as a venue for advancing governance change will be a challenge for the foreseeable future. The Doha Round of trade talks (named for the city in Qatar in the Arabian Gulf where the negotiations began) have been deadlocked almost from the moment they were launched. The talks reached a stalemate in July 2008, and we do not expect a conclusion to the negotiations until well into the new U.S. administration. This is an opportunity, not a tragedy. The Doha Round's ICT agenda has focused on solving the trade problems of the past; the current agenda merely attempts to improve commitments obtained in the WTO basic telecom agreement in the mid 1990s. That agreement was rooted in the realities of the de-monopolization, deregulation, and divestiture movement of the late 1980s. The goal was to open formerly closed monopoly wireline networks to competition. The agreement included commitments on other technologies, including wireless and satellite, but was intellectually grounded in the communications network invented in the late nineteenth century. Thus, although the Doha Round will likely take additional months (or years) to conclude, this is not a bad thing. The time can be used to create an ICT

Table S.2

An agenda.

Encouraging build-out of competitive broadband infrastructure

Promote business models that allow user cooperatives to build out competitive infrastructure: Governments could commit to permit network sharing among users and to permit shared user networks to interconnect to backbone networks on non-discriminatory terms.

Encourage flexible use of spectrum for new broadband networks and flexible services and architectures: A country can commit to service and technology neutrality for spectrum licensing and use and commit to commercial resale of spectrum.

Encouraging technological innovation while dealing with the challenges of the next generation of interconnection policy

Allow networks to establish legitimate security requirements for networks with which they peer while restricting the use of illegitimate security requirements for anti-competitive purposes: Governments could commit to set functional security requirements for networks, but be technology neutral on how they are fulfilled. In addition, governments could commit to the rule that functional requirements will be transparent and least burdensome for trade.

Foster competition in the provision of security functions: Governments could allow third party suppliers (i.e., value added service suppliers) to provide security functions for networks.

Encourage innovation on mobile broadband networks: Governments could commit to freedom of terminal attachment and terminal software for mobile broadband networks.

Encouraging liberalization and globalization of audio-visual content markets while allowing national rules to encourage localism, pluralism, and diversity of content

Recognize the need to respect the societal and cultural aspects of media: Governments could commit to limiting domestic regulation to rules that encourage localism, pluralism, and diversity of content.

Establish the principle that content rules should not unnecessarily restrict Internet delivery of audio-visual content: Governments could make commitments that distinguish between push (i.e., broadcast) and pull (i.e., Internet audio-visual downloads) technologies for audio-visual services by accepting market liberalization commitments for audiovisual services delivered through pull technologies.

Provide transparent means of subsidy for the production and distribution of content: Governments could commit to ensure that subsidy regimes are least burdensome for trade (e.g., a bit tax on data flows that supports national content producers subject to rules of national treatment)

Encouraging harmonization of core national policies on personal data

Recognize the vital importance of privacy policies: Governments could commit to transparent rule making and rules on binding consumer rights regarding control of their personal data.

Establish the right for consumers to move their personal data from a website operated by a telecom carrier to a third-party web portal (e.g. from NTT to Google): Governments could commit to assure a consumer's right to portability of his/her personal data that is equivalent to number portability for telecommunications services.

---

negotiating agenda that responds to the demands of the changing ICT technological and innovation landscape. This new agenda can serve as a blueprint for the future.

The advent of the Internet and of modularity demands the establishment of a new framework for global ICT governance and a WTO deal on ICT that points the way forward. We favor a more aggressive agenda that takes into account the evolving modularity of ICT and is based on the principles and norms promoted in this chapter. Table S.2 illustrates how trade agreements could advance the policy framework advocated here. It employs specific language from existing trade commitments to show how new agreements could be written. Even if avenues other than trade agreements end up as the most immediate vehicles for reorganizing global market governance of ICT, these initiatives could ultimately relate to a trade agenda. Moreover, the language of trade obligations pervades agreements in other international forums.

We believe that the agenda laid out in table S.2 is attainable in future trade negotiations because governments have a strong interest in trying to harness the destabilizing impact of technological change rather than inheriting a set of rules that have little relevance in political or economic terms to the emerging marketplace. Government policy makers and regulators would rather enter into difficult trade talks than accept that technological change circumvents their choice of regulatory actions or policy options. There are strong political and economic motives to act, and so governments will influence the ICT infrastructure in some important ways. The challenge of the $4 trillion market for global communications and information industries is that political economy will stall policy change or push policies down unproductive paths. We began this book by arguing that the goal of governments should be "pretty good" governance. Achieving this outcome in a rapidly changing marketplace with high commercial stakes will require astute risk taking by policy makers.

7. Even a little bandwidth can go a long way. Innovation in the use of wireless networks in rural areas of China suggests a different pattern of use and development is possible and highly valuable. See "Rural push boosts China Mobile profit," *Financial Times*, August 16, 2007.

8. By 2007, GPS navigation systems for cars had evolved to introduce constantly updated information on road congestion based on real-time feedback from other GPS systems on the road and data analysis made possible by a hybrid of cellular data networks. See "Navigating with feedback from fellow drivers," *New York Times*, October 18, 2007.

9. For a report on recent spending, see Cara Garretson, "Venture funding reaches five-year high in Q1: Investors empty pockets as start-ups eye public markets," *Networked World* (http://www.networkworld.com), April 24, 2007.

10. Social scientists call the outcome to be explained the *dependent variable*. Market governance and its consequences are the dependent variable in this study.

11. There is still worry in some quarters that competing jurisdictions create a "race to the bottom" in the quality of regulation, but there is little evidence to support this general proposition.

Chapter 2

1. IBM was late to the party. In 1977, the Apple II, Commodore International's PET, and Tandy's TRS 80 were the first successful pre-built minicomputers. The Computer History Museum identifies the Kenbak-1 (introduced in 1971) as the first personal computer, but only about 40 were ever built.

2. The FCC unanimously found that the AT&T tariff preventing interconnection was illegal and ordered AT&T and other phone companies to allow interconnection of devices to their networks that did not cause actual harm. See Gerald W. Brock, *Telecommunication Policy for the Information Age* (Harvard University Press, 1994), pp. 84, 85.

3. Electronic switching began to supplant mechanical switches. The first digital electronic switch, an AT&T 4ESS, was put into service in Chicago on January 16, 1976 (source: http://www.corp.att.com.)

4. The advent of satellite communications services in the 1960s led to great improvement in long-distance telephone service and, later, broadcast transmission into the home. At first such services did little for data transmission. Fiber-optic transmission began to enter the network in 1977, when AT&T installed fiber telephone systems in Chicago and GTE began providing service in Boston (source: http://www .fiber-optics.info).

5. AT&T licensed the transistor to other companies in 1952. In 1959, Texas Instruments and Fairchild introduced the integrated circuit. During the 1960s, integrated

circuits became microprocessors. In 1971, Intel created the microprocessor. IBM introduced its Personal Computer in 1981. In 1986, Cisco introduced the TCP/IP router. Source: Alfred D. Chandler Jr., *Inventing the Electronic Century* (Free Press, 2001), pp. 262–265.

6. The 1956 antitrust decree created the IBM "plug compatible" industry worldwide. In 1963, the Digital Equipment Corporation made its first meaningful impact in the marketplace with a mini-computer that made putting computers on the factory floor practical. Source: Chandler, *Inventing the Electronic Century*, p. 104.

7. Prices might have decreased more precipitately if the regional Bell Companies initially had been allowed to provide long-distance services. See Robert W. Crandall, *After the Breakup* (Brookings Institution, 1991), p. 48.

8. Even with increased transmission capacity, most Quality of Service guarantees were done on specialized network overlays (virtual private network or private network). Megabits and megabytes are frequently confused. In most instances bits are used to talk about data transfer rates. Bytes generally are used to talk about storage size calculations. Specifically, 1 kilobit = 1,000 bits, 1 byte = 8 bits, 1 kilobyte = 1,024 bytes, and 1 megabyte = 1,024 kilobytes. If an Internet provider offers a "1-Mb" connection, it is megabits, not megabytes. To determine approximately how much is being downloaded, divide by 8—for example, a speed of 1 megabit per second will result in downloads of 128 kilobytes of data. Source: http://wiki .answers.com.

9. On personal computers, see Chandler, *Inventing the Electronic Century*; Charles H. Ferguson and Charles R. Morris, *Computer Wars* (Times Books, 1993).

10. This trend, praised by most leading analysts, occurred in both the US and the EU. See Pamela Samuelson and Susan Scotchmer, "The law and economics of reverse engineering," *Yale Law Review* 11 (2002), no. 7: 1577–1633.

11. Tim Berners-Lee, *Weaving the Web* (Harper, 1999).

12. Shane Greenstein, "Markets, standardization, and the information infrastructure," *IEEE Micro, Chips, Systems, and Applications* 13 (1993), no. 6: 36–51.

13. The global electronics market and the telecommunications equipment market were under pressure from Japanese and later Taiwanese and Korean exporters that relied on scale economies. The semiconductor challenge moved the US closer to industrial policy than at any time except wartime. The strategy was to shore up US firms by two strategies. First, the US tried to increase its firms' market penetration in Japan, so they could build scale economies and pressure Japanese price margins at home. This was the point of the US-Japan Semiconductor Agreement. The second goal was to share the cost of maintaining the supplier infrastructure for integrated American chip producers. The proposed idea was Sematech, a consortium jointly funded by industry and the US government. On the US-Japan Semiconductor Agreement, see Peter Cowhey and Jonathan Aronson, *Managing the World Economy*

(Council on Foreign Relations, 1993), pp. 139–145. See also Leslie Berlin, *The Man Behind the Microchip* (Oxford University Press, 2005).

14. John Richards and Timothy F. Bresnahan, "Local and global competition in information technology," *Journal of the Japanese and International Economies* 13 (1999), no. 4: 336–371.

15. The effort in the late 1990s to force incumbent local-service carriers to share their network elements on an unbundled, cost-related basis was the ultimate effort to achieve disintegration through government intervention. Competition in most countries diverged from the US model of splitting the local and long-distance elements of the monopolist. Those with vigorous regulators, such as the EU, did focus on these carriers' local-service networks as the most enduring part of their former market control.

16. For example, Korea and Taiwan used industrial policies to steer high national savings rates into subsidies for specialized entry into capital intensive and lower return segments of the memory chip industry. Source: *International Production Networks in Asia*, ed. M. Borrus et al. (Routledge, 2000). See also Michael Borrus, *Competing for Control* (Ballinger, 1988).

17. Eric von Hippel, *Democratizing Innovation* (MIT Press, 2005).

18. In Japan, this innovation storm—driven by lower costs, flexible networking, and user co-invention—was absent. Japan continued to favor vertical integration anchored on the technological planning of the dominant carrier, NTT. Although Japan also introduced telecom services competition, it limited the impact of competition by placing all new entrants under a micro-managed price umbrella set by NTT. Network expansion plans need ministry approval because the government wished to sustain its subsidy scheme for electronics firms Japan required the licensing of value-added networks. It did not license a network embracing Internet protocols until 1992. Sources: Roger Noll and Frances Rosenbluth, "Telecommunications policy: Structure, process, and outcomes," in *Structure and Policy and Japan and the United States*, ed. P. Cowhey and M. McCubbins (Cambridge University Press, 1995); Shane Greenstein, "The evolution of market structure for Internet access in the United States," draft, Northwestern University, 2005; Robert E. Cole, "Telecommunications competition in world markets: Understanding Japan's decline," in *How Revolutionary Was the Digital Revolution?* ed. J. Zysman and A. Newman (Stanford University Press, 2006).

19. Peter Cowhey, "Telecommunications," in *Europe 1992*, ed. G. Hufbauer (Brookings Institution Press, 1990); Computer Science and Telecommunications Board, *Realizing the Information Future* (National Research Council, 1994), pp. 270–277.

20. OECD Information and Communication Technology, "OECD broadband statistics to June 2007," at http://www.oecd.org. Broadband data related to penetration,

usage, coverage, prices, services and speed are updated regularly and are available at http://www.oecd.org. Comparable figures are not kept for large corporate and research center users of large broadband, but the US remains dominant in this market segment.

21. Peter Cowhey and Mathew McCubbins, eds., *Structure and Policy and Japan and the United States* (Cambridge University Press, 1995); Roger Noll and Frances Rosenbluth, "Telecommunications policy: Structure, process, and outcomes," in ibid.; Charles R. Shipan, *Designing Judicial Review* (University of Michigan Press, 2000).

22. In political science this is called a *veto point*. See George Tsebelis, *Veto Players* (Princeton University Press, 2002).

23. The split between presidential and parliamentary systems on incentives for delegation of authority is fundamental. However, the systems differ in their behavior based on such factors as the design of electoral voting systems. And some countries use hybrids systems. See Royce Carroll and Matthew Søberg Shugart, "Neo-Madisonian Theory and Latin American Institutions," in *Regimes and Democracy in Latin America*, ed. G. Munck (Oxford University Press, 2007).

24. A final form of control over the FCC is the division of some of its powers with other branches of the government. The most important of these is the shared power over competition policy with the Antitrust Division of the Justice Department. In view of the strength of US antitrust laws, both political parties are sensitive to the possibility of the rival party politicizing competition policy when it controls the federal government. As a result, the career officials in the Antitrust Division enjoy a relatively high level of protection from routine political oversight. Decisions on the general criteria for when to prosecute are subject to guidance by a political appointee, but the president is generally circumspect on antitrust matters. The shared power of Justice and FCC over telecom mergers leads the FCC to be careful not to conflict with Justice. It can happen, however, as the late 2006 ATT–SBC merger decisions show.

25. For a candid account by a point person for the Clinton administration, see Reed Hundt, *You Say You Want a Revolution* (Yale University Press, 2000).

26. Noll and Rosenbluth, in *Structure and Policy and Japan and the United States*, ed. Cowhey and McCubbins. Between 1900 and 1933, as national industrial and network markets took form, state authorities used antitrust actions to shelter local competitors from national competitors that held advantages over them. Most senators from these states were wary of nationally dominant firms. America's veto-oriented system and Congress's distrust of sweeping regulatory powers dampened impulses toward national economic planning. Industrial policy that might have concentrated firms into a few national champions was difficult to pass.

27. Peter Cowhey, "States and politics in American foreign economic policy," in *Blending Economic and Political Theories*, ed. J. Odell and T. Willett (University of Michigan Press, 1990).

28. James Cortada reports various estimates of ICT as the costs of the largest banks (*The Digital Hand*, volume 2, Oxford University Press, 2005, pp. 33 and 89–90). His estimates are in the range of 7–15% of the total costs of the banks. As late as 1992, after networking costs had declined dramatically from the 1970s, networking costs were 10% of the total. Interviewing and documents supplied to the authors in the 1980s showed that during the 1970s networking costs were much higher.

29. As described in chapter 3, these changes were part of the broader transition to a service economy that eventually made sophisticated manufacturing into a part of service product schemes, as clearly has happened in ICT since 2000.

30. Gerald Brock, *Telecommunication Policy for the Information Age* (Harvard University Press, 1994), pp. 65–74.

31. Cowhey, "States and politics in American foreign economic policy."

32. Large customers sought volume discounts and customized service packages for internal private networks. Computer services, including networking, were profitable but were on a smaller scale than today. Sales of IBM computers in 1984 were $22.2 billion. The combined revenue of the top five computer services firms was $3.4 billion. (Computed from Datamation figures reported on pp. 118–119 of Chandler, *Inventing the Electronic Century*.) On the high level of oligopsony in communications use, see Peter F. Cowhey, "The International Telecommunications Regime: The political roots of regimes for high technology," *International Organization* 44 (1990), no. 2: 169–199.

33. Eventually, the FCC ordered AT&T to create a separate subsidiary for terminal equipment because of issues about cross-subsidies in the competitive equipment market. The FCC did not think that these decisions would cause local phone rates to balloon. See Brock, *Telecommunication Policy for the Information Age*, pp. 79–98.

34. Linda Cohen and Roger Noll, *The Technology Porkbarrel* (Brookings Institution, 1991). The funding of research leading to the Internet was not an exception. Nobody saw the Internet as commercial data architecture until late in its deployment.

35. We thank Gerry Faulhaber for this point.

36. Brock, *Telecommunication Policy for the Information Age*, p. 118.

37. Steve Coll, *The Deal of the Century* (Athenaeum, 1986), pp. 18–19, 169–171.

38. Stephen Breyer, *Regulation and Its Reform* (Harvard University Press, 1982).

39. The classic account of White House thinking in this matter is Coll, *The Deal of the Century*.

40. All major telecom carriers, including the new entrants, were unionized. Thus, a decline in employment at AT&T was partly offset by new employees at MCI and other firms. This reduced the resistance of organized labor, a major constituency of the Democrats.

41. The Bells got the licenses from AT&T as a sop at the breakup. See Leslie Cauley, *End of the Line* (Free Press, 2005), pp. 36–37.

42. R. Preston McAfee and John McMillan, "Analyzing the airwaves auction," *Journal of Economic Perspectives* 10 (1996), no. 1: 159–175.

43. We thank Reed Hundt for this observation.

44. The Democrats also wanted to distinguish new forms of subsidy for consumers from programs identified with the welfare of the Bells. Despite grumbling from the Republican Congress, the FCC used its discretion to institute a new fee for telecom services to fund the establishment of Internet access for schools, libraries, and hospitals. This was a conscious decision to meet the political demands to keep service widely distributed to all areas, but the Democrats designed the subsidy so that it went as much to poor urban neighborhoods as it did to rural areas. Inevitably, coverage of middle class areas was part of the political bargain.

45. There were divisions in each party, but the median point of each party's congressional caucus was significantly different. Conservative Republicans cast this as enhancing competition by taking regulatory shackles off the Bells. Clinton Democrats stressed enhancing competition by letting new entrants attack the local transmission bottleneck on the network.

46. Representative critiques: Thomas Willett, "The political economy of cable 'open access,'" working paper 00-09, AEI-Brookings Joint Center, 2002; Jerry A. Houseman and J. Gregory Sidak, "Does mandatory unbundling achieve its purpose? Empirical evidence from five countries," working paper 04-40, MIT Department of Economics, 2004. For a nuanced analysis, see chapter 5 of Jonathan E. Neuchterlein and Phillip J. Weiser, *Digital Crossroads* (MIT Press, 2005).

47. The collapse of Global Crossing after it completed fiber-optic submarine cables linking the US and Asia allowed for the outsourcing revolution in India and elsewhere. See Thomas L. Friedman, *The World Is Flat* (Farrar, Strauss and Giroux, 2005), pp. 103–106.

48. Timothy F. Bresnahan and Shane Greenstein, "Technological competition and the structure of the computer industry," *Journal of Industrial Economics* 47 (1999), no. 1: 1–40.

49. For a review, see Gerald R. Faulhaber, "Policy-induced competition: The telecommunications experiments," *Information Economics and Policy* 15 (2003), no. 11: 73–97.

50. For instance: How much time should be required for quality children's programming? How much control local broadcast content should be mandated?

51. This section relies on several sources. Neuchterlein and Weiser succinctly analyze broadcast policy in chapters 11 and 12 of *Digital Crossroads*. Also see Mark Robichaux, *Cable Cowboy* (Wiley, 2005), pp. 72–74 117–119, and 208–278. For an opinionated, erratic, but fascinating polemic, see Stephen Keating, *Cutthroat* (Johnson Books, 1999).

52. Another effort to promote international competition was the decision to introduce competition in satellite communications. Intelsat, formed in 1964 at US instigation to manage global satellite communications, was a "monopoly of monopolies" for international satellite services. Each national telecom monopolies owned a share of Intelsat proportionate to its international use. The US was a partial exception. It created a private national satellite monopoly, Comsat, to represent its interests instead of tapping AT&T. But in 1983, as domestic deregulation was gaining momentum in the US, a new venture, Orion Satellite Corporation sought permission from the FCC to launch a transatlantic satellite service in competition with Intelsat. Overcoming fierce opposition by Comsat and Intelsat, in late 1984 President Reagan determined "that separate international communication systems are required in the national interests," but promised it would consult and coordinate with Intelsat to make entry smooth. The FCC then ruled that private firms should be allowed to provide international satellite communication services in competition with Comsat and Intelsat. In 1988 PanAmSat finally broke the Intelsat/Comsat stranglehold on international satellite services. For a detailed account, see Aronson and Cowhey, *When Countries Talk* (Ballinger, 1988), pp. 116–135.

53. An ongoing battle between the Ministry of Post Telecommunications (MPT) and the Ministry of International Trade and Industry (MITI) eventually prompted the Japanese government to mandate facilities competition. (The Diet passed new telecom laws in December 1984 that went into effect on April 1, 1985.) See Chalmers Johnson, Laura D'Andrea Tyson, and John Zysman, *Politics and Productivity* (Harper Business, 1989), pp. 211–215.

Chapter 3

1. See "Winner-take-all: Google and the third age of computing" at http:www .skrenta.com.

2. Nicholas Carr, *The Big Switch* (Norton, 2008). Carr sees Google as an epitome of the change, but not as a potential monopoly.

3. There are disputes over the definitional lines. We use "the Grid" to indicate an architecture that joins multiple computing platforms within a predefined organization. It is a subset of "the Cloud," a virtual "on demand" approach that allows decentralized users to tap networked computing and storage as needed. Interfaces

must be open but we do not assume that they must be produced by open-source code. See Heinz Stockinger, "Defining the Grid: A snapshot on the current view," *Journal of Supercomputing* 42 (2007), no. 1: 3–17.

4. Marketing is still moving faster than execution. "Virtualization" of blades is still imperfect—as of early 2008, three well-financed start-ups were trying to close this performance gap according to our interviews. Yet the impetus for the vision is clear. Since the early 1980s large companies' use of powerful computers has increased more than tenfold and perhaps as much as a hundredfold because they assigned a separate server to each new application. Consequently, these companies use only 10–15% of the effective capacity of their computers. Large financial institutions are key early adopters of the Grid. See Alan Cain, "Silver bullet or snake oil—is grid computing a money-saver?" *Financial Times* September 20, 2006 8; Alan Cain, "Virtualisation can bring an end to 'server sprawl'," *Financial Times,* September 20, 2006 8.

5. Enterprises are operating in more heterogeneous environments (hybrid Windows/ Linux environments, with some mainframe and Unix flavors added) that rely on huge amounts of data in enterprise resource planning (ERP) and other systems. During the 1990s, SAP, PeopleSoft (Oracle), and related systems were deployed. Recently enterprise buyers focused on efforts to broaden the impact of these investments across the business. Customer demands for data interoperability and ease of use required changes in products and approach from software vendors. The use of xml file formats in Microsoft Office 2007 is one example of this trend. System vendors to enterprises have to support at least three major operating systems with the Web browser as the common interface.

6. Robert Cringely argues that Google holds more fiber-optic capacity rights than any other US organization and is building new giant data centers. Industry interviews suggest that Google's extensive fiber holdings do not come close to large cable operators like Comcast. But its server growth is stunning. See Cringely, "When being a verb is not enough: Google wants to be YOUR Internet," at http://www.pbs.org.

7. Robert Hahn and Robert Litan have noted that dominance might emerge because scale is a barrier to effective rivals for online ads ("Some Internet mergers deserve a careful look," AEI-Brookings Joint Center, 07-17, 2007).

8. We thank Michael Kleeman for showing us how this might be done.

9. "Nokia sets sights on Google," www.telecoms.com.

10. Rishad Tobaccowala, cited in "Deal that may create more, not less, competition," *New York Times*, February 2, 2008.

11. The effort to promote a "Google phone" does not foresee the phone as a significant source of profit, but as a commodity whose chief value is driving traffic to the Google search engine and related online services.

12. Robert A. Burgelman and Andrew Grove, "Strategic dissonance," *California Management Review* 38, no. 2 (1996): 8–28.

13. This builds on Joseph Farrell and Philip Weiser, "Modularity, vertical integration and open access policies: Towards a convergence of antitrust and regulation in the Internet age," *Harvard Journal of Law and Technology* 17 (2003), no. 1: 85, 100–105. Modularity is an idealized characterization of several important underlying properties. Today, some end systems, like personal computers, approximate the pure ideal. So the overall vector of the ICT networked infrastructure is toward modularity. Pierre de Vries pointed out to us that a purely modular architecture for ICT would be partial (no module is self-sufficient for the end service), separable (each module is self-contained and detachable), and substitutable (another module can be substituted). Andrea Ottolia and Dan Wielsch, "Mapping the information environment: Legal aspects of modularization and digitalization," *Yale Journal of Law and Technology* 6 (2003–04), no. 174: 176–276.

14. There are both production and consumption externalities in digital environments. The quotation is from D. Evans, A. Hagiu, and R. Schmalensee, "A survey of the economic role of software platforms in computer-based industries," RIETI discussion paper 04-E-032, 2004. Assuming that the platform can manage the price structure, it has incentives to avoid many traditional anti-competitive strategies found in vertical markets, such as foreclosure. See Jean-Charles Rochet and Jean Tirole, "Two-sided markets—An overview," March 12, 2004, at http://faculty.haas.berkeley.edu. Thinking on multi-sided platforms overlaps with the Farrell-Weiser analysis of complementary efficiencies in their discussion of modularity and on the concept of complementary products. See Antonio Ladron de Guevara, Anita Elberse, and William P. Putsis, "Diffusion of Complementary Products With Network Effects: A Model and Application," April 24, 2007, at http://www.people.hbs.edu. For a critical analysis of the related "serial monopoly" hypothesis, see Gerald R. Faulhaber, "Bottlenecks and Bandwagons: Access Policy in the New Telecommunications," in *Handbook of Telecommunications Economics*, ed. S. Majumdar et al. (Elsevier, 2005), pp. 506–510.

15. On shifts in Microsoft's strategy, see Suzanne Scotchmer, *Innovation and Incentives* (MIT Press, 2004), pp. 302, 303.

16. Microsoft Windows was a multi-sided platform, but Windows, according to antitrust complaints, had an essential facility that gave it power over others, the incentive to exploit this advantage, and an active strategy to profit from the centrality of the platform. The litigation ultimately produced a major antitrust consent decree requiring changes in Microsoft's conduct. For a sophisticated review of the state of "predation" analysis, see Joseph Farrell and Michael L. Katz, "Competition or predation? Consumer coordination, strategic pricing and price floors in network markets," *Journal of Industrial Economics* 53 (2005), no. 2: 203–231.

17. Voice-over-Internet is commonly called VoIP. The abbreviation stands for "Voice-over-Internet Protocol."

18. Slash Lane, "Google iPhone usage shocks search giant," *AppleInsider* (http://www.appleinsider.com), February 14, 2008.

19. Christian Hogondorn, "Regulating vertical integration in broadband open access versus common carriage," *Review of Network Economics* 4 (2005), no. 1: 19–32.

20. Examples include the iPod Nano (which maintains a cloud store that the user chooses a subset to "sync" with the tiny Nano) and Amazon's Kindle (which comes pre-configured with your Amazon account information for easy access to additional content).

21. Rich Karlgaard coined the phrase in "The big cheap chance," *Forbes*, April 28, 2003. We have extended the categories covered by the phrase.

22. For summaries of changes in terminals that illustrate our interview data, see *The Economist*, November 30, 2006. See also "The phone of the future" and "What's a cellphone for?" *Wall Street Journal*, March 26, 2007.

23. RFIDs and sensor chips are lumped together for convenience sake. However, RFIDS are more driven by the economics of specialized printing while sensors respond directly to Moore's Law. A RFID's average cost (about 20 cents in 2006) was forecast at 10 cents by 2007. RFIDs allow trucks, trains, ships, and planes to be treated as moving warehouses by yielding precise information about the time and location of inventory. Smaller firms can operate global supply chains using companies that can outsource this function because of less expensive information networks provided by innovations like RFIDs. See "A Survey of Logistics," *The Economist*, June 17, 2006, p. 17. We learned of the one-cent goal in interviews, but note the skepticism of Eric Haseltine, "RFID: How the next big thing could be small," Strategic News Service, August 1, 2007.

24. To eliminate paperwork and speed delivery, a partnership of Heineken and IBM along with Dutch, British, and US custom agencies plans to use RFIDs combined with satellite and cellular networks to track and document shipments. The OECD estimates the current shipping system generates thirty different documents per cargo container. This effort would cut the number significantly. See Brad Smith, "IBM brews with Heineken," *Wireless Week*, October 27, 2006.

25. We thank Larry Smarr for this example.

26. John Hagel III and John Seely Brown, *The Only Sustainable Edge* (Harvard Business School Press, 2005), p. 12. In 1981, 256 megabytes of memory cost $200,000 (in 1981 dollars). In 2001, that capacity sold for less than $50 (in 2001 dollars). Source: http://www.littletechshoppe.com.

27. By 2009, household markets for storage of 500 gigabytes and above is expected to soar, led by the North American market. See "Consumer network storage: heavy hitters enter market" at http://www.instat.com.

28. For many in the developing world, the first experience of the Web will be on phones, not personal computers.

29. Lisa Endlich, *Optical Illusions* (Simon and Schuster, 2004). Dan Bieler estimates that the one European carrier's 1.5 billion Euro investment in next generation networks will save several hundred million dollars in operating expenses each year starting in 2010 ("KPN's next-generation network takes shape," at http://www.ovum.com).

30. Martin Cave, Luigi Prosperetti, and Chris Doyle, "Where are we going? Technologies, markets and long-range public policy issues in European communications," *Information Economics and Policy* 18 (2006): 242–255. The minimum capacity of broadband for home users will permit high-definition video downloading (around 12 megabits per second) and significant upstream speeds in the medium term.

31. Using 2004 cost data published by NTT, and allowing a 20% margin on NTT's average monthly revenue per user for fiber service, it would take NTT more than 8 years to recoup its capital costs. NTT's data for 2004 are reported at http://www.rbbtoday.com. Interviews in November 2007 confirmed the decreasing price of fiber to the curve. But NTT scaled back its plan to extend fiber to the home in 2007 by one third because it would take more than 8 years to recoup capital costs based on NTT pricing in 1997. Analysts question the financial viability of Verizon's residential fiber scheme. See "Big thinking on small caps: Cable's new technology roadmap," Bernstein Research, September 28, 2007.

32. "AT&T has done the deals. Now it needs results," *New York Times*, March 27, 2007.

33. In conversation François Bar suggested to us that functional characteristics like latency and reliability, not broadband speed, initially might be most crucial for ubiquitous networks.

34. According to interviews we conducted in 2007, early deployment of "battlefield of the future" systems being prepared by Boeing will require an average throughput capacity of 70 megabits per second to provide stable rich depictions of tactical developments for each unit in combat.

35. MSV, a new satellite system, combines satellite and terrestrial wide band wireless to serve these regions and target markets with broadband. An incumbent, Inmarsat, is planning a similar system.

36. On the John Deere tractor, see Jessie Scanlon, "The way we work: On the farm," *Wired*, May 2003, p. 40. Another example is the discussion of remote monitoring

of bridges and other infrastructure in the wake of the collapse of a bridge in Minnesota in July 2007.

37. Optimizing traffic may lead many of these sensors to be in local peer-to-peer relationships that do not lead to traffic on the general Internet backbone. See David D. Clark et al., "Making world (of communications) a different place," *ACM SIGCOMM Computer Communication Review* 35 (2005), no. 2: 91–96. Also see Exploring the Business and Social Impacts of Pervasive Computing, report on a conference organized jointly by IBM Zurich Research Laboratory, Swiss Re Centre for Global Dialogue, and TA-SWISS, 2006.

38. Krishna Nathanson, "From RFID to the Internet of things: Bridging the gap between research and business in the on demand era," presentation to EU IST Conference, 2006.

39. European Commission, "Radio frequency identification (RFID) in Europe: Steps toward a policy framework," COM(2007) 96 final and [SEC(2007) 312].

40. The motes currently operate on the 900-megahertz and 2.4-gigahertz unlicensed bands (source: http://www.dustnetworks.com). Many sensors can now do a preliminary assessment of the data to see if performance is within acceptable parameters. A "smart sensor," according to the IEEE, "provides extra functions beyond those necessary for generating a correct representation of the sensed quantity." See F. L. Lewis, "Wireless Sensor Networks," in *Smart Environments*, ed. D. Cook and S. Das (Wiley, 2004); David Culler, Deborah Estrin, and Mani Srivastava, "Overview of sensor networks," *IEEE Computer* 37 (2004), no. 8: 41–49.

41. Neil Gershenfeld and Danny Cohen, "Internet 0: Interdevice internetworking—End-to-end modulation for embedded networks," *Circuits and Devices Magazine* 22, no. 5 (2006): 48–55.

42. CalIT2 director Larry Smarr notes that this is essentially a dedicated light wave, a revolution in architecture compared to the shared system of the Internet. It represents the ability of a packet-switched network to create a virtual circuit switched route on demand. See http://www.nlr.net.

43. Gershenfeld and Cohen, "Internet 0."

44. Launched in 1984 at 56 kilobits per second, it reached 1.5 megabits per second in 1988 and topped 44 megabytes per second (a T-3 capacity) in 1992. Japan and Korea deployed ADSL for consumers at 45 megabits per second by 2005. Histories of NSFNET are available at http://communication.ucsd.edu and at http://www.livinginternet.com.

45. The architecture of the Internet may have to evolve to take full advantage of the transmission capacity. See Geoff Huston, "Gigabit TCP," *Internet Protocol Journal* (http://www.cisco.com) 9, no. 2.

46. Data use now exceeds voice use on the network. Data use includes surges in peak demand tied to peer-to-peer media applications downloaded by human users. Still, there is a limit to how many data search requests and YouTube videos anybody can absorb. Although "human in the loop" traffic will be important, new forms of "last stop is human" and "no human in the loop" applications will emerge to drive data traffic. Pilot deployments of the latest network-centric war-fighting applications suggest that large data requirements will emerge in which machines generate traffic without humans in the loop at all times. New traffic management systems have car GPS systems provide real-time feedback to traffic monitors on congestion and speeds that is then aggregated and displayed to individual drivers.

47. Figure 2.6 extrapolates from 2005, but interviews in 2007 corroborate the continuing trend.

48. This is a central observation of James W. Cortada's study of the use of ICT. See especially *The Digital Hand*, volume 2 (Oxford University Press, 2005).

49. In contrast, in the IBM mainframe era and in the Windows era, developers wrote applications designed to run in a specific operating environment. Thus, Win32 APIs were strategic for Microsoft and generated huge backward compatibility efforts so that no applications "broke" as Windows upgrades were released. More focused standards, like SIP for Internet Messaging and efforts to deliver "Services Oriented Architecture" inside the corporate firewall also contributed to more modular software infrastructure and solutions.

50. "Web 2.0" is an imprecise term that refers to the growing ability of the Web to support interactive user communities through such arrangements as social networks, hosted services, and wikis. Another key feature is that mash-ups use content from multiple sources to create a new service. Examples can be found at www .programmableweb.com and at http://googlemapsmania.blogspot.com. Also see "The mash-ups will let companies get creative with data," *Financial Times*, September 5, 2006.

51. A description of RSS is available at http://en.wikipedia.org.

52. The best-known ad network is Google's AdSense, but there are others (Yahoo, Microsoft, and various specialized networks), and there is a vibrant start-up community in "ad networks" for more specialized applications and end points (i.e., mobile). At a press conference on October 10, 2006, Sun Microsystems cited Second Life as an example of what it is now "calling the Participation Age, and the next evolution of the network as the computer."

53. Enthusiasts argue that the open-source communities lower the cost of entry barriers for operating systems, particularly through the creation and use of Linux. Some Linux applications offer cheaper and easier delivery. Yet as of 2006 Linux was more important for cannibalizing the pre-existing Unix market than challenging

proprietary software. Still, open-source models inevitably will impact platforms and applications development. See Steven Weber, *The Success of Open Source* (Harvard University Press, 2004).

54. On "Slingbox Mobile," see http://us.slingmedia.com.

55. Spencer Reiss, "Here comes trouble," *Wired*, February 2007: 94–99.

56. Anita Elberse, "A taste for obscurity: An individual-level examination of 'long tail' consumption," working paper 08-008, Harvard Business School, 2007.

57. Some analysts claim that Google is pessimistic about having effective search algorithms for video, so its purchase of YouTube was a switch in direction for search engines. It will rely on social networking to "search" video. See "Two Kings Get Together," *The Economist*, October 14, 2006, pp. 67–68. On a different approach to people-search, see www.spock.com.

Chapter 4

1. Don Tapscott and Anthony Williams believe that IBM primarily seeks to leverage its programmers by embracing open-source innovations. This may be a collateral benefit, but neutralizing rivals at the customer interface could be a powerful driver. See Tapscott and Williams, *Wikinomics* (Portfolio Press, 2006).

2. In 2008 a senior executive of a major competitor to IBM in this market showed us an analysis of his firm's margins (about 7% on sales) and their analysis of likely returns for IBM and other rivals. His point was that desired levels of profitability came off items like hardware, not most of the systems services and integration businesses. This confirmed other industry interviews in the preceding year.

3. "Good enough" refers to a line of thinking that argues that most end users only require some small subset of the features and capabilities delivered in current (or past) software solutions—suggesting that there is little need to upgrade to the latest or more complex offerings because that what users are already using is "good enough" to meet most needs. On the "good enough" point, see Steven Baker, "Why good enough is good enough," *Business Week*, September 3, 2007. Industry interviews confirmed that this is IBM's view—even in areas where they cooperate with leading Web-based vendors they view these primarily as short-term opportunities to learn but not as real threats to more complex requirements of critical IBM customers.

4. The mobile phone handset business is the closest to the fashion industry today. For example, in 2005 the fastest-selling phone in the UK during the Christmas season was the Motorola Razr in pink.

5. In 2008, for example, Microsoft announced the Internet Explorer 8 would adhere to important Internet standards, something that had not been the case in previous versions.

6. The Cloud also changes the economics of distribution in ways that help smaller firms. "Software as a Service," an alternative to packaged software, gradually emerged as a driver in enterprise ICT because of the ease of deployment and management. No new client code is necessary to manage and upgrade it because the data and application logic reside primarily on a Cloud server.

7. Amazon has a strategy that invests in building innovative infrastructure (its development tools are prized in the software community) so as to build an ecology that can sustain rapidly updated services in a state-of-the-art e-commerce marketplace. Amazon resells its infrastructure and development tools to others, thereby defraying costs. Amazon's Web services bandwidth now exceeds the bandwidth used for all of its global commercial portals—an indication of significant size, according to Josh Catone, who argues that the primary customers are small to medium-size Web firms ("Amazon Web services: Bigger than Amazon," at http://www.readwriteweb.com).

8. Level 3 was the most successful of the first-generation carriers with different financial and technology models. We think that hybrid network models will expand if policy is favorable. See Robert Cringely, "Oh Brother Where Art Thou?" at http://www.pbs.org.

9. Sources: interviews by the authors with various industry sources, 2007 and 2008.

10. See "Apex code: The World's First On-Demand Programming Language," at http://www.salesforce.com.

11. Analysts use the analogy to the fashion industry to explain why Motorola's Razr V3 phone declined from a status symbol sold at $500 to a $30 commodity in slightly more than 2 years ("Cellphone envy lays Motorola low," New York Times, February 3, 2007). It was no longer unique and fresh. Industry interviews in 2007 revealed that Motorola was losing money net on the Razr.

12. For a discussion of the supply chain for personal computers, see "Inside Lenovo's search for the perfect laptop," Business Week, February 14, 2008.

13. Even though we think that modularity encourages multi-sided platforms, Apple specifically rejected this approach for the iPod. Apple made a strategy decision to make it "one-sided" by controlling every aspect of the platform and thus beat rivals using a multi-sided approach.

14. In 2007 the Norwegian consumer ombudsman declared iPod's DRM scheme illegal because it restricted the hardware that could be used to play legally obtained music. Some speculate that Steve Jobs' public protests against the insistence on DRM schemes by record companies is to show that content providers force the restrictions on Apple. See http://www.buzzbums.com/buzz/norway-declares-itunes-illegal; "Europe cool to Apple's suggestions on music," New York Times, February 8, 2007.

15. The labels may state that it is acceptable to move a user's iTunes Store music collection from an iPod to a competing device, but Apple still must grant permission. This may be one reason that EMI and Universal are moving away from a DRM to an MP3 format. Otherwise Apple could control the retail channel so that as users bought more Apple music the cost to switch to a competitor's device soars. We thank Cory Doctorow for this point. The rapid adaptation to the iPod strategy by the record labels, however, contributes to the potential of new rivals to iPod. We thank Cory Ondrejka for this observation.

16. Michael Borrus, *Competing for Control* (Ballinger 1988); Dieter Ernst, "The new mobility of knowledge: Digital information systems and global flagship networks," in *Digital Formations*, ed. R. Latham and S. Sassen (Princeton University Press, 2005).

17. ODMs are just one part of what is now a distributed and complex value chain that delivers almost all components necessary for new entry. Consider the highly specialized, proprietary technology shops that design components for systems producers and systems users. These companies control system segments characterized by fast innovation, deep intellectual property, and extreme specialization. Some firms, like Qualcomm, are pure specialists. Others players are divisions of larger conglomerates like Samsung's operations on large display systems. Samsung may choose to control its own display panel manufacturing, but this is a strategic choice, not a necessity for a specialized innovation strategy. Qualcomm is a purer example than Samsung of a technology input specialist because it does not also sell end-product systems.

18. For a complementary line of analysis, see John Zysman, "Creating value in a digital era: How do wealthy nations stay wealthy?" in *How Revolutionary Was the Revolution?* ed. J. Zysman and A. Newman (Stanford University Press, 2006).

19. Integration creates network effects and lock-in. Even cheating on digital rights management is easier in the iPod-to-iPod transfer world. Only a technological or business model shift will knock off a dominant leader that holds 80% of the US digital music market. Ad services, like Universal's SpiralFrog, offer one approach, but its users must renew downloads monthly on Universal's system. In Asia the growth of mobile phone music systems may rival Apple through cell phones. See "Apple's sound strategy can keep the iPod as number one," *Financial Times*, September 2–3, 2006.

20. See "NBC, Fox launching video site Hulu.com" at http://www.usatoday.com.

21. The Big Three suppliers (Nokia, Ericsson-Sony, and Motorola) in the $70 billion handset market (2006 estimate) were critical to the major carriers' innovation and marketing plans. They dominated a complex design and manufacturing business. But original design manufacturers like BenQ, Arima, and Compal of Taiwan are

eroding their edge. They supply Ericsson, Motorola, Siemens-Sony, and Toshiba. The ODMs' market share grew from 9% in 2002 to about 30% in 2005. Customized ODM phones for Orange allowed tighter hardware-applied service integration for Orange in France and raised revenues by $18 per month. ODMs also allowed Microsoft to circumvent the Big-3 backed Symbian operating system. Since mobiles have key open standards at the network layer, the industry may be heading to a model like that of the automobile industry, where a "system integrator" like Honda may combine horizontal layers of value added so no player dominates any layer. See "Mobile phones battling for the palm of your hand," *The Economist*, May 4, 2004, pp. 71–73.

22. These include desktop computers, cellular phones set up for television or, much anticipated, "free" ad-funded hardware.

23. Modularity also allows new online ways to sell and place ads and permits more rapid choices of dynamic delivery platforms. A US trade association earmarked $50 million to set up such a market for ads. See "Silicon Valley prepares to take the revolution offline," *Financial Times*, May 24, 2006.

24. "In raw world of sex movies, high definition could be a view too real," *New York Times*, January 22, 2007.

25. Hal R. Varian, Joseph Farrell, and Carl Shapiro, *The Economics of Information Technology—An Introduction* (Cambridge University Press, 2004), pp. 74–77.

26. For Apple's position, see http://www.apple.com/hotnews/thoughtsonmusic/.

27. For example, the Indian TV and film industry is experiencing a golden era. The potential for local storylines and content serve a growing national audience—even if a large part of this "national audience" is part of a global diaspora. See "In India, the golden age of television is now," *New York Times*, January 11, 2007.

28. See *Personal, Portable, Pedestrian*, ed. M. Ito et al. (MIT Press, 2005).

29. Source: http://www.video-games-survey.com.

30. "World of Warcraft Reaches New Milestone: 10 Million Subscribers," at http://www.blizzard.com.

31. Among US Internet users, 79% (100 million) use social network sites. The Korean market is growing at 45% annually. See "Korean site tackles might of MySpace," *Financial Times*, September 1, 2006, p.16.

32. YouTube had more than 83 million unique visits in July 2006, an increase of nearly 2200% over July 2005. The second largest site for video was iTunes, with about 56 million visits but a much lower annual growth rate ("Wal-Mart sets stage for digital action," *Financial Times*, September 13, 2006, p. 17). In early 2007, YouTube accounted for about 43% of all video views on the Internet ("Xeep Video on the Net," at http://www.xeep.net).

33. Traditional television programs devote substantial time to support user forums where community content about the show becomes part of its value. Fan magazines are not new. What is new is the ease and scale of consumer feedback and complementary programming.

34. New media face substantial monetization challenges. The management of intellectual property rights on YouTube remains controversial; see, e.g., "Viacom tells YouTube: Hands off," *New York Times*, February 3, 2007.

35. Chris Anderson, *The Long Tail* (Hyperion, 2006).

36. Korean subscribers to SK Communications' Cyworld number 18 million, or 40% of the population. More than 90% of all users in their twenties are registered on Cyworld which reported sales of $168 million and a profit of $21 million in 2005. It generates 80% of its revenue from sales of digital items decorating its members' home pages. It launched ventures in China, Japan, the US, and Taiwan, and established a joint ventures to enter Europe. Global expansion required customization of the avatars and navigation tools. Cyworld withdrew from Europe in March 2008, citing cultural differences. Immediately, Korea's Pandora TV, the dominant firm for video sharing in Korea (about 10 times more Web hits than YouTube in Korea) announced plans to launch in Japan, China, and the US with local language services. See "Korean site tackles might of MySpace." *Financial Times*, September 1, 2006; "Pandora sees hope in global labyrinth," *Korea Times*, March 13, 2008.

37. On March 18, 2007, Eric Schmidt, CEO of Google, suggested that language translation programming was likely to be a disruptive force in the coming years. See "Eric Schmidt, CEO of Google, on iinnovate" at http://www.youtube.com.

38. Source: www.entertainmentasia.com.

39. John Hagel traces the origins of the term to a 1971 article in which Herbert Simon noted that "a wealth of information creates a poverty of attention" (Hagel, "The economics of attention," at http://edgeperspectives.typepad.com).

40. Interviews with industry participants suggest that the rates paid by most standard ad networks cannot deliver the ad revenue required to build and deliver more sophisticated online applications.

41. Michael Arrington. "These crazy musicians still think they should get paid for recorded music," at http://www.techcrunch.com.

42. On aggregation, see "How to create your own TV channel," *Business 2.0*, February 12, 2007.

43. We thank Paul Maritz for his observations.

44. It also changes the architecture of corporate ICT networks. See David Strom, "How instant messaging is transforming the enterprise network," *Internet Protocol Journal* (http://www.cisco.com) 9, no. 2.

45. See Robert McMillan, "Corporate data slips out via Google calendar," at http://www.computerworld.com.

46. GPS on phones will allow routine updating of plans. In 2007, Nokia announced plans to embed GPS in all cell phones ("Nokia plans to install GPS chips in all handsets," at http://www.dailytechrag.com). Nokia is pushing the idea of "augmented reality," which uses GPS to locate a building and bring up third-party information on its "content" ("What's New in Wireless," *Wall Street Journal*, March 26, 2007). See also "Nokia to buy Navteq for $8.1 billion," *New York Times*, November 16, 2007.

47. http://www.motoqwiki.com/index.php?title=Motorola_Q_Wiki.

48. On Yahoo's purchase on online applications provider Zimbra, see "Yahoo buys e-mail software firm Zimbra" at http://www.news.com.

49. There are already rules governing some aspects of privacy in the workplace, most notably EU Framework Data Protection Directive (95/46/EC). The Directive on Privacy and Electronic Communications (2002/58/EC). The latter requires an opt-in system by users before direct marketers with email can solicit them. This could be handled by a PNP. Social networking data, another element of a PNP, has also drawn European regulatory attention (EurActiv, "EU Web security watchdog sets sights on MySpace," at http://www.euractiv.com).

50. We thank Michael Borrus for suggesting this phrasing.

51. See "China Mobile's hot signal," *Business Week*, January 25, 2007.

52. Anderson, *The Long Tail*.

53. We thank Cory Doctorow for this insight. He also cites the parallel case of the London transport system which "now charges a 100% premium to ride the bus on an anonymous cash fare, and will not sell" passengers a weekly or monthly pass unless they agree to use an RFID card that can be used to keep track their travel forever.

54. The movement to online medical records raises substantial privacy challenges, as HIPAA compliance rules are not required once individuals have granted permission to non-medical providers to store and share their data. See "Google Health makes its pitch" at http://healthcare.zdnet.com.

55. Eric Haseltine, "RFID: How the next big thing could be small," Strategic News Service, August 1, 2007.

56. Important privacy and related issues must be resolved to make this a reality.

57. Wikipedia defines "bleeding edge" as "a term that refers to technology that is so new (and thus, presumably, not perfected) that the user is required to risk reduc-

tions in stability and productivity in order to use it. It also refers to the tendency of the latest technology to be extremely expensive."

58. David E. Culler and Hans Mulder, "Smart sensors to network the world." *Scientific American* 290 (2004), no. 6: 85–91.

59. Markus Endler, "Large scale body sensing for infectious disease control," position paper submitted to Sentient Future Competition, Department of Informatics, Pontifícia Universidade Católica do Rio de Janeiro, 2005.

60. Haseltine, "RFID: How the next big thing could be small."

61. Robert Litan, "Catching the Web in a net of neutrality," http://www .washingtonpost.com.

62. Tapscott and Williams, *Wikinomics*, pp. 24–27, 163–168.

63. These may include electric load management forecasts, pricing the cost of an auto trip on new toll roads, or water systems in drought-stricken countries.

64. Report from NSF Sponsored Workshop, Environmental Cyberinfrastructure Needs for Distributed Networks, Scripps Institution of Oceanography, August 12–14, 2003. See Tim Wark et al., "Transforming agriculture through pervasive wireless sensor networks," *IEEE Pervasive Computing* 6 (2007), no. 2: 50–57.

65. Von Hippel, *Democratizing Innovation*, chapters 8 and 11; William J. Baumol, Robert E. Litan, and Carl J. Schramm, *Good Capitalism, Bad Capitalism, and the Economics of Growth and Prosperity* (Yale University Press, 2007).

66. There are many other challenges in these countries, especially the lack of skilled IT labor forces and laws that impair ICT-focused business. But this is not the focus of our study. For an overview, see Ernest J. Wilson III, *The Information Revolution and Developing Countries* (MIT Press, 2004).

67. Source: interviews conducted by the authors.

68. Source: interviews conducted by one of the authors in 2005 and 2006.

69. See Memorandum and Order of AT&T Inc and BellSouth Corporation, FCC 06-189, December 29, 2006, paragraph 36. See also Simon Wilkie Ex Parte on behalf of ACTEL June 14 2005, FCC dockets 05-65 and 05-75.

70. In November 2007, Bernstein Research estimated that even on triple-play customers Verizon runs a negative present value on fiber to the home. Strategists for a major fiber-optic carrier suggested the pattern of cable and Bell upgrade strategies to us.

71. Joseph Farrell and Philip Weiser, "Modularity, vertical integration and open access policies: Towards a convergence of antitrust and regulation in the Internet age," *Harvard Journal of Law and Technology* 17 (2003), no. 1: 85, 100–105; Eli Noam,

"How telecom is becoming a cyclical industry, and what to do about it," working paper, Columbia University, 2002; Cave et al., "Where are we going?"

72. The European road traffic system is an example of a vertically integrated solution that relies on low turnover infrastructure and a narrow solution. Turnover is low because transaction costs are high. Building agreement on a system is politically complex. Initially, competition may be inefficient in many comparable niches. See Peter F. Cowhey and Jonathan David Aronson, "Wireless standards and applications—Industrial strategies and government policy," Annenberg Research Network on International Communication, 2004.

73. Although asset specific solutions for business processes may be stable in particular niches, controlling an expensive, hard to replace facility may not be enough to guarantee this result. Consider the situation of telecom carriers that still control local transmission facilities. Despite this control, prices of voice packages are decreasing and likely will continue to do so. The reasons are that there is substitution among modes of communications to provide the specific user service (a phone call) and that multi-sided platform economics makes the phone call into just one of several uses and prices on the platform. However, new entrants leverage modular software and the installed capital stock to deliver tailored multi-sided platform offerings quickly. For a general treatment, see Varian et al., *Economics of Information Technology*, pp. 21–28.

74. There are ways of attacking complex legacy systems. For example, the software code for telephone switches was costly to create. Once established, the code that permitted reliable phone service was huge and difficult for competitors to understand. Vendors still sell this equipment at huge discounts in anticipation of customer lock-in for service and upgrades because it was so hard to crack the code. Today more powerful computational devices offer service applications built on relatively open software standards, like the marriage of routers to VoIP software, thereby pressuring traditional producers of network equipment.

75. We thank Robert Pepper for pointing out the parallel between the Ofcom and FCC concerns. Holders of key content, like ESPN, may prefer to make an exclusive deal with the dominant network. So the government cannot bank on some form of countervailing strategy on the content side. See Christian Hogondorn and Ka Yat Yuen, "Platform competition with must have components," working paper, Wesleyan University, 2006.

76. Lawrence Lessig, *Free Culture* (Penguin, 2004); Jonathan D. Aronson, "Protecting International Intellectual Property Rights," in *Power, Interdependence, and Nonstate Actors in World Politics*, ed. H. Milner and A. Moravcsik (Princeton University Press, 2008).

77. An early exploration was examined by Anne Wells Branscomb in *Who Owns Information?* (Basic Books, 1994). Also see Viktor Mayer-Schönberger, "Beyond copy-

right: Managing information rights with DRM," *Denver University Law Review* 84 (2006), no. 1: 181–198.

Chapter 5

1. Europe taken as a whole is a larger market than the United States. Although there is unity in some spheres, others remain contentious.

2. Moore's Law focuses on silicon capacity, throwing little light on how semiconductor firms entice customers to their more powerful chips. See Amar Bhidé, "Venturesome consumption, innovation and globalisation," presented at CESifo and Centre on Capitalism and Society conference, Venice, 2006.

3. Hundt, *You Say You Want a Revolution*, pp. 134–136.

4. For a typical list of examples including 3G and RFIDs, see "Changing China—Will China's Technology Standards Reshape Your Industry?" Global Technology, Media and Telecommunications Industry Group. Ernst and Young.

5. Scott Kennedy, "The political economy of standards coalitions: Explaining China's involvement in high-tech standards wars," *Asia Policy* 2 (2006): 41–62.

6. Calculated from data provided on pp. 76–78 of OECD, *ICT Report 2007*.

7. Accounting for these markets is imprecise. See Andrew Bartels and Andrew Parker, "European enterprise IT spending 2006 to 2007: Looking up, still lagging behind the US," Forrester Research, October 2, 2006.

8. Sources: "Digital Planet 2004" (September 2005) and "Digital Planet 2006" (WITSA, May 2006); data provided by Global Insight.

9. Based on table of "gross domestic expenditures on R&D" in OECD Factbook 2007: Economic, Environmental and Social Statistics.

10. Data on the capital stock and the role of US multinationals are from Nick Bloom, Raffaella Sadun, and John Van Reen, "Americans do IT better," Stanford Institute for Economic Policy Research Policy Brief, 2007, available at http://siepr .stanford.edu.

11. Source: http://ww.jetro.go.jp.

12. We thank Cory Doctorow for pointing out that the rules governing liability for network content are constantly being contested and that an inappropriate set of rules could offset other US advantages in regards to content markets.

13. "US jumps to 24th in worldwide broadband penetration," at http://www .websiteoptimization.com. However, the 23 higher-rated countries include Monaco, Macau, Guernsey, and Luxembourg.

14. OECD Directorate for Science, Technology and Industry, "OECD broadband statistics to December 2006," at http://www.oecd.org.

15. "Mobile phones battling for the palm of your hand," *The Economist*, May 4, 2004, pp. 71–73.

16. "Mobile set to become a trillion dollar industry in 2008," at http://www .cellular-news.com.

17. Mobile video reaches 2% of US subscribers, which is dwarfed by Japan and South Korea. In-Stat predicts that by 2010 mobile video will reach $3.1 billion market in Asia. The major US carriers are now launching video services on large scale. Source: "What's new in wireless," *Wall Street Journal*, March 26, 2007.

18. Information and Communication Technologies, *OECD Communications Outlook 2007*, p. 76.

19. Manuel Castells noted to us that the language of national competition is more and more outdated. Global network competition matters greatly now and will only increase. Still we believe that for reasons of history and structure the US will remain the critical player in efforts to shape global agreements at least until 2025.

20. Merrill Lynch, "Beyond subscriber growth," *Global Wireless Matrix, 3Q 2007* (December 24, 2007), pp. 54, 57.

21. Reuters, "In 2008 there are close to 300 million subscribers to 3G technologies worldwide," March 3, 2008.

22. Interviews with executives of wireless start-ups and venture capitalists, San Diego and Silicon Valley, fall 2006.

23. Although the broader obligation to interconnect with any network also was challenged, the primary focus of concern was unbundling. See Howard Shelanski, "Adjusting regulation to competition," *Yale Journal on Regulation* 24 (2007): 56–105.

24. Analysts associated with the Democratic Party, including Rob Atkinson, president of the Information Technology and Innovation Foundation, eventually came to praise this restraint. For a sample of opposing views, see *Antitrust Policy and Vertical Restraints*, ed. R. Hahn (AEI-Brookings, 2006).

25. After accounting for the largest users of ICT infrastructures (e.g., the Fortune 500), the level of competitive provision of fiber decreases significantly. See Simon Wilkie Ex Parte on behalf of ACTEL, June 14 2005m FCC dockets 05-65 and 05-75.

26. At the end of 2007, the 19 largest US cable and telephone firms, accounting for 94% of the broadband market, had 61.9 million subscribers. Telcos had 28.4 millions subscribers and cable companies had 33.5 million broadband subscribers. Source:

Multichannel News (http://www.multichannel.com), "Broadband connects with 8.5 million US customers in 2007," March 3, 2008.

27. Shelanski, "Adjusting regulation to competition"; Mark L. Del Bianco, "Voices past: The present and future of VoIP regulation," *ComLawConspectus* 14 (2006): 365–401.

28. Other technologies, including the use of electric power lines for communications transmission, were highlighted but had less commercial focus than wireless.

29. A related goal was to permit "underlay" networks that used idle capacity in licensed bands, including the "guard bands" that buffered a band from interference. This was accomplished through the use of "smart terminals" and some government mandates of best practices (performance requirements) for devices. See Neuchterlein and Weiser, *Digital Crossroads*. On the debate over the use of white space on television demands, see Pierre de Vries, "Populating the vacant channels the case for allocating unused spectrum in the digital TV bands to unlicensed use for broadband and wireless innovation," working paper 14, New America Foundation, 2006.

30. The FCC retained network sharing and interconnection obligations for traditional telephone networks and ADSL. See "Appropriate framework for broadband access to the Internet over wireline facilities," FCC docket 02-33 September 23, 2005.

31. "Microsoft urged the FCC to allocate additional spectrum below 2 GHz and at 5 GHz for unlicensed broadband uses. It argued that such spectrum could supplement cable and DSL services and 'jump-start' the creation of competitive wireless US broadband networks. Cingular, Cisco, the Consumer Federation of America, Ericsson, the Information Technology Industry Council, Motorola, Proxim, the Rural Telecommunications Group, and the Wireless Ethernet Compatibility Alliance also expressed support for additional unlicensed spectrum. In their joint reply comments, the New America Foundation, Consumers Union, et al. state that there is tremendous support in the record for the allocation of additional frequency bands of spectrum for unlicensed use, particularly to facilitate broadband wireless networking." Federal Communications Commission, Spectrum Policy Task Force, "Report of the unlicensed devices and experimental licenses." Working Group 11, November 15, 2002.

32. This assumes that some technological issues involving VoIP and wireless systems are overcome. See John Blau, "T-Mobile CEO: VOIP will have no major impact," *InfoWorld* (http://www.infoworld.com), February 13, 2007.

33. FCC, Broadband Wireless Network as an Information Service, March 22, 2007.

34. Jon M. Peha, "Emerging technology and spectrum policy reform," ITU Workshop on Market Mechanisms for Spectrum Management, Geneva, 2007. See also Thomas Hazlett, "Assigning property rights to radio spectrum users: Why did FCC

license auctions take 67 years?" *Journal of Law and Economics* 41 (1998), no. 2: 529–578; Yochai Benkler, "Overcoming agoraphobia: Building the commons of the digitally networked environment," *Harvard Journal of Law and Technology* 11 (1997–98): 287; De Vries, "Populating the vacant channels"; William Lehr, "Economic case for dedicated unlicensed spectrum below 3 GHz," available at http://itc.mit.edu.

35. There is well-established precedent for this approach as well. Part 15 spectrum is "unlicensed." Anyone who complies with the conditions of operations can transmit and operate in this spectrum with appropriate certified devices that do not cause harmful interference to others. They also must accept interference. Operators in Part 15 spectrum obtain no superior rights; while anyone may use the spectrum, no one may exclude others from using the spectrum. In terms of property rights, this spectrum is a "commons." Source: "Wireless:: WiFi: Unlicensed: Part 15," at http://www.cybertelecom.org.

36. The most important legislation came when a Republican Congress and a Democratic president extended immunity from liability for content posted on websites to Web portals under section 230(c) of the Communications Decency Act of 1996. This mirrored the broad protections that common carriers in telecom traditionally enjoyed. For liberal Democrats this was free speech. For conservative Republican this was defense of the marketplace from litigation. For both it catered to the virtually unanimous demands of the Internet commerce industry.

37. Robert D. Atkinson and Phillip J. Weiser, "A 'Third Way' on Network Neutrality," Information Technology and Innovation Foundation, 2006. Available at http://www.itif.org.

38. Cisco is prominent in this arena, but other companies and equipment segments also are pursuing these strategies.

39. Christian Hogondorn, "Regulating vertical integration in broadband open access versus common carriage," *Review of Network Economics* 4 (2005), no. 1: 19–32.

40. "Video road hogs stir fear of internet traffic jam," *New York Times*, March 13, 2008.

41. Matthew Lasar, "Comcast, net neutrality advocates clash at FCC hearing." *ars technica* (http://arstechnica.com), February 25, 2008. The perception of the issue might have been quite different if Comcast had waited until customer complaints about slow service mounted before they acted to filter content.

42. "Comcast paid to pack FCC hearing," *New York Post*, February 27, 2008.

43. Mark Cooper ("The Economics of Collaborative Production in the Spectrum Commons," working paper, Stanford University Center for Internet and Society, 2006) argues that this opens the way to a peer-to-peer community and policy coalition to gain the benefits of collaborative productive. Our point is narrower. Regard-

less of battles over the precise contours of copyright or peer-to-peer video distribution, mainstream, IPR-oriented industries have bet on a new ICT infrastructure model.

44. The Open Internet Coalition does not object to tiered pricing for consumers based on bandwidth. Google, Amazon, Yahoo, eBay, and IAC finance this broad coalition in support of network neutrality.

45. "[T]he FCC's Policy Statement fails to address a critical issue: discrimination by broadband providers against unaffiliated Internet content, services, and applications. ... [AT&T] 'shall not discriminate in their carriage and treatment of Internet traffic based on the source, destination or ownership of such traffic.' ... [This would] prohibit tiering schemes that impose additional surcharges on Web companies to 'deliver' Internet content. ..." (comments of The Open Internet Coalition, "In the Matter of AT&T Inc and BellSouth Corporation applications for approval of transfer of control," FCC WC docket 06-74, filed October 24, 2006. This proposal allowed for network prioritization based on type of traffic and nondiscriminatory network management. Also see Kodak Corporation, "Net neutrality: Principles," in Advisory Committee to the Congressional Internet Caucus, Briefing Book, June 8, 2006.

46. Testimony of Gary R. Bachula, Vice President, Internet2, Before the US Senate Committee on Commerce, Science and Transportation, Hearing on Net Neutrality, February 7, 2006. Bachula endorsed a national goal of 100 megabits per second in 5 years and 1 gigabit per second in 10 years for households. Tim Berners-Lee and Larry Lessig were among the prominent researchers. For a critique of relying solely on bandwidth, see Michael Kleeman, "Point of disconnect: Internet traffic and the US communications infrastructure," policy brief, Center for Pacific Economies, University of California, San Diego, 2007.

47. The Department of Justice had approved the merger without conditions. Because one commissioner disqualified himself to avoid the appearance of a conflict of interest, Republicans were unable to muster the three votes needed for FCC approval.

48. The House Commerce Committee Chair and Senators Byron Dorgan (D) and Olympia Snowe (R) introduced bills backing net neutrality. See Marc S. Martin, Henry L. Judy, and Benjamin Oxley, "Update: Net neutrality back on the political agenda," *E-Commerce Law and Policy*, January 2007: 10–11.

49. Former FCC Chairman Michael Powell promoted these goals as the "Four Freedoms" of networking. The fourth freedom was the customer's right to obtain full information on the service plan. The FCC advanced these goals in a non-binding policy statement. Nicholas Economides questions the likelihood of these competitive risks in "The economics of the Internet backbone," in *Handbook of Telecommunications Economics*, volume 2, ed. S. Majumdar et al. (North-Holland, 2005).

50. This is Carterfone revisited. (The Carterphone case was the policy battle on connecting third-party terminals to the AT&T network that in 1968 led the FCC to

open the way to connect non-AT&T devices to the network.) See Gerald Brock, *Telecommunication Policy for the Information Age* (Harvard University Press, 1994), pp. 84–85.

51. TechNet, a coalition of tech CEOs, strongly urged the FCC to endorse non-discrimination on access to content and websites. It also argued that broadband networks should be required to enable websites to prioritize delivery of their content according to the plans of websites. But it supports tiered pricing and other network options to enhance the delivery of services and finance the network. Large users in the financial industry are cautious about committing on net neutrality. (Source: http://www.hillnews.com)

52. For strong evidence that competitive local exchange carriers (CLECs) differentiated themselves from incumbents, see Shane Greenstein and Michael Mezzo, "The role of differentiation strategy in local telecommunication entry and market evolution: 1999–2002," *Journal of Industrial Economics* 54 (2006), no. 3: 323–350.

53. Marguerite Reardon, "FCC approves AT&T-BellSouth merger," CNET News.com, December 29, 2006. After months of partisan deadlock, the Federal Communications Commission approves the merger valued at roughly $86 billion.

54. Scott Moritz ("Cisco Shreds 'Net Neutrality,'" TheStreet.com, January 4, 2007) suggested that Cisco decided that the FCC principles did not block its network security offerings that would prioritize packets after deep packet inspection.

55. John Blau, *InfoWorld*, February 2007.

56. Timothy Wu, "Wireless Carterfone," *International Journal of Communication* 1 (2007), February: 389–426. Also see Skype, "Petition to confirm a consumer's right to use Internet communications software and attach devices to wireless networks," submitted to FCC February 20, 2007.

57. In many countries, consumers routinely buy a phone and the SIM card of their preferred service provider as two different purchasing decisions.

58. Janice Obuchowski (R) and Reed Hundt (D) were the bipartisan team's leaders. See Comments of Frontline Wireless LLC, FCC Public Safety proceeding, February 26, 2007. The company failed in these efforts, and in January 2008 it went out of business.

59. Frontline's proposal contained detailed provisions about preemption of the private network capacity for public safety when necessary. It also allowed the licensee to make secondary, preemptive use of the public-safety network.

60. There were also disputes about the FCC auction rules. If not properly designed, auctions can allow incumbents to foreclose new entrants by making it easier for incumbents to bid a premium to foreclose entrants. Critics of the rules claimed that the FCC rules enabled the foreclosure strategy although FCC economists try to avoid

such risks. We based this section on discussions with participants involved in the auction.

61. This policy episode also shows the risks of policy innovation. The FCC set a high minimum bid for the winner to show that this was not a political giveaway. Then, the 2008 auction began just as the credit market meltdown took place. Frontline could not secure its financing and declared bankruptcy. No other bidder was willing to meet the FCC's reserve price.

62. Anne Broache, "Google lobbies for open wireless networks," CNET Networks (http://news.com), June 14, 2007; Elizabeth Woyke, "Google likely out, and happy," www.forbes.com, February 6, 2008.

63. See Farrell and Weiser, "Modularity, vertical integration and open access policies," *Harvard Journal of Law and Technology* 17 (2003), no. 1: 85, 100–105. Dominant firms may value long-term profits from maintaining their market power; see Dennis W. Carlton and Michael Waldman, "Why tie an essential good?" in *Antitrust Policy and Vertical Restraints*, ed. R. Hahn.

64. In *Digital Crossroads* Neuchterlein and Weiser show why pricing freedom may not lead to the predicted behavior of efficient network sharing, but pricing irrationalities make the problem less tractable.

65. Someone will profit. VeriSign, for example, is building a business by operating the Object Name Server, the new root directory for Electronic Product Codes, that is vital to the growth of RFIDs as a commercial application.

66. Simon Moores, "Prepare for some 'digital tension,'" September 27, 2006, at http://silicon.com.

67. Bill Gates, testimony before US Senate Committee on Health, Education, Labor and Pensions, March 12, 2008, available at http://www.computerworld.com. Gates said: "The federal government needs to increase funding for basic scientific research significantly.... We should seek to increase funding for basic research by 10% annually over the next 7 years. Congress should consider other innovative ideas as well, such as (1) new research grants of $500,000 each annually to 200 of the most outstanding early career researchers; (2) a new National Coordination Office for Research Infrastructure to manage a centralized research infrastructure fund of $500 million per year; (3) establishing and providing funding for Advanced Research Projects Agencies in various departments, similar to DARPA of the 1970s; and (4) ensuring that research projects are communicated to the private sector so that companies can collaborate more effectively with recipients of public research funds."

68. This included favorable regulations for VoIP. See Del Bianco, "Voices Past"; Robert E. Cole, "Telecommunications competition in world markets: Understanding Japan's decline," in *How Revolutionary Was the Digital Revolution?* ed. Zysman and

Newman; Martin Fransman, "Introduction," in *Global Broadband Battles*, ed. M. Fransman (Stanford University Press, 2006).

69. Shun Sakurai, "Japan's best practice for telecommunications market," presentation to WTO, February 20, 2008. Sakurai is a senior official in Japan's Ministry of Internal Affairs and Communications.

70. Ibid.

71. Interviews in Tokyo, June 2007.

72. Phedon Nicolaides, "The political economy of multi-tiered regulation in Europe," *Journal of Common Market Studies* 42 (2004), no. 3: 599–618.

73. On unbundling network components in order to stimulate DSL roll-out, see W. Distaso, P. Lupi, and F. Manenti, "Platform competition and broadband uptake," *Information Economics and Policy* 18 (2006), no. 1: 87–106. The cable infrastructure is greater in the UK due to regulatory policy in the 1980s. The German cable infrastructure is extensive (passing nearly 60% of households), but it is technically obsolete. German regulatory restrictions make it hard to invest in upgrading. Italy's broadcasters successfully managed to stunt the growth of cable. France Telecom owns a significant share of the cable television industry in France. Martin Fransman.

74. Martin Cave and Pietro Cicioni, "Does Europe Need Network Neutrality Rules?" *International Journal of Communication* 1 (2007): 669–679; J. Scott Marcus, "Is the US Dancing to a Different Drummer?" *Communications and Strategies* no. 60, fourth quarter, 2005: 39–58; Tom Kiedrowski, "Remarks on net neutrality," CEPS–PFF Conference, February 22, 2007.

75. See the discussion of the European Commission on the priority for embedding broadband policy into a broader ICT policy in order to correct the EU's weaknesses in global competition (available at http://europa.eu/i2010).

76. Nicolas Economides, "Commentary of the EU Microsoft antitrust case," at http://www.stern.nyu.edu.

77. For a historical review, see Paul Goldstein, *Copyright's Highway* (Stanford University Press, 2003).

78. Coherence does not mean vast power. For example, the formidable lobbying power of local television broadcasters required a congressional decision on the deadline for turning back the 700-MHz band spectrum held by broadcasters as they rolled out high-definition television services.

79. Of course, other parts of the US government, including the Office of the US Trade Representative and the Department of Commerce, actively argue for strict intellectual property protection for American movies, music, and other cultural

industries. The US also provides significant funding for public broadcasting and public radio.

80. Eli Noam, "What regulation for Internet TV? Telecommunications vs. Television Regulation," 2006. Available at http://www.london.edu.

81. This also leads to softening of news content. See James T. Hamilton, *All the News That's Fit to Sell* (Princeton University Press, 2004).

82. The EU Parliament reacted to broadcasting on the Net with alarm. They worry about its impact on the Audiovisual Media Services directive. The 1989 Television without Frontiers directive helped ensure free flow of programs and broadcast while protecting consumers. New proposals may include online gaming and delivery of content to mobiles. Britain's Ofcom thinks that may include video-blogging and content on YouTube. Critics charge that a proposed EU directive would ban ads as downloadable specialized programs (such as cooking shows downloaded from food company website). See "A truly nonsensical law for television," *Financial Times*, September 6, 2006.

83. In 2007, Google held 74% of the French search market. Google's plan to put English books online was last straw for President Jacques Chirac. He directed his Culture Minister and the head of the national library to create a similar project for French books with a new search engine that rejects Google's premise of ranking by popularity. The French effort will rely on a committee of experts to guide search links. Source: "Google a la française," *The Economist*, April 2, 2005, pp. 45–46.

84. The US is engaged in a long-standing WTO dispute over online gambling. It won the right to ban Internet gambling for public welfare reasons, but was found to be in violation of WTO rules for allowing some exceptions solely for US providers. On IP TV regulation, see Noam, "What regulation for Internet TV?"

85. Changing pricing schemes might entail charging more for content without embedded digital rights management (DRM). Some claim that various DRM systems can reduce the availability or dissemination of copyrighted material.

86. A notable example was "The Grey Album," the work of a music producer named Brian Burton who went by the name Danger Mouse. He never asked permission to use material from the Beatles that he mixed with material by the rapper Jay-Z. Although Jay-Z's material was copyrighted, it was released for the implicit purpose of encouraging mash-ups and remixes.

87. Bruce Abramson, *Digital Phoenix: Why the Information Economy Collapsed and How It Will Rise Again* (MIT Press, 2005), p. 221. This is inducing innovations like the Copyright Clearance Center's plan to charge a single per-student fee annually to universities for the unlimited use of copyrights controlled by its licensing control. See Brock Read, "Copyright Center will let colleges pay blanket fees to reuse print material," *Chronicle of Higher Education*, June 29, 2007.

88. Scotchmer, *Innovation and Incentives*, pp. 182–185.

89. Source of data: http://www.techcrunch.com.

90. See "Mix08: Kawasaki grills Ballmer in lively Q&A" at http://www
.computerworld.com.

91. Tim O'Reilly, "What is Web 2.0: Design patterns and business models for the
next generation of software," 2005, at http://www.oreillynet.com.

Chapter 6

1. Similarly, a clear danger of over-fishing global fisheries exists, but it is difficult for
each nation to restrain its own fishing industry if others refrain. Indeed, the fishing
fleet would do better in the short run if it kept fishing while everyone else limited its
catches. In short, often it is logical not to cooperate even if there are long-term gains
to be realized.

2. For game theorists these examples represent the prisoners dilemma tied to collective goods and the "battle of the sexes" problem in regard to coordination. See
Stephen D. Krasner, "State power and the structure of international trade," *World
Politics* 28 (1976): 317–347; "Global communications and national power: Life on
the Pareto frontier," *World Politics* 43 (1991): 336–366. The literature introduced
other important distinctions about collective goods, externalities, and strategic
behavior reflected informally in this book. See Duncan Snidal, "The Limits of hege-
monic stability theory," *International Organization* 39 (1985), no. 4: 579–614; Lisa
Martin, "The Political Economy of International Cooperation," in *Global Public
Goods*, ed. I. Kaul et al. (Oxford University Press, 1999).

3. Even in the US Congress it is the power to block new initiatives that is the strongest form of agenda control for the majority party. See Gary Cox and Mathew
McCubbins, *Setting the Agenda* (Cambridge University Press), 2005

4. Bargaining theorists use the concepts of bargaining trees and "spatial models" of
decision making. The tree starts at the end in a bargaining game and then works
inductively backwards. Implicitly or explicitly, strategic actors think about the end
game and shape current decisions in light of it. Spatial models consider policy
choices in one or two dimensions (e.g., more or less money and more or less centralization of authority) and then map player preferences on them. The decision
rules (does a player have a veto, for example) plus the preference clustering allow
predictions about the range of outcomes. This analysis uses these insights
informally.

5. Sophie Meunier, *Trading Voices* (Princeton University Press, 2005).

6. Ancient Greece and China are examples. See David Landes, *The Wealth and
Poverty of Nations* (Norton, 1998).

7. John Zysman, "Creating value in a digital era: How do wealthy nations stay wealthy?" in *How Revolutionary Was the Revolution?* ed. Zysman and Newman.

8. Jeffrey Legro, *Rethinking the World* (Cornell University Press, 2005); Judith Goldstein and Robert O. Keohane, eds., *Ideas and Foreign Policy* (Cornell University Press, 1994); Peter Haas, "Social constructivism and the evolution of multilateral environmental governance," in *Globalization and Governance*, ed. J. Hart and A. Prakash (Routledge, 1999); William J. Drake and Kalypso Nicolaides, "Ideas, interests, and institutionalization: 'Trade in services,'" *International Organization* 46 (1992), winter: 37–100.

9. Ideas combined with transnational social networks are an important variant of this argument. See Margaret E. Keck and Kathryn Sikkink, *Activists Beyond Borders* (Cornell University Press, 1998); Kathryn Sikkink, *Mixed Message* (Cornell University Press, 2004).

10. Thomas Schelling, "The legacy of Hiroshima: A half-century without nuclear war," *Philosophy & Public Policy Quarterly* 20 (2000), no. 2/3, available at http://www.puaf.umd.edu.

11. The cost of ignoring a good idea can be high. Communism stumbled badly because Marxist economists never accounted properly for the cost of capital.

12. For a classic early work on interest groups, see Mancur Olson, *The Rise and Decline of Nations* (Yale University Press, 1982). On bureaucratic politics, see I. M. Destler, *Presidents, Bureaucrats, and Foreign Policy* (Princeton University Press, 1972).

13. Economists and policy makers differ about how to conceive of these interests. Should the focus be on specific companies like Microsoft vs. Google, on industry segments such as computers versus telecommunications, on sectors of the economy (like agriculture versus services versus high tech), or on the factors of production (labor, capital, and land)? See Jeffry Frieden, "Invested interests: The politics of national economic policies in a world of global finance," *International Organization* 45 (1991), no. 4: 425–451; Michael J. Hiscox, *International Trade and Political Conflict* (Princeton University Press, 2002).

14. Another version of bureaucratic politics views governments as large complex organizations with fallible but possibly improvable operating procedures and problem solving capabilities. Bureaucrats, at their best, champion rationality or uphold shared values and beliefs that might improve public welfare. See John Kingdon, *Agendas, Alternatives and Public Policy* (Harper Collins, 1995).

15. With modifications these concepts apply to non-democratic countries. Political scientists refer to "voters" within Communist Parties (members of the Central Committee) as the "selectorate" and then examine rules for winning dominance within the selectorate. See Susan Shirk, *The Political Logic of Economic Reform in China*

(University of California Press, 1993); Philip G. Roeder, *Red Sunset* (Princeton University Press, 1994).

16. A more formal theory would point to any major disruptive influence, including war or global depression. But we simplify our exposition by sticking to the disruptive force most important for these markets.

17. Robert O. Keohane and Joseph S. Nye Jr., *Power and Interdependence*, third edition (Little, Brown, 2001).

18. Based on our experiences as consultants in the 1980s and 1990s even when telecom companies pursued large global accounts before 2000, they really meant upgrades on a service structure that provided no cohesive infrastructure, cost structures that were inefficient, and price discounts that reduced margins from the exorbitant to the lucrative.

19. The high salience of the issue and the relatively small number involved (a few dozen firms dominating a few hundred firms, compared to millions of consumers) makes mobilization for political action easier than for many actors (such as household consumers) which have a smaller proportional stake in the issue. See Sam Peltzman, "Toward a more general theory of regulation," *Journal of Law and Economics* 19 (1976), no. 2: 211–240.

20. A central feature of the modern study of political parties is that they are policy entrepreneurs seeking to invest in building positions to build their reputations to appeal to voters and interest-group stakeholders.

21. John Zysman, *Governments, Markets, and Growth* (Cornell University Press, 1983); Herbert P. Kitschelt, "Industrial Governance Structures, Innovation Strategies, and the Case of Japan," *International Organization* 45 (1991), no. 4: 453–493; Peter Hall, *Governing the Economy* (Oxford University Press, 1987); Jonah Levy, ed., *The State after Statism* (Harvard University Press, 2006).

22. This is policy diffusion. EU market leadership exerted a powerful influence on wireless policy globally. China may become the source of future unilateral disruptive change. See Beth Simmons and Zachary Elkins, "The globalization of liberalization in the international political economy," *American Political Science Review* 98 (2004), no. 1: 171–189.

23. International arrangements may induce domestic political actors to enforce and advance international commitments to cooperate. See Xinyuan Dai, "Why comply? The domestic constituency mechanism," *International Organization* 59 (2005), no. 2: 363–398.

24. Larger numbers of smaller market powers facing disruption might successfully push for change using cleverly organized collective action. This route is complicated, but international institutions may facilitate such initiatives. The proper specification

of the power hypothesis is that a single dominant or a small number of major market powers can more easily initiate change than many small market countries. The success of a large coalition of small countries probably depends more on the ability of international institutions to facilitate their coordination.

25. Robert Keohane, *After Hegemony* (Princeton University Press, 1984). See also Stephen Krasner, ed., *International Regimes* (Cornell University Press, 1983); Mark Zacher with Brent A. Sutton, *Governing Global Networks* (Cambridge University Press, 1995); Lisa Martin, "The Rational state choice of multilateralism," in *Multilateralism Matters*, ed. J. Ruggie (Columbia University Press, 1993).

26. International NGOs can play a role in building publicity and pressure that may sometimes influence powerful governments. The anti-landmine treaty was one example. Prominent NGOs played major roles in the governance of the Internet. Still, the general proposition should hold true.

27. David Lake and Mathew D. McCubbins, "Delegation to international agencies," in *Delegation and Agency in International Organizations*, ed. D. Hawkins et al. (Cambridge University Press, 2006).

28. One exception to this rule occurs when one stumbles upon a virtual "free lunch" where efficiency gains are huge and costs are trivial. An example was the original "hot line" agreement. Khrushchev proposed the idea. Kennedy asked a Department of State staffer to draft language. Kennedy sent the draft language back to the USSR, which accepted it without changes. The agreement was signed and implemented in 1963.

29. Andrew Mertha and Robert Pahre, "Patently misleading: Partial imperfection and bargaining leverage in Sino-American negotiations on intellectual property rights," *International Organization* 59 (2005), no. 3: 695–729.

30. This reduces uncertainty and informational asymmetries. For example, the OECD gathers reams of market data to clarify the real interests of governments regarding complex issues. The WTO has elaborate conventions on how to make "market access" offers for communications services to reduce uncertainty about what is pledged.

31. Competition was introduced to Intelsat during the 1980s; it was privatized in July 2001.

32. Barbara Koremenos, Charles Lipson, and Duncan Snidal ("The Rational Design of International Institutions," *International Organization* 55, 2001: 761–799) distinguish between soft and hard legal arrangements among countries depending on the governance challenge.

33. Hawkins et al. (*Delegation and Agency in International Organizations*, p. 11) distinguish between international cooperation as either a mutual adjustment of

national authorities or as a delegation (conditional grant of power) from governments to an international institution.

34. Helen Milner and Marc Austin, "Product standards and international and regional competition," *Journal of European Public Policy* 8 (2001), no. 3: 411–431; George Tsebelis and Xenophon Yataganas, "Veto players and decision-making in the EU after Nice: Policy stability and judicial/bureaucratic discretion," *Journal of Common Market Studies* 40 (2002), no. 2: 283–308.

35. Shane Greenstein, "Markets, standardization, and the information infrastructure," *IEEE Micro, Chips, Systems, and Applications* 13 (1993), no. 6: 36–51.

36. Miles Kahler, "Multilateralism with small and large numbers," *International Organization* 46 (1992), no. 3: 681–708.

37. Sometimes bureaucrats are foolish, corrupt, or pig-headed. Still, in most industrial democracies they are in control. They respond to well-developed mandates of an earlier era that were deliberately entrusted to bureaucrats to insulate them from easy modification by future skeptics.

38. These arrangements are called "fire alarms" in the literature. See Mathew McCubbins, Roger Noll, and Barry Weingast, "Political control of the bureaucracy," at http://mccubbins.ucsd.edu.

39. Problem-solving communities are sometimes called epistemic communities because social scientists love jargon with ancient Greek origins.

40. Theorists disagree about how to account for the "learning" that goes on globally within effective governance arrangements. Is there direct or indirect coercion? Do poorer nations learn how to adapt to the conventions of the strong, as during the spread of the Napoleonic code throughout Europe? Or do actors learn from competitive pressures to match rivals or emulate respected peers? Do social and institutional networks enhance "channeled learning"? These causal strands intertwine in complex ways. The argument here resembles "channeled learning" but is agnostic about the precise mix. For an overview of the literature, see Beth Simmons, Frank Dobbin, and Geoffrey Garrett, "The international diffusion of liberalism," *International Organization* 60 (2006), no. 4: 781–810.

41. Max Weber highlighted the importance of organizing principles for efficiency.

42. Lawrence Lessig pushed this logic in *Code and Other Laws of Cyberspace* (Basic Books, 2000), arguing that in a digital era the software contains the "code" for the marketplace. His analysis is insightful, but it is not necessary to go as far as he does for the point to hold true.

43. This follows from theories of delegation.

44. It can also alter the power of national governments or the degree of decision making equality among states, among other outcomes. But this analysis is interested in the impact on markets.

45. Cowhey, "Telecommunications," p. 177.

46. Gary Libecap defines property rights as "the social institutions that define or delimit the range of privileges granted to individuals to specific assets" (*Contracting for Property Rights*, Cambridge University Press, 1989, p. 1).

47. The discussion of property rights draws on the following works: John Richards, "Toward a Positive Theory of International Institutions: Regulating Postwar International Aviation Markets," *International Organization* 53 (1999), no. 1: 1–37; Hendrik Spruyt, *The Sovereign State and Its Competitors* (Princeton University Press, 1994); Douglas C. North and Barry R. Weingast, "Constitutions and Commitment: The Evolution of Institutions Governing Public Choice in 17th Century England," *Journal of Economic History* 49 (December 1989) 803–832; Kal Raustiala and David Victor, "The regime complex for plant genetic resources," *International Organization* 58 (spring 2004): 277–309.

Chapter 7

1. On why the introduction of trade in telecom services was transformative for the traditional trade regime, see Jonathan D. Aronson, and Peter F. Cowhey, *When Countries Talk* (Ballinger, 1988). But that is not the primary focus here.

2. See Peter Cowhey and John Richards, "Building global service markets: Economic structure and state capacity," in *The State after Statism*, ed. J. Levy (Harvard University Press, 2006); Frances Cairncross, *The Death of Distance* (Harvard Business School Press, 1997). On the different perspectives of the US and Japan, see Sylvia Ostry, "Convergence and sovereignty: Policy scope for compromise," in *Coping with Globalization?* ed. A. Prakash and J. Hart (Routledge, 2000).

3. This is generally true when negotiating partners have divergent national regulatory and legal traditions. See Ostry, "Convergence and sovereignty."

4. Many trade economists disdain unilateral action. See Jagdish Bhagwati and Anne O. Krueger, *The Dangerous Drift to Preferential Trade Agreements* (AEI Press, 1995).

5. Some argue that domestic liberalization meant that the WTO deal was only a token ratification of de facto international liberalization. We believe that domestic competition inevitably leads to some form of greater international competition. What was unclear was how much competition would occur, when, and with what limitations. The WTO deal meant much more liberalization now and with fewer limits. See William J. Drake and Eli M. Noam, "Assessing the WTO agreement

on basic telecommunications," in *Unfinished Business*, ed. G. Hufbauer and E. Wada (Institute for International Economics, 1997).

6. On the breakdown of the traditional cartel, see Aronson and Cowhey, *When Countries Talk*; Cowhey, "The International Telecommunications Regime."

7. Everything is relative. Customers of local phone services might have paid less if competition and cost-based services existed than if they had subsidized monopoly services. Developing countries argued that international competition undermined development objectives because it made domestic network build-out more difficult. Their arguments resemble AT&T's assertions about the US domestic network in the 1970s. On AT&T positions, see Peter Termin with Louis Galambos, *The Fall of the Bell System* (Cambridge University Press, 1988). For a critique of this position, see Peter Cowhey, "FCC benchmarks and the reform of the international telecommunications Market," *Telecommunications Policy* 22 (1998), no. 11: 899–911.

8. Cowhey, "The International Telecommunications Regime."

9. Screen time quotas for films are exempted in GATT Article III. No other services were touched upon in the founding documents. The GATT focused exclusively on trade on goods until the Tokyo round when services required to facilitate trade in goods were touched upon for the first time. Trade in services first made it on to the negotiating agenda in the Uruguay Round during the late 1980s.

10. Leonard J. Schoppa, *Bargaining with Japan* (Columbia University Press, 1997); Bruce Stokes, "Divergent paths: US-Japan relations towards the twenty-first century," *International Affairs* 72 (1996), no. 2: 281–291.

11. Government-owned PTTs traditionally operated and regulated the monopoly telecom service provider. On monopolists' plans to offer an Integrated Service Digital Network (ISDN), see Aronson and Cowhey, *When Countries Talk*, pp. 186–204.

12. On the Uruguay Round, see Jeffrey J. Schott, *The Uruguay Round* (Institute for International Economics, 1994); John Whalley and Colleen Hamilton, *The Trading System After the Uruguay Round* (Institute for International Economics, 1996); Barry Eichengreen and Peter Kenen, "Managing the world economy under the Bretton Woods system: An overview," in *Managing the World Economy*, ed. P. Kenen (Institute for International Economics, 1994). For a history of trade in services, see William J. Drake and Kalypso Nicolaides, "Ideas, Interests, and Institutionalization: 'Trade in Services,'" *International Organization* 46 (1992), winter: 37–100. On NAFTA, see Frederick M. Abbot, "The North American integration regime and its implications for the world trading system," in *The EU, the WTO and the NAFTA*, ed. J. Weiler (Oxford University Press, 2000); Richard Feinberg. *Summitry in the Americas* (Institute for International Economics, 1997), pp. 42–48.

13. Asian countries sought binding dispute regulation to temper US use of anti-dumping and countervailing subsidies. For different reasons, the US wanted binding

dispute settlement. By placing agriculture and textiles prominently on the agenda developing countries were induced to cooperate on services, intellectual property, and investment.

14. The US telecom industry initially needed substantial coaching on the GATT. They thought that they could advance their purposes better in bilateral trade negotiations by using unfettered threats of sanctions by the US government against those not opening their market sufficiently. The shift to the GATT reflected the larger political agenda for multilateral trade.

15. The leading US bureaucratic proponent and strategist of including trade in services on the Uruguay GATT/WTO agenda was Geza Feketekuty, at the time the Senior Assistant Trade Representative at USTR. His strategy relied on international fact finding to demonstrate the relevance and logic of applying trade disciplines to services. See Jonathan D. Aronson, "Negotiating to launch negotiations: Getting trade in services onto the GATT agenda," Pew Case Study 125-92-R, 1988 (revised 1992).

16. Mexico also wanted to demonstrate its commitment to free trade at a time when the Salinas Administration was negotiating Mexican membership in the OECD.

17. Mexico's 1990 reforms allowed the privatization of Telmex, the dominant carrier, with minority foreign ownership. Mexico decided to end Telmex's monopoly on long-distance services after 1996. The growth of heterogeneous demand in Mexico had generated marketplace conditions that favored entry by focused firms to fill specific demand niches. This situation provided domestic support for reform in Mexico and incentives for US specialized players to back regional liberalization. On why heterogeneous demand matters in developing countries, see Roger Noll, "Telecommunications reform in developing countries," in *Economic Policy Reform*, ed. A. Krueger (University of Chicago Press, 2000).

18. The important distinction made in NAFTA, and reconfirmed in the 1994 and 1997 WTO agreements, was between services made widely available to the public and those that satisfied specific needs of telecommunications (private networks or value-added networks). See A. Acedo, "Opportunities in Mexico," presented at International Telecom Competition Seminar," Seattle, 1997. The NAFTA deal ensured the provision of private leased circuits on a flat-rate basis, the key to allowing a computer network to get a cheap, fixed rate for transmission capacity and then use advanced engineering to carry more data than the typical telecom circuit. Unlike NAFTA, the 1997 WTO offer included public networks; see Peter Cowhey and John Richards, "Deregulating and liberalising the North American telecommunications market: Explaining the US approach," in *Trade, Investment and Competition Policies in the Global Economy*, ed. P. Guerrieri and H.-E. Scharrer (Momos, 2002).

19. Except for narrow exceptions, US rules forbade the regional Bell operating companies from owning equipment suppliers. Lucent was, until it was spun off in the

1990s, part of AT&T. The US had unilaterally liberalized the competitive supply of customer premises equipment.

20. Before NAFTA, the US equipment market was relatively open. US suppliers pushed for telecom equipment liberalization in NAFTA. On NAFTA equipment agreement, see Ronald A. Cass and John R. Haring, *International Trade in Telecommunications: Monopoly, Competition, and Trade Strategy* (MIT Press, 1998), p. 123.

21. The new criterion for network interconnection for equipment was a guarantee of "no harm to the network." Previously equipment had to conform to idiosyncratic, national design standards. This fundamental reform was implemented by a rule that allowed countries to recognize one another's certification of the safety of equipment (mutual recognition agreements). Mutual recognition promised to relieve equipment suppliers from slow and expensive procedures to get technical certification for their products in each individual country. Implementation of these agreements was often contentious, as was the case with Mexico.

22. World Trade Organization, Information Technology Agreement—Introduction, at www.wto.org.

23. NAFTA also created a complex dispute settlement mechanism that elicited divergent reviews. (Abbot, "The North American integration regime and its implications for the world trading system.") US companies later criticized Mexico's performance under its WTO telecom obligations. They preferred the WTO dispute-resolution system.

24. Settlement rates apply to switched international traffic offered on the public telephone network. Services like traditional phone calls require the use of telephone network switches. (Here the adaptation to VoIP and similar technological innovations is omitted.) If settlement rates sound arcane, the system was more complicated in all its bureaucratic glory. As a matter of economic analysis it is simpler and more accurate to focus on the settlement rate. For the full complexities, see Peter Cowhey, "FCC benchmarks and the reform of the international telecommunications market," *Telecommunications Policy* 22 (1998), no. 11: 899–911.

25. The FCC created "proportionate return" rules to block the "whipsawing" of competitive US carriers negotiating with a foreign monopolist. The rule mandated that each US carrier be entitled to the same share of incoming switched international traffic from a country as it sent to the country. See Peter Cowhey, "Building the global information highway: Toll booths, construction contracts, and rules of the road," in *The New Information Structure*, ed. W. Drake (Twentieth Century Fund, 1995).

26. The FCC's International Bureau staff based this estimate on settlement rate data published by the FCC. See Jim Lande and Linda Blake, "Trends in the US interna-

tional telecommunications industry. Industry Analysis Division," Common Carrier Bureau, FCC, 1997.

27. The FCC acquiesced to balance-of-payments deficits that occurred in efficiently priced markets.

28. In 1995 the FCC formalized its rules governing foreign entry into the US market for basic telecommunications services in the form of the Effective Competitive Opportunities (ECO) test. It believed this test was fairer than past practices and could permit substantial opening. It still considered this route to be inferior to a multilateral trade agreement. Foreign governments disliked the test. They saw it as an intrusive examination of their domestic regulatory practices. However, the ECO tests foreshadowed the regulatory principles adopted in the subsequent WTO agreement on telecommunications services. The Commission intentionally cast ECO in a manner designed to signal the rules it would consider necessary for a satisfactory WTO agreement. See Federal Communications Commission, "In the matter of market entry and regulation of foreign-affiliated entities, report and order," IB docket 95-22, November 28, 1995.

29. Federal Communications Commission, "Regulation of international accounting rates, phase ii, fourth report and order," 11 FCC Rcd 20063, 1996 (the "Flexibility Order").

30. At that time less than a half dozen countries (including Canada, the UK, and Sweden) qualified for flexibility without special waivers from the FCC.

31. Put differently, settlement rates that far exceeded costs created the possibility of anti-competitive behavior in the provision of US international services. This would harm consumers and erode market efficiency over time. The FCC provided an operational definition of two forms of anti-competitive behavior. On the problems and the remedies, see Federal Communications Commission, "In the matter of international settlement rates, report and order," IB docket 96-261, 1997, paragraphs 211–259. Also see Thomas Krattenmaker, Richard Lande, and Steven Salop, "Monopoly power and market power in antitrust law," Georgetown Law Journal 76 (1987): 241–253.

32. Many worrisome tactics were variations on the strategy of "one-way bypass." This occurred if the home market of a foreign carrier licensed to provide services in the US required US carriers to terminate at the settlement rate while the foreign carrier terminated traffic into the US at the rates prevailing under "flexibility." Thus, country X might charge 39 cents as the settlement rate to terminate US traffic while its carrier could terminate traffic into the US at 6 cents using leased transmission lines without paying a settlement rate. This would drive up US net settlement payments and escalate the price of international services for US consumers. A WTO agreement made this scenario probable if the US agreed to liberalize licensing of

international leased circuits, but most WTO countries had not. For details, see Cowhey, "FCC benchmarks."

33. By contrast, carriers from less competitive markets worried that trade reforms would cut into their large profit margins from international services. Therefore, these carriers also lobbied their home governments to resist liberalization of competition in international telephone services.

34. The WTO negotiation had some parallel issues involving the specialized market for satellite communications services. Discussion is omitted because it is a logical subset of the problem discussed here. See Laura B. Sherman, "'Wildly enthusiastic' about the first multilateral agreement on trade in telecommunications services," *Federal Communications Law Journal* 51 (1998), no. 1: 62–100.

35. The U.S. unilateral and multilateral initiatives had many critics. For a representative critique, offered by an ardent admirer of traditional market governance, see Jill Hills, *Telecommunications and Empire* (University of Illinois Press, 2007).

36. This is based on Peter Cowhey's notes from negotiating sessions between the US and the EU. Japan supported the WTO negotiations but waited to see what the two main players could agree on before making its best offer.

37. The US understanding reflected its difficulties in using bilateral negotiations to liberalize global telecom markets in the early 1990s.

38. On the division of powers and credibility, see Peter Cowhey, "Domestic institutions and the credibility of international commitments: The cases of Japan and the United States," *International Organization* 47 (1993): 299–326; Charles Lipson, *Reliable Partners* (Princeton University Press, 2003).

39. The EU, based on experience, believed the US promise that compliance by its state regulatory commissions would be forthcoming after the passage of the 1996 Telecommunications Act mandated competition in local telephone services.

40. Similarly, divided powers increased the required scope for liberalization of international aviation markets. See John Richards, "The domestic politics of international regulatory policy: The regulatory institutions for trade in aviation services," Ph.D. dissertation, University of California, San Diego, 1997.

41. Peter Cowhey and Mathew McCubbins, eds., *Structure and Policy in Japan and the United States* (Cambridge University Press, 1995). The EU may face this problem in the future. The French Fifth Republic and many of the Eastern European members admitted to the EU after this period are better described as semi-presidential systems that draw on both presidential systems and parliamentary systems.

42. On the relationship between the division of powers and judicial action on environmental rules, see Kal Raustiala, "The sources of state interests: British and

American policy towards international environmental cooperation, 1983–1993," Ph.D. dissertation, University of California, San Diego, 1996.

43. On how the structure and process of regulatory agencies matters for policy outcomes, see Mathew McCubbins, Roger Noll, and Barry Weingast, "Administrative Procedures as Instruments of Political Control," *Journal of Law, Economics, and Organization* 3 (1987): 243–276.

44. EU member states ratify a tentative trade pact each time they authorize a new offer in a WTO negotiation. The Congress ratifies the US trade offer only at the conclusion of a negotiation. The Executive branch tries to anticipate congressional preferences.

45. This contrasted strongly with the impasse on WTO negotiations on aviation services, in which nobody believed in the end that Washington or Brussels would make credible commitments to make essential facilities (e.g., more landing gates at local airports) available.

46. See Maria Behrens and Raymund Werle, "Lobbying for global telecommunication markets? The political activities of dominant providers in the EU and the US during the basic telecommunication negotiations of the WTO," paper presented at ECPR Conference, Marburg, 2003.

47. Peter Cowhey and Laura Sherman, "The FCC and the reform of the international telecommunications services market," *Euromoney*, winter 1998; Laura Sherman, "Introductory note on reference paper to the telecommunications annex to GATS," *International Legal Materials* 36 (1997): 354; Peter Cowhey and Mikhail M. Klimenko, "The WTO agreement and telecommunications policy reform," World Bank policy research working paper 2601, 2001. Some scholars who opposed US telecommunications policy in the 1990s feared that the reference paper would force the rest of the world to replicate US errors. See Jeffrey H. Rohlfs and J. Gregory Sidak, "Exporting telecommunications regulation: The US-Japan negotiations on interconnection pricing," *Harvard International Law Journal* 43 (2002), no. 2: 317–360.

48. The European Union left its market access commitments on the table when negotiations stalled. It argued that a deal could go forward without the US. But it is doubtful that this would have happened.

49. MFN treatment, a fundamental trade concept, requires that the same degree of market opening must be provided to all WTO members.

50. WTO members promise not to discriminate in favor of domestic firms over foreign-owned ones. The WTO rule on non-discrimination requires national policy measures to provide equal treatment of firms of WTO members and of local firms.

51. Even for developing countries (e.g. Mexico) that were committed to the timely introduction of competitive international services, the rents generated by settlement

rates were so high that the government designed measures to ensure their retention for several years.

52. The diplomatic dialogue is simplified to clearly emphasize the bottom line. Other issues are ignored that might have prevented agreement.

53. As hopes for a deal improved, the US government upgraded the level of political contacts used to press industrializing countries. Cabinet officers and senior White House officials began to call their foreign counterparts to request careful political attention by top officials to the WTO negotiation.

54. The benchmarks averaged cost data gathered by the FCC for each income tier of countries. The FCC used World Bank data on income tiers. The FCC allowed for a transition period to achieve the price cap, providing poorer countries more time. Industrial countries had one year to reach 15 cents per minute. The cap for middle-income countries was set at 19 cents with a two or three year transition period. Low-income countries needed to reach 23 cents in 4 or 5 years. See FCC, "In the matter of international settlement rates, report and order." Also see Cowhey, "FCC benchmarks and the reform of the international telecommunications market." The US was optimistic that benchmarks would work and not be overturned by trade challenges at the WTO. See Peter Cowhey and John Richards, "Dialing for dollars: The revolution in communications markets," in *Coping with Globalization*, ed. J. Hart and A. Prakash (Routledge, 2000).

55. For a summary, see Jonathan D. Aronson, "Telecom agreement tops expectations," in *Unfinished Business*, ed. G. Hufbauer and E. Wada (Institute for International Economics, 1997).

56. The waiver of the foreign ownership restriction applies only to companies from WTO members. The FCC rules adopted in fall 1997 to implement the WTO agreement created a presumption in favor of entry for foreign carriers into the US market. The FCC also used its discretion under the Communications Act of 1934 to eliminate discrimination against foreign ownership. The 1934 act restricts the FCC from waiving the limits on direct foreign ownership, but the differences between direct and indirect ownership are a matter of legal form. See Federal Communications Commission, "Rules and policies on foreign participation in the US telecommunications market, report and order," IB dockets 97-142 and 95-22. For an analysis that correctly attacks the original foreign investment limits but misses how the FCC reformed them effectively in 1997, see Gregory Sidak, *Foreign Investment in American Telecommunications* (University of Chicago Press, 1997).

57. See Ben Petrazzini, *Global Telecom Talks* (Institute for International Economics, 1996).

58. Laura B. Sherman, "Clarifying the Meaning of WTO Telecommunications Obligations: Mexico—Measures Affecting Telecommunications Services," *Info* 7 (2005), no. 6: 16–32.

59. James Hodge, "WTO negotiations in telecommunications: How should SADC countries respond?" *Spitjerm Africa Update* 18 (2003): 1–4.

60. International Telecoms Intelligence, "South Africa—Market intelligence report," 2007. Also see "South Africa: Let's talk," Economist Intelligence Unit, Global Technology Forum, 2007.

61. Robert Pepper, presentation at WTO Services Symposium on WTO Basic Telecommunications Negotiations, Geneva, 2008.

62. Even Japan ritualistically protested that Japanese carriers could not afford to terminate US traffic for less than 50 cents per minute. Nobody believed this claim, including the Japanese government. Today, US traffic terminates in Japan for a few cents per minute.

63. Cowhey, "FCC benchmarks and the reform of the international telecommunications market."

64. The ITU reports that in 2007 only 54% of international traffic gateways are fully liberalized (and 17% partly liberalized), a big jump from 1997 but an indication of how many countries try to protect these price margins by monopoly. See Susan Schorr, "Ten years of regulatory trends," WTO Services Symposium on WTO Basic Telecommunications Negotiations, 2008, available at http://www .wto.org.

65. Telegeography Research, "Map of Major Internet Routes, 2005"; Scott Wallsten, "An Econometric Analysis of Telecom Competition, Privatization, and Regulation in Africa and Latin America," *Journal of Industrial Economics* 49 (2001), no. 1: 1–19; Scott Wallsten et al., "New Tools for Studying Network Industry Reforms in Developing Countries: The Telecommunications and Electricity Regulation Database," *Review of Networked Economics* 3 (2004), no. 3: 248–259.

66. Schorr ("Ten years of regulatory trends") reports that approximately 18 countries had general telecom competition and 50 had some mobile competition in 1995. By 2006, 110 countries had general competition and 150 had mobile competition (usually with multiple competitors).

67. Vanessa Gray, "ICT market trends," presentation to WTO Services Symposium on WTO Basic Telecommunications Negotiations, 2008.

68. Tim Wu, "The world trade law of censorship and Internet filtering," 2007, available at http://papers.ssrn.com.

69. On trade and cultural issues at the WTO, see J. P. Singh, *Negotiation and the Global Information Economy* (Cambridge University Press, 2009); Mu Lin, "Changes and consistency: China's media market after WTO entry," *Journal of Media Studies* 17, no. 3 (2004): 177–192.

70. We thank Don Abelson for pointing out this distinction to us.

Chapter 8

1. Neuchterlein and Weiser, *Digital Crossroads*, p. 230.

2. Social scientists cannot provide definitive assessments on the technical merits of competing technology proposals. Luckily, the debate is not central to this argument. See Johan Lembke, "Global Competition and Strategies in the Information and Communications Technology Industry: A Liberal Strategic Approach," *Business and Politics* 4 (2002), no. 1 (available at http://www.bepress.com). For insightful efforts to examine decision making in standards bodies, see Mark Lemley, "Intellectual property rights and standard-setting organizations," *California Law Review* 90 (2002): 1889; Joseph Farrell and Garth Saloner, "Economic issues in standardization," working paper 393, MIT Department of Economics, 1985.

3. The EU created a new telecommunications standards organization, ETSI, partly out of frustration with the ITU process. See Walter Mattli and Tim Buthe, "Setting international standards: Technological rationality or primacy of power?" *World Politics* 56 (2003), no. 1: 1–42.

4. The Euro-Japanese alliance was primarily coordinated by industries with similar business interests. Once these ties were forged, they had implications for the options of governments and regulatory bodies. See Lembke, "Global Competition."

5. Robert Iannucci, Chief Technology Officer, Nokia presentation at Supernova Conference, San Francisco, June 16, 2008.

6. Calculating total 3G subscribers is confusing because sometimes, as in this case, CDMA 2000 1× RTT customers are counted as if they were 3G customers. "Using CDMA2000 and WCDMA (UMTS) technologies, commercial 3G networks are providing service to more than 486 million paying subscribers. As of July 31, 2007, KDDI in Japan had recorded more than 27.8 million CDMA2000 subscribers after 5 years of service. NTT DoCoMo in Japan now has more than 38.7 million WCDMA subscribers. SoftBank Mobile surpassed 10 million 3G subscribers. Korea has accumulated more than 40 million CDMA2000 subscribers through July 2007, more than 17.5 million of which are EV-DO." Source: Wireless Intelligence, http://www.3gtoday.com.

7. Where network externalities exist, networks become more valuable to individual users as more people use or are connected to the network. See Bruce Owen and Gregory Rosston, "Spectrum allocation and the Internet," SIEPR discussion paper 01-09, 2001.

8. Once a carrier has installed a supplier's network equipment, it is locked in and the vendor is unlikely to be displaced. Because global carriers prefer suppliers with global support capabilities, this limits entry for a network and, to a lesser extent, to handset equipment. (Based on interviews with European and Asian suppliers, November and December 2002.)

9. Stanley M. Besen and Joseph Farrell, "The role of the ITU in standardization," *Telecommunications Policy* 15 (1991): 311–321; Carl Shapiro and Hal R. Varian, *Information Rules* (Harvard University Press, 1998).

10. Eli Noam, *Telecommunications in Europe* (Oxford University Press, 1993).

11. Helen Milner and Marc Austin, "Product standards and international and regional competition," *Journal of European Public Policy* 8 (2001), no. 3: 411–431; George Tsebelis, *Veto Players* (Princeton University Press, 2002).

12. Shane Greenstein, "Markets, standardization, and the information infrastructure," *IEEE Micro: Chips, Systems, and Application* 13 (1993), no. 6: 36–51.

13. Johan Hjelm, "Research applications in the mobile environment," in *Designing Wireless Information Services* (Wiley, 2000).

14. The absence of private property rights partly reflects the high transaction costs of assigning and monitoring individual property rights in the early days of radio technology. See Thomas Hazlett, "The wireless craze, the unlimited bandwidth myth, the spectrum auction faux pas, and the punch line to Ronald Coase's big joke," *Harvard Journal of Law & Technology* 14 (Spring 2001): 335–567. Philip J. Weiser and Dale Hatfield, "Spectrum Policy Reform and the Next Frontier of Property Rights," *George Mason Law Review* 15 (2008): 549–609.

15. The laws of physics make bands differ in their radio propagation characteristics, so spectrum is not equally tractable for all tasks. For example, spectrum bands over 100 MHz permit straight-line transmissions that can be power efficient.

16. In most industrial countries the military controls about 30% of the spectrum.

17. The political process is arcane and fiercely contested. Advocates debate what would constitute a threat of interference and the plans for reallocating different pieces of spectrum to different uses. These proceedings raise enormous informational problems for government decision makers. The glacial process indirectly favors incumbents.

18. Owen and Rosston, "Spectrum allocation and the Internet."

19. See Peter Cowhey, Jonathan D. Aronson, and John E. Richards, "Property rights and 3G wireless standards," in *How Revolutionary Was the Revolution?* ed. Zysman and Newman.

20. Shankar Jagannathan, Stanislav Kura, and Michael J. Wiltshire, "A help line for telcos," *McKinsey Quarterly*, no. 1 (2003): 87–98.

21. Ovum Data, as reported in "Wireless Briefing," *Red Herring* (March 2002): 68–69.

22. In the late 1990s, when the serious decisions about the transition to 3G were made, consistent regional and global roaming across national borders remained rare

except within Western Europe and parts of Asia. The temptation to create viable global footprints was huge, despite gigantic investment costs. Economies of scale in purchasing for a single technology would reduce costs.

23. The global ITU standards process is formally organized around and fed by, leadership out of the major regional standards bodies. (The ITU was created in 1865. In March 2008 it had 191 member states, 565 sector members, and 141 associates.)

24. Significant consensus on the outline of the standard was reached by 1987. Initially, the European Conference of Posts and Telecommunications (CEPT) was the principal player. It created the GSM MOU (Memorandum of Understanding). This evolved into a global organization for promoting GSM. Source: Zixiang Tan, "Comparison of wireless standards-setting—United States versus Europe," draft paper, 2001.

25. National and regional standard-setting processes varied. Effective participation required a significant commercial presence and the ability to fund staffers who could spend extensive time on the standard-setting process. Voting, if used, often was weighted according to market revenues and required super-majorities of 60% or more. In contrast to the one company-one vote principle used by the US Telecommunications Industry Association, the ETSI used weighted voting. Market revenues mattered significantly in the weighting. Manufacturers dominated the voting. In 1997, 49.5% of the members were manufacturers, 15.8% were public network operators, 9.18% were national government authorities, and 12.4% were research bodies. See Heather Hudson, *Global Connections* (Van Nostrand, 1997).

26. It took the Japanese suppliers several years to acquire the IPR licensing agreements. The delay gave the major European firms a significant lead. See Rudi Bekkers, Bart Verspagen, and Jan Smits, "Intellectual property rights and standardization. The case of GSM," *Telecommunications Policy* 26 (2002), no. 3–4: 171–188.

27. The EU used a combination of spectrum and standards policy to ensure a common approach to 2G. For an excellent discussion of government intervention to make standards setting credible, see Jacques Pelkmans, *European Integration* (Prentice-Hall, 2001).

28. Japan eventually opened its procurement policy to international scrutiny by agreeing to extend the GATT procurement code to the NTT.

29. Michael Mastanduno, "Do relative gains matter? America's response to Japanese industry policy," *International Security* 16 (1991), summer: 73–113; Leonard J. Schoppa, *Bargaining with Japan* (Columbia University Press, 1997).

30. The economic reasoning involved in the FCC policy of technology neutrality is discussed in Farrell and Saloner, "Economic issues in standardization." Also see chapter 8 of Neuchterlein and Weiser, *Digital Crossroads*.

31. Johan Lembke, "Harmonization and globalization: UMTS and the single market," *Info* 3 (2001), no. 1: 15–26.

32. The most important dispute involved Qualcomm and Ericsson in litigation that began in 1995. This was resolved in an agreement announced on March 25, 1999, that included cross-licensing of patents and Ericsson's purchase of Qualcomm's terrestrial infrastructure business. Vitally, from the viewpoint of Qualcomm, the agreement included a stipulation that licensing would be done for all three proposed versions of 3G. This settlement allowed commercialization to proceed but other patent battles continued through 2008 that pitted Qualcomm against Broadcom and Nokia on control of patents and licensing terms. See Hjelm, "Research applications in the mobile environment."

33. Traditionally, some standard-setting organizations, including the ITU, demanded "royalty-free licensing." Many others now require "reasonable and nondiscriminatory" licensing. This discussion relies on Patterson 2002. In 2000 the ITU Telecommunication Standardization Bureau stated: "The patent holder is not prepared to waive his rights but would be willing to negotiate licenses with parties on a nondiscriminatory basis on reasonable terms and conditions." The bureau does not set precise criteria for these conditions and leaves it to negotiations among the parties. The relevant factors for setting royalties include development and manufacturing costs plus profits. See Mark R. Patterson, "Invention, Industry Standards, and Intellectual Property," *Berkeley Technology Law Journal* 17 (2002), no. 3: 1053–1054 and n. 40.

34. In 2002 another group of European vendors announced that it would set an absolute cap, at a relatively low level, on royalties charged for W-CDMA technology use. Qualcomm quietly rejected the cap and observed that it held about 50% of the IP on W-CDMA, thus making any royalty offer that it did not agree to meaningless. Other companies rejected Qualcomm's estimate of its holdings. This set the stage for royalty disputes extending through 2008.

35. For data on the large role still played by 2G in 2003 and the estimate for 2005 see table 14.2 of Cowhey, Aronson, and Richards, "Property rights and 3G wireless standards." Concern over 2G sales was why neither side followed the economic logic of compromise to grow the market size set out in Shapiro and Varian, *Information Rules*. In 2006 Japan became the first country in which 3G accounted for the majority of terminal sales. Source: "W-CDMA goes top in Japan five years after launch," www.cellular-news.com, November 14, 2006.

36. The collective approach of numerous industrial actors sought to ensure compatibility across markets for preferred methods of technology. For more on how the objectives of both firms and national level actors were driven by regional interests, see Lembke, "Global Competition."

37. Neil Gandal, David Salant, and Leonard Waverman, "Standards in wireless telephone networks," *Telecommunications Policy* 27 (2003): 325–332.

38. The W-CDMA initiative emerged from a successful negotiation on common interests among the largest expected winners in Europe: DoCoMo, Nokia, and Ericsson. In *Brave New Unwired World* (Wiley, 2002), Alex Lightman notes that if the ITU had standardized only around W-CDMA specifications, the chip rate in the system would have been incompatible with seamless upgrading from 2G CDMA systems.

39. Irene Wu, *From Iron Fist to Invisible Hand: Telecommunications Reform in China* (Stanford University Press, 2008); Kenji Erik Kushida, "Wireless Bound and Unbound: The Politics Shaping Cellular Markets in Japan and South Korea," *Journal of Information Technology and Politics* 5 (2008).

40. Lembke, "Global Competition."

41. Qualcomm notified the standards bodies involved in 3G that it held essential patents on all proposed versions of 3G. It offered to license, on reasonable and nondiscriminatory terms, a single converged ITU standard for 3G or its own proposed standard. Qualcomm declared that it would not license other versions of 3G, such as the EU's W-CDMA standard. Sources: "Qualcomm supports converged standard for IMT-2000," press release, June 2, 1998, available at http://www.cdg.org.

42. There was no comparably dominant wireless incumbent in the US. AT&T was a TDMA carrier, as were the wireless groups of several regional Bell operating companies. Verizon and Sprint ran the flagship CDMA networks. So the carriers quarreled bitterly over the US position in the ITU on standardization.

43. For example, on October 13, 1999, US Commerce Secretary William Daley, US Trade Representative Charlene Barshefsky, and FCC Chairman William Kennard released a letter to EU Commissioner Erkki Liikanen protesting EU policy.

44. Most low-income developing markets rely more on European suppliers of network equipment than on North American suppliers. European companies, seeking larger markets, attempted to enter these markets before their American counterparts.

45. See figure 14-3 in Cowhey, Aronson, and Richards, "Property rights and 3G wireless standards."

46. Qualcomm collects IPR royalties on all versions of CDMA.

47. In November 2002, China appeared to tilt in this direction by setting aside spectrum reserved for this technology. The US and the EU raised issues about mandatory standards with China.

48. Hudson, *Global Connections*.

49. John Zysman and Wayne Sandholtz, "1992: Recasting the European bargain," *World Politics* 42 (1989), no. 1: 95–128; Peter Cowhey, "Telecommunications," in

Europe 1992, ed. G. Hufbauer (Brookings Institution Press, 1990); Pelkmans, *European Integration.*

50. Developing countries benefited enormously from 2G for reasons discussed in chapter 2 above. See Peter F. Cowhey and Mikhail M. Klimenko, "The WTO agreement and telecommunications policy reform," World Bank policy research working paper 2601, 2001.

51. Source: US Congress, Office of Technology Assessment, The 1992 World Administrative Radio Conference: Technology and Policy Implications," OTA-TCT-549, May 1993, pp. 108–115.

52. Commission of the European Communities, "Amended proposal for a European parliament and council decision on the coordinated introduction of mobile and wireless communications in the Community," 98/C 276/04; Council of the European Union, "Council decision on the coordinated introduction of third generation mobile and wireless communications system (UMTS) in the community," 128/1999/EEC.

53. Opponents included the politically powerful UHF television broadcasters.

54. Some dual-band and dual-mode phones could handle both 3G modes. This increases production costs in markets where consumers demand low prices.

55. CDMA carriers (Alltel, Sprint, Verizon) focused on the large North American market, while GSM and TDMA carriers (AT&T Wireless, Cingular) sought alliances with non-US carriers. Vodafone owned a minority share of Verizon. Deutsche Telekom (now called T-Mobile as a wireless provider) waited until 2000 before becoming the first foreign carrier to act, buying VoiceStream.

56. Gandal, Salant, and Waverman, "Standards in wireless telephone networks."

57. Based on 2004 an analysis done by Lehman Brothers that was provided to the authors.

58. The licensing system required large resources and usually was designed to produce one or two new entrants. See Paul Klemperer, "How (not) to run auctions: The European 3G telecom auctions," *European Economic Review* 46 (2002), no. 4–5: 829–845. Klemperer argues that the merits of auction designs of countries varied considerably. High price alone did not prove than an auction was poorly designed.

59. The Netherlands and France waived some auction fees or provided the winning bidders with financial aid. The UK and Germany granted relief by allowing carriers to share the build out of certain network infrastructure. This reduced the financial burden on all bidders by as much as 30% of capital costs. For evidence and details, see Cowhey, Aronson, and Richards, "Property rights and 3G wireless standards."

60. Most former British colonies in Asia (Hong Kong, Singapore, Australia, and New Zealand) tilted toward auctions with varying degrees of success. Hong Kong had four carriers. See John Ure, "Deconstructing 3G and reconstructing telecoms," *Telecommunications Policy* 27 (2003): 187–206.

61. Noll and Rosenbluth, "Telecommunications policy: Structure, process, and outcomes."

62. Japan did not consider increasing the number of competitors until mid-2005.

63. Michelle Donegan, "Tata unleashes WiMax in India," at www.unstrung.com.

64. Source of GSM data: 3G Americas, a trade group of GSM carriers and vendors. Source of data on spending and deployment of 3G and CDMA: CDG white paper.

65. "3G and 4G wireless blog," at http://3g4g.blogspot.com.

66. Global Mobile Suppliers Association, "3G/WCDMA launches worldwide," at http://www.gsacom.com.

67. See the discussion of EDGE in Morgan Stanley, "Telecom services and equipment: Cross-industry insights," February 1, 2005.

68. NTT DoCoMo dominates the wireless data revenues rankings with over $3.4B in data services revenue in Q1 2008. In he first quarter of 2008 data services accounted for 35.7% of its revenues. Source: Chetan Sharma Consulting, "US wireless data market update, Q1 2008," May18, 2008. www.chetansharma.com/.

69. Morgan Stanley Equity Research, *3G Economics a Cause for Concern,* February 1, 2005.

70. It is part of a generation of 802.16 that relies on one of two variants of orthogonal frequency division multiplexing. The 802.16-2004 standard relies extensively on "OFDM" to provide fixed wireless service, either to small businesses or as backhaul for cellular networks. This garnered considerable attention in 2004 but it is incompatible with 802.16e, the center of attention for Intel and Samsung, which relies on "OFDMA" to serve mobile users. The standard was not yet fully specified in 2007 and there was bitter fighting in the US standards group working on the 802.16e with Intel and Qualcomm exchanging complaints over the group's work.

71. At the end of 2006, WiBro only had about 1,000 subscribers on the Korean Telecom network. KT was looking for ways to invigorate growth while SK Telecom took a wait and see policy. Source: "In-Stat, WiBro in Korea: Ambitious launch—turbulent take off," May 17, 2007. www.instat.com/.

72. Bill Ray, "WiMAX gets EU harmonization at 2.6 GHZ," *The Register*, May 9, 2008. "European Commission decides to give 3.5 G.5-GHz WiMAX spectrum 'Mobility' status," *RFDESIGN*, June 10, 2008.

73. Some variants are fixed wireless systems that will compete against WiMAX.

74. George Gilder, "The wireless wars," *Wall Street Journal Online*, April 13, 2007.

75. Jeff Orr, "Mobile broadband: 4G 4Play," at www.lightreading.com.

76. Based on the authors' interviews with equipment vendors, network carriers, and government officials in the US and Japan in June 2007.

77. Some features of the contract in places like China may provide limited advantages for massive volume.

78. Qualcomm is also one of the largest producers of all forms of 3G chipsets. Qualcomm has faced legal complaints that it manipulated its IPR to favor its chip-making operation over its rivals. Complaints by Nokia, Ericsson, Broadcom, Texas Instruments, NEC, and Panasonic were filed with European, Korean, and the US competition and trade authorities that Qualcomm is trying to vertically leverage its IPR, much as Microsoft did. Qualcomm denies this. They have also filed suits claiming Qualcomm violated their patents. In 2006 Nokia and Qualcomm deadlocked on cross-licensing GSM and CDMA technology patents. The stakes were large. Business analysts estimated that Nokia could end up paying $1 billion per year in royalties if terms did not change. In 2007 Qualcomm had several setbacks in these legal battles although the severity of the losses remained unclear. See "Cellphone crusader to divide and conquer," *Financial Times*, June 12, 2006.

79. In August 2007, Nokia, the last end-system producer still trying to produce the bulk of its own chips, decided to rely predominantly on outside suppliers. See "Nokia to outsource chip development," *Financial Times*, August 8, 2007.

80. A further complication is the possibility that Qualcomm has tied up essential IPR in important technologies for alternative approaches to 3G. It purchased Flarion in 2006 to reinforce its IPR.

81. Martin Cave, "Review of radio spectrum management, report for the UK department of trade and industry," at http://www.ofcom.org. Also see "Oftel's response to the Independent Spectrum Review of Radio Spectrum Management," at http://www.ofcom.org.

82. "EU telecom ministers agree state aid inappropriate," *Wall Street Journal Online*, December 5, 2002.

83. Many governments still try to micro-manage competing interests and particular technology plans. India, for example, decided to designate WiMAX as the technology to expand broadband rural connectivity. And, in late 2006 Colombia awarded 55 WiMAX licenses, favoring long-distance carriers that were struggling, but it did not issue 3G licenses to mobile carriers that were prospering. Sources: "Gartner: India to remain niche market for WiMAX," *Fierce Broadband Wireless*, May 27, 2008; "MinCom assigns 55 WiMax licenses," at http://www.wimax-industry.com; Alec

Barton, "Colombian ministry receives 161 WiMax license applications, allocates 55," at http://www.developingtelecoms.com.

84. In-Stat, "The road to 4G: Will LTE, UMB and WiMax just be stops along the way?" (Product Number IN0703689GW), August 2007, www.instat.com.

85. William Lehr and Lee W. McKnight, "Wireless Internet access: 3G vs. WiFi," *Telecommunications Policy* 27 (2003): 351–370.

Chapter 9

1. This chapter draws substantially on Peter Cowhey and Milton Mueller, "Delegation, Networks and Internet Governance," in *Networked Politics: Agency Power and Governance*, ed. M. Kahler (Cornell University Press, 2009).

2. John Perry Barlow argued that the Internet is beyond governments. Chapters 2 and 4 spelled out the regulatory realities omitted by this claim.

3. Some see large swaths of international agreements on commerce and human rights as parts of Internet governance. We follow the more restrictive definition suggested by John Mathiason et al. in an Internet Governance Project research paper titled "Internet governance: The state of play" (available at http://www .internetgovernance.org).

4. One could add a fourth layer, referring to policies, laws, and regulations governing the *use* of the Internet by people. This would include rules about crime, fraud, security, privacy, intellectual property, and content that attempt to govern *conduct* rather than the way the Internet and its resources are structured. These problems are not unique to the Internet, and are too inchoate to analyze here.

5. This point is stressed in the literature. See Wolfgang Reinicke, *Global Public Policy* (Brookings Institution, 1998).

6. One sign of the entrenched status of these principles was their central role in the proposal of the European Union on modifying Internet governance (Proposal for addition to chair's paper Sub-Com A Internet Governance on paragraph 5 'Follow-up and Possible Arrangements,'" document WSIS-II/PC-3/DT/21-E, 2005, available at http://www.itu.int). The access goal is embraced as an educational mission by the Internet Society in "The strategic operating plan of the Internet Society," 2005 (available at www.isoc.org).

7. Despite the tortuous and convoluted working of global resolutions, all but the second norm (which is subject to an ambiguous compromise throughout the text) are embraced in the World Summit on the Information Society's Declaration of Principles: Building the Information Society: a global challenge in the new Millennium, document WSIS-03/Geneva/Doc/4-E, available at http://www.itu.int.

8. Important goals of the Internet Society's strategic plan include the ability to innovate and to share.

9. Its name changes, but its mission remains pretty much the same. The Advanced Research Projects Agency (ARPA), created on February 7, 1958, was responsible "for the direction or performance of such advanced projects in the field of research and development as the Secretary of Defense shall, from time to time, designate by individual project or by category." On March 23, 1972, its name was changed to Defense Advanced Research Projects Agency (DARPA). On February 22, 1993, it was renamed Advanced Research Projects Agency (ARPA). On February 10, 1996, its name was changed again to Defense Advanced Research Projects Agency (DARPA). To avoid confusion, we use DARPA, the current name, throughout. The quotation is from the DARPA history available at http://www.darpa.mil.

10. Often the DoD paid a premium of close to 100% to get desired performance and weight margins. See Leslie Berlin, *The Man Behind the Microchip—Robert Noyce and the Invention of Silicon Valley* (Oxford University Press, 2005), p. 130.

11. Peter Cowhey, "The Politics of US and Japanese Security Commitments," in *Structure and Policy in Japan and the United States*, ed. Cowhey and McCubbins.

12. For a vivid account, see Reed Hundt, *You Say You Want a Revolution* (Yale University Press, 2000). Anthony M. Rutkowski ("Multilateral cooperation in tele-communications: implications for the great transformation," in *The New Information Infrastructure*, ed. W. Drake, Twentieth Century Fund, 1995) notes the increase in importance given to ICT technology during the Clinton administration.

13. The World Wide Web Consortium ("W3C") deals with certain applications software issues that are pertinent to the transport software. For simplicity's sake this is omitted from this discussion. The section that follows draws heavily on Milton Mueller, *Ruling the Root* (MIT Press, 2002). Also see Daniel Benoliel, "Cyberspace technological standardization: An institutional theory retrospective," *Berkeley Technology Law Journal* 18 (2003): 1259–1339; Mathiason et al., "Internet governance: The state of play"; Bernd Holznagel and Raymund Werle, "Sectors and strategies of global communications regulation," *Knowledge, Technology and Policy* 7 (2004), no. 2: 19–37.

14. See the discussion of standards in chapter 8.

15. It had several earlier names and structures, and by 1990 it had evolved into the Internet Society, but the continuity is substantial enough to justify referring to the IETF throughout this discussion.

16. Janet Abbate, *Inventing the Internet* (MIT Press, 1999), pp. 144–145.

17. Benoliel, "Cyberspace technological standardization," p. 28.

18. Internet standards may contain corporate intellectual property, but only if licensed on a reasonable and non-discriminatory basis. Many standards have no intellectual property protection.

19. This motif included an informal process emphasizing expert participation open to all (unlike most standards bodies) that relied on a "request for comment" and feedback system to design standards, applied field tests to validate them, and relatively quick decision making. Tinkering over the years tried to ensure that the process was opened to a broader range of participants in the computer community. See Abbate, *Inventing the Internet*, pp. 206–207.

20. The "constitution" of these communities is the architecture of the Internet. There is agreement that central design principles of the Internet will be upheld in the implementation of standards. Even as ISOC membership and administration has come to reflect greater influence of corporate executives they participate in their private capacity and adhere to the "constitutional rule."

21. The ITU was an early participant in the effort to create data networking. Caught up in a system of slower inter-governmental decision making and largely driven by the interests of telephone companies, its approach failed commercially. See Abbate, *Inventing the Internet*, pp. 150–151.

22. The theory of delegation does not require a formal act of deliberative delegation by a principal. Rather, it is common that the principal can find itself newly interested in an arena (such as credentialing doctors or certifying the safety of consumer products) where there is a pre-existing "agent." See Hawkins et al., *Delegation and Agency in International Organizations*, p. 7.

23. For communications networks governments retain the right to dictate technical standards, and so their forbearance is an important restraint on standards-setting bodies. This influenced the dynamic of Internet standard setting. The IETF is treated as a "virtual agent," not created by governments but requiring a decision by governments not to displace it by more traditional institutions with overlapping jurisdiction. This potential for governments to change IETF's effective jurisdiction had implications for its operations. In contrast, the arrangement for governing Internet address was a classic act of formal delegation.

24. Abbate, *Inventing the Internet*, pp. 167–177. The OSI model also failed because it relied on traditional face-to-face, bureaucratic mechanisms. By contrast the IETF relied on virtual collaboration and a fusion of users and developers. The IAB was created in part to solidify this advantage. See Rutkowski, "Multilateral cooperation in telecommunications."

25. In 1992 the CCITT was renamed the ITU Telecommunication Standardization Sector (ITU-T), but since most activities cited here took place before 1992, we use CCITT throughout. The Open Systems Interconnection Basic Reference Model,

usually referred to as the OSI Model, describes communications and computer network protocol design. It is sometimes known as the OSI seven-layer model. From top to bottom, the OSI Model consists of the Application, Presentation, Session, Transport, Network, Data Link, and Physical layers. Each layer is a collection of related functions that provides services to the layer above it and receives service from the layer below it.

26. Abbate, *Inventing the Internet*, pp. 174–176.

27. Shane Greenstein, "Markets, Standardization, and the Information Infrastructure," *IEEE Micro, Chips, Systems, and Applications*, Special Issue on Standards, 13 (December 2003), no. 6: 36–51.

28. As late as 1990 there were factions in the US government that supported OSI over the TCP/IP protocols. See Petri Mahonen, "The standardization process in IT—Too slow or too fast," in *Information Technology Standards and Standardization*, ed. K. Jakobs (IGI Publications, 2000). On a major dispute that arose between the IAB and IETF when the IAB proposed to incorporate an OSI standard into Internet protocols, see Andrew L. Russell, " 'Rough consensus and running code' and the Internet-OSI standards war," *IEEE Annals of the History of Computing* 28 (2006), no. 3: 48–61.

29. Shane Greenstein ("The economic geography of Internet infrastructure in the United States," in *Handbook of Telecommunications Economics*, volume 2, ed. S. Majumdar et al., North-Holland, 2005) suggests that in this case no one had a superior position on IPR and all would benefit from strong network externalities. In addition, the Internet architecture made it possible to co-exist with other proprietary architectures as long as was necessary, thus reducing the costs for "losers" to the Internet protocols.

30. Based on Cowhey's notes as a participant in the US government team that planned for the G-8 meeting.

31. This logic became clearer when standard setting for the software enabling the World Wide Web was institutionalized. The World Wide Web Consortium develops standards recommendations for the Web. The Consortium was founded when commercial interest in the creation of the Web was strong, as was government attention. Tim Berners-Lee, the key architect of the Web, writes that the desire of all players to avoid capture of key tools and design guidelines by any one company (i.e., Microsoft) made it easier for the Consortium to operate as an open standards-setting body. (See T. Berners-Lee, *Weaving the Web*, Harper Business, 2000.) Unlike the IETF, the W3C has membership dues and does some centralized development work of design tools.

32. The three conditions for any delegation were proposed by Lake and McCubbins in "Delegation to international agencies."

33. See Request For Comments 4071, documenting changes in administrative support relationship between the Internet Society and the IETF, at http://tools.ietf.org. The World Wide Web Consortium is another hybrid model that some advocate for the IETF.

34. Actually $N(N - 1)/2$, not quite the square but close. See Milton Mueller, "The switchboard problem: Scale, signaling and organization in the era of manual telephone switching, 1878–1898," *Technology and Culture* 30 (1989), no. 3: 534–560.

35. An illustrative case is the (so far) lagging transition from IPv4 to IPv6. We thank Pierre de Vries for this observation.

36. Increasing bandwidth in the age of copper required expanding the diameter and weight of the copper cables, while extending their geographic scope meant adding more physical electronics devices such as loading coils or repeaters to boost the signal. See Neil H. Wasserman, *From Invention to Innovation* (Johns Hopkins University Press, 1985). A hierarchical control system for routing and centralized, integrated network management procedures conserved these scarce resources and allowed redundant routing options to increase reliability.

37. A central principle of the Internet, "end-to-end" connectivity, stipulates that the "end devices" (terminals) on the network contain much of the network intelligence instead of centralizing intelligence in a central telephone switch.

38. François Bar, Stephen Cohen, Peter Cowhey, Brad Delong, Michael Kleeman, and John Zysman, "The Next Generation Internet," in *Tracking a Transformation*, ed. S. Weber (Brookings Institution Press, 2001); Roger Noll, "Resolving policy chaos in high speed Internet access," policy paper 01–013, Stanford Institute for Economic Policy Research, 2002.

39. A classic paper by David Parnas on systems software ("On the criteria to be used in decomposing systems into modules," *Communications of the ACM* 15 (1972), no. 12: 1053–1058 identifies another variant of the question of scarcity and hierarchy by pointing out that the time and effort to change code correctly are themselves scarce resources. Network designs differ on how they handle this problem. Parnas observes that hierarchy is one solution for conserving time and effort (one module orders the others) and, if done properly, hierarchy may actually make the lower level functions in the network more resistant to disruption. Chopping off the head does not hurt the rest of the body, only the highest level reasoning. The Internet's domain name system (DNS) handles the problem of assigning unique names in precisely this way.

40. For a good description of what they do and why they are needed, see National Research Council, *Signposts in Cyberspace* (National Academy Press, 2005).

41. This corresponds with Parnas's discussion referenced earlier.

42. For an excellent description of the root server system, see chapter 3 of *Signposts in Cyberspace*.

43. The software, known as BIND, is open-source software developed and maintained by the Internet Systems Consortium (ISC) in Palo Alto, California.

44. See Mueller, *Ruling the Root*; Michael Froomkin, "Wrong turn in cyberspace: Using ICANN to route around the APA and the Constitution," *Duke Law Journal* 50 (2000): 17–184; Robert Shaw, "Internet domain names: Whose domain is this?" in *Coordinating the Internet*, ed. B. Kahin and J. Keller (MIT Press, 1997).

45. Using a carefully negotiated compatibility among co-equal, hierarchic organizations, can coordinate the domain name system, but this raises the same strategic bargaining issues associated with telecommunications interconnection noted before. See Milton Mueller, "Competing DNS roots: Creative destruction or just plain destruction?" *Journal of Network Industries* 3 (2002): 313–334; also see *Signposts in Cyberspace*.

46. For a comparable case involving the International Monetary Fund, see J. Lawrence Broz and Michael Brewster Hawes, "Congressional Politics of Financing the International Monetary Fund," *International Organization* 60 (2006), no. 2: 367–399.

47. As a non-profit corporation, ICANN is subject to US law and courts. This further roots it in US sensibilities, which raises some concerns for non-US interests. The delegation to ICANN also makes its deliberations exempt from the Administrative Procedures Act, a concern for some US critics. See Viktor Mayer-Schönberger and Malte Ziewitz, "Jefferson rebuffed: The United States and the future of Internet governance," *Columbia Science and Technology Law Review* 8 (2007): 188–228; Jonathan Weinberg, "ICANN and the problem of legitimacy," *Duke Law Journal* 50 (2000), no. 1: 187–260.

48. The first is a Memorandum of Understanding (MoU) between the US Department of Commerce and ICANN. The second is a contract between ICANN and the US government. The third is a Cooperative Agreement between the US Department of Commerce and VeriSign.

49. The root zone is the top level of the Domain Name System hierarchy for any DNS system.

50. Contrary to the original intentions of the US Department of Commerce, most of the root server operators still have no contractual relationship with ICANN or any government. The relationship between the US government and the nongovernmental root server operators is one of co-existence. Consistent with delegation theory, however, should one of these operators within the US take actions that go beyond certain political parameters—e.g., seriously undermining the ICANN regime or the stability of the Internet—it likely would trigger action by the government.

51. Mueller, *Ruling the Root*; *Signposts in Cyberspace*.

52. ICANN resembles "discretion-based" delegation where uncertainty concerning the task and expertise of the agent lead to a significant grant of discretion. In view of the enormous influence of the US and the task of getting enough consent from the rest of the world's stakeholders to be viable, ICANN has the implicit mandate of setting the policy at a point that precludes being overturned. See Hawkins et al., *Delegation and Agency in International Organizations*, pp. 27–28.

53. ICANN soon promoted competition by facilitating entry into the market for registering .com names in competition with VeriSign. However, the US negotiated the initial contract with VeriSign as it set up ICANN. This contract set the framework for the initial bargaining options for the movement to competition.

54. The policy is available at http://www.icann.org. See also Jonathan Weinberg, "ICANN, 'Internet stability,' and the new top level domains," in *Communications Policy and Information Technology*, ed. L. Cranor et al. (MIT Press, 2002).

55. "At-large" delegates elected on the basis of geographic representation system were replaced by candidates selected by the board who were geographically diverse in their nationalities. See Hans Klein, "Global Internet Democracy," *Info* 3 (2000), no. 4: 255–257.

56. The US decision to keep control was partly reversed by a decision to phase it out over a three-year period. This won praise from the EU. See Associated Press, "EU praises ICANN on role in Internet," November 2, 2006. For an excellent review of WSIS, see Mayer-Schönberger and Ziewitz, "Jefferson rebuffed."

57. The report of the Working Group on Internet Governance states in paragraph 48 that "no single government should have a pre-eminent role in relation to international Internet governance."

58. Hawkins et al., *Delegation and Agency in International Organizations*, pp. 21 and 27.

59. NTIA statement, June 30, 2005.

60. Mayer-Schönberger and Ziewitz, "Jefferson rebuffed."

61. Principles for the Delegation and Administration of Country Code Top Level Domains, ICANN Governmental Advisory Committee (GAC), 2000, available at http://gac.icann.org.

62. The sovereignty principle with respect to ccTLDs was formally recognized in the June 30, 2005 principles issued by the US government. For technical and political reasons, the continuing growth of the Internet has led to more resource assignment functions occurring at specialized regional authorities, such as those for North America, Africa, and Latin America. For example, this discussion omits detailed discussion of the role of regional address registries and other functional elements of the Internet. However, these arrangements fit in with the concept of a chain of

delegation and with the general US policy of internationalization through privatization. The two most important non US-based address registries (for Europe and Asia-Pacific) were delegated to external nonprofits before the creation of ICANN. In both cases, delegations of address resources to non-US actors was a conscious part of an attempt to promote the spread of Internet protocol by reassuring foreign actors that the US was willing to share control.

63. National Science Foundation, The National Research and Education Network Program," "A Report to Congress in response to a requirement of The High Performance Computing Act of 1991," (P.L. 102–194) December 1992. The privatization of the backbone was nudged forward by the effort to boost the US computing industry whose various public policy organizations (among them the Computer Systems Policy Project) saw high-speed networking for computing as a major advantage in competing against Japan. The High Performance Computing Act of 1991, sponsored by Senator Al Gore (D-Tennessee), created the National Research and Education Network. For a candid and opinionated review of the players and their interests at the time, see "The National Research and Educational Network—Whom shall it serve?" (available at http://thecookreport.org).

64. Charles Ferguson, *High Stakes, No Prisoners* (Three Rivers Press, 1999), p. 48.

65. Greenstein, "The economic geography of Internet infrastructure in the United States."

66. Traditional telephone networks were hierarchical. The data transport market had two main layers. One provided local access and transport by an ISP in, for example, a city. The other layer was the backbone, long haul transport. On how regulation influenced strategies about local access, but long haul is most relevant for Internet governance, see Greenstein, "The economic geography of Internet infrastructure in the United States."

67. Because of this, there was no systematic ability to withhold capacity to raise prices on a sustained basis or limit the ability of others to enter the market (Greenstein, "The economic geography of Internet infrastructure in the United States; Economides, "The economics of the Internet backbone." For a summary of the views of those worried that a competitive problem was ignored, see Jay P. Kesan and Rajiv C. Shah, "Fool Us Once Shame on You—Fool Us Twice Shame on Us: What We can Learn from the Privatizations of the Internet Backbone Network and Domain Name System," *Washington University Law Quarterly* 79 (2001): 89–220; Benoliel, "Cyberspace technological standardization."

68. The US government prevented one merger and required the divestiture of backbone transport to a third company in another merger.

69. The system prevailing before 1998 drove up prices and discouraged technological efficiency.

70. The individual contracts differed, but one common practice in the late 1990s particularly angered foreign carriers. Worldcom and other US carriers asked, for example, an Australian carrier to transport all of the Web traffic for Worldcom to and from Australia for free in return for Worldcom providing free transport within the US for the Australian carrier accessing US websites. See Peter Cowhey, "Accounting Rates, Cross-Border Services, and the Next WTO Round on Basic Telecommunications Services," in *The WTO and Global Convergence in Telecommunications and Audio-Visual Services*, ed. D. Geradin and D. Luff (Cambridge University Press, 2004); *Telegeography 2001* (Telegeography, 2004), pp. 58–59.

71. International Charging for Access to Internet Services (ICAIS) was a major issue at the ITU's Study Group 3 that dealt with "tariffing" issues and then at the ITU's World Telecommunications Standardization Assembly in 2000.

72. Cowhey, "Accounting Rates."

73. For examples of the divided editorial comment on this outcome, see Kieren McCarthy, "Breaking America's grip on the net," *The Guardian*, October 6, 2005; Adam Thierer, and Wayne Crews, "The World Wide Web (of Bureaucrats?)", OpinionJournal.com, October 9, 2005.

74. International development institutions might fund special facilities to aggregate the regional traffic of, say, West Africa before peering with a global network. Larger traffic volumes should improve the terms for peering. Another idea would place renewed focus on the high prices charged for international transport by the poorest countries because the prices reduced the growth of their traffic. See Russell Southwood, "Africa: Local IXPs and Regional Carriers, Balancing Act," at http://www.balancingact-africa.com; Michael Jensen, "Open access—Lowering the cost of international bandwidth in Africa," Association for Progressive Communications issues paper, 2006, available at www.apc.org.

75. Jack Goldsmith and Timothy Wu, *Who Controls the Internet?* (Oxford University Press, 2006). David W. Drezner, *All Politics is Global: Explaining International Regulatory Regimes* (Princeton University Press, 2007).

Summary and Conclusions

1. Although competition and universal service challenges remain, this era should emphasize minimizing the transaction costs for mixing and matching the diverse modular resources of the emerging infrastructure and production system.

2. Strong and clear property rights generally are desirable for market efficiency, but rights can be beneficial or perverse depending on their precise terms.

3. The Next Generation Network (NGN) is "a multi-service network based on IP technology [that] provides an open architecture by uncoupling services and net-

works and allowing them to be offered separately. In this context, the services can be developed independently regardless of the network platforms being used." (Working Party on Telecommunication and Information Services Policies, Next Generation Network Development in OECD, Paris, 2004, paragraphs 13 and 14) ITU-T Study Group 13 leads this work at the ITU. The IETF works on protocols that allow intersection with NGN, such as ENUM for allowing telephone numbering to intersect with VoIP and multimedia in new ways.

4. Our goal is to suggest common approaches that promote global negotiations but also allow for significant variance in national policies.

5. Jonathan Zittrain, *The Future of the Internet* (Yale University Press, 2008); Gerald Faulhaber, "Net Neutrality: The Debate Evolves," *International Journal of Communications* 1 (2007), February: 680–700.

6. This is true because major buyers and the major ICT vendors assume a heterogeneous network and IT stack.

7. Farrell and Weiser, "Modularity, vertical integration and open access policies."

8. Japan, Korea, and other countries are engaged in similar exercises. We use some elements of the European search for principles to illustrate this wider range of thinking.

9. For a concise summary of the EU thinking, see J. Schwarz da Silva, "Converged networks and services," paper presented at NSF/OECD Workshop on Social and Economic Factors Shaping the Future of the Internet, Washington, 2007.

10. A hybrid that can be effective under certain circumstances is a transgovernmental network of specialized national bureaucracies. See Mette Eilstrup-Sangiovanni, "Varieties of cooperation: Government networks in international security," in *Networked Politics*, ed. M. Kahler (Cornell University Press, 2008).

11. Privacy exchanges that follow this model are described later in this chapter.

12. Del Bianco, "Voices past."

13. On the Wireless Grid and other developments, see the following papers, presented at the NSF/OECD Workshop on Social and Economic Factors Shaping the Future of the Internet (Washington, 2007): Lee W. McKnight, "The future of the Internet is not the Internet: Open communications policy and the future wireless grid(s)"; David Clark, "Defining a future network: A new research agenda"; J. Schwarz da Silva, "Converged networks and services."

14. Brenden Kuerbis and Milton Mueller, "Securing the root: A proposal for distributing signing authority," Internet Governance Project, Syracuse University, 2007.

15. Many fear market manipulation through mandatory standards in big national markets. However, China and others will usually fail to achieve major global wins if they set compulsory local standards. Modularity makes it harder to leverage vertical layers into broader successes. To the contrary, successful global standards rely more on ubiquity and speed of deployment. Nonetheless, government mandates could harm consumer welfare.

16. The focus here is more on the theory that these markets are prone to "tipping" and bundling of capabilities around platforms than on complaints aimed at specific forms of illegal competitive conduct.

17. For a sophisticated comparison, see Katarzyna A. Czapracka, "Where Antitrust Ends and IP Begins," *Yale Journal of Law and Technology*, 9 (2007), Fall: 44–108; Nicholas Economides and Ioannis Lianos, "The Elusive Antitrust Standard on Bundling in Europe and in the United States at the Aftermath of the Microsoft Cases," *Antitrust Law Journal* (2008).

18. Robert Hahn, ed., *Antitrust Policy and Vertical Restraints* (AEI-Brookings Joint Center for Regulatory Studies, 2006).

19. Remaining foreign direct investment restrictions are documented in *OECD Communications Outlook 2007* (Information and Communications Technologies, 2007). See p. 29 and table 2.6 on pp. 43–44.

20. For example, a global telecom carrier concluded in 2007 that China simply would not let it make a meaningful investment regardless of its telecom commitments at the WTO. Source: meetings with corporation's executives, October 2007.

21. As we noted in chapter 8, strategic game playing over spectrum is routine. The same game is being played out between 3G and WiMAX advocates today. Spectrum should be flexible. See Eric Sylvers, "Wireless: Seeking a voice in future of WiMax," *International Herald Tribune*, October 10, 2006.

22. Modularity also allows for efforts to relieve "scarcity" by pricing. Real-time bidding for spectrum bands if there is crowding (most of the time spectrum is idle) is possible with smart terminals. See Eli Noam, "What regulation for Internet TV? Telecommunications vs. television regulation," at http://www.london.edu.

23. In some countries the license comes with many terms and conditions. Paring these conditions down is also optimal.

24. Private clearinghouses for spectrum, for example, can improve transactional efficiency by distributing the compensation needed to clear existing spectrum for new uses, subject to regulatory oversight. The FCC selected the CTIA Spectrum Clearinghouse to serve this purpose for the 2.1-GHz band. Source: "CTIA Spectrum Clearinghouse Announces Launch of New website," at http://www.ctia.org.

25. Similar models exist in poor countries. Microfinance institutions, such as the Grameen Foundation's "Village Phone" program, have built a successful business model for the poor by lending them the capital to buy a cell phone, minutes on a phone card, an antenna booster, and a car battery with recharger to resell services to their villages.

26. "Editor's corner," Fierce Broadband Wireless, September 17, 2007; Natasha Lomas, "Urban wireless networks set to surge," Silicon.com, July 26, 2007; "Wireless Internet for all, without the towers," *New York Times*, February 4, 2007; Hernan Galperin and François Bar, "The Microtelco Opportunity: Evidence from Latin America," *Information Technologies and International Development* 3 (2006) no. 2: 73–86.

27. We thank Carlos Casasus for drawing our attention to the work of Bill St. Arnaud of CANARIE Inc., a Canadian Internet 2 firm. St. Arnaud points to Montreal as a model city for these policy initiatives. This paragraph draws heavily on his "New Media and Infrastructure Issues in Canada." Atkinson and Weiser suggest in "A 'third way' on network neutrality" that tax incentives for broadband build out may be more desirable than more rigid regulations to ensure network neutrality.

28. Private communication.

29. One backbone carrier has a pricing option that is a variant on the club model. It has a lead user pay a premium price to get initial fiber service. As others sign up for the fiber, the lead user's price declines. In effect, the user most valuing the fiber bears the upfront risk but benefits as others join the "club."

30. We agree with Michael L. Katz and Howard A. Shelanski, "'Schumpeterian' competition and antitrust policy in high-tech markets," *Competition* 14 (2005): 47p. that there is still a need for antitrust policy, but think that the inflection point narrows the focus and changes the mix of tools used for the policy.

31. The EU member states have agreed on a limited number of subsectors in the electronic communications sector that are subject to "ex ante" procedures. They must notify the European Commission of these procedures.

32. The US mix might include simpler ex ante rules built around a stronger presumption that competitive harm is difficult. Properly designed, such rules might pair with somewhat quicker enforcement mechanisms to provide a rough equivalent to "light touch" regulation.

33. Howard Shelanski, "Adjusting regulation to competition," *Yale Journal on Regulation* 24 (2007): 56–105.

34. The USC Annenberg Center Principles were developed during an off-the-record seminar among representatives of stakeholders in February 2006. The goal was to

provide a simple, clear set of guidelines addressing the public Internet markets for broadband access. We have slightly modified them by eliminating the call for competitive facilities (see our earlier discussion) and adding the requirements on wholesale and terminal equipment and applications. Atkinson and Weiser suggest comparable guidelines based on their independent analysis of the challenges.

35. Network operators providing basic access should not insert themselves in the traffic stream by blocking or degrading traffic. Traffic should be carried regardless of content or destination, and operators should not give preferential treatment to their own content in the basic access service.

36. The specific parameters (speed and latency) of this service could be reviewed on a quadrennial basis. In 2006 speeds exceeding 1 megabit per second downstream and less upstream were deemed acceptable. In time the idea is to move increasingly symmetric bandwidth at higher speeds in the future.

37. There are issues that are central to broadband competition in developing country markets that this package does not address. For example, many developing markets have competition but carriers with significant market power dominate the wholesale market and often refuse to deal with newcomers. Such situations may require additional measures.

38. Michael Kleeman, "Point of disconnect: Internet traffic and US communications infrastructure," *International Journal of Communication* 1 (2007): 177–183.

39. The economic negotiation over peering based on roughly reciprocal volumes of traffic is purely a commercial decision. This discussion applies only to "technical" issues influencing peering.

40. In April 1996 WTO members agreed in the Fourth protocol to specific commitments and exceptions to the WTO's agreement concerning basic telecommunications.

41. Assem Prakash and Matthew Potoski, "Racing to the bottom? Trade, environmental governance and ISO 14001," *American Journal of Political Science* 50 (2006), no. 2: 350–364.

42. For one view, see http://www.wired.com/wired/archive/12.01/mpaa.html.

43. "Draft non-paper on the WIPO Treaty on the Protection of Broadcasting Organizations," Draft 1.0, March 8, 2007, available at http://www.wipo.int.

44. The non-linear category still is subject to more restrictions that we would prefer, as explained in this passage in an analysis funded by Ofcom, the UK regulator: "Where the viewer actively requests the individual video file on demand. . . . [It] would be regulated according to minimal standards, lighter than linear 'broadcasting' regulation, but still encompassing a wide range of prohibitions against particu-

lar types and durations of advertising, other commercial communications, different types of expression, and so on. The definitions do not exclude video blogs, interactive computer games or delivery of video over mobile telephone networks." (*Assessing Indirect Impacts of the EC Proposals for Video Regulation*, Rand Europe, 2006, p. v).

45. In "What Regulation for Internet TV?" Eli Noam lists eight factors that lead to infrastructure regulation as the nexus for Internet television regulation: least mobile, fewest participants, market power, existing sophisticated regulatory tools, enforcer of content restrictions, effective revenue source, source of in-kind contributions, and customization of regulation.

46. Clay Shirky, *Here Comes Everybody* (Penguin, 2008).

47. For a smart outline of why draconian reinforcement of the status quo will not sell, see Gigi B. Sohn, "Don't mess with success: Government technology mandates and the marketplace for online content," *Journal of Telecommunications and High Tech Law* 5 (2006), fall: 73–86.

48. Abramson, *Digital Phoenix*, pp. 29–44.

49. Ibid., pp. 29–35. Lawrence Lessig is one of the many critics of this position; see his 2001 book *The Future of Ideas* (Random House).

50. Cass R. Sunstein and Richard H. Thaler, "Liberal paternalism is not an oxymoron," *University of Chicago Law Review* 70 (2003), no. 4: 1159–1202.

51. All that is necessary for this is for copyright holders to use an equivalent of Google Alerts to monitor their IPR and for the copyright office to post notices of obsolete contact information on their websites. This approach differs in spirit from the WIPO privacy convention that the US recently signed, although the agent system could provide for privacy. One obstacle for this system is making sure that a synthesis of DRM and a trading system does not lead to an unwarranted expansion of copyright claims; see Pamela Samuelson, "Digital rights management {and, or, vs.} the law," *Communications of the ACM* 46 (2003), no. 4: 41–45.

52. The options on Creative Commons licenses allow up to eleven different combinations for licenses. As of October 2008, licenses were available in 46 countries and under development in 18 more. Source: http://creativecommons.org.

53. Suzanne Scotchmer has shown that private mechanisms for implementing market rights and capabilities, like ASCAP's system of collecting royalties for broadcasts of copyrighted music, require monitoring.

54. Set forth in the Health Insurance Portability and Accountability Act of 1996.

55. See Douglas MacMillan and Paula Lehman, "Social Networking with the Elite," at http://www.businessweek.com.

56. Furthermore, some personal rights may be treated as impossible to waive. Distinguishing these fundamental rights from other layers of protection is one task for policy making.

57. For Microsoft's policy, see http://privacy.microsoft.com/en-us/fullnotice.aspx. On Ask.com, see http://www.informationweek.com/news/showArticle.jhtml? articleID=201200282.

58. The report can be found at http://www.privacyinternational.org. On recent calls for international regulation, see "Google calls for international standards on internet privacy," *Washington Post*, September 15, 2007.

Index